The
Eclectic
Gourmet
Guide to
San Francisco
& the Bay Area

Also available from MENASHA RIDGE PRESS

The Eclectic Gourmet Guide to Los Angeles,
  by Colleen Dunn Bates
The Eclectic Gourmet Guide to New Orleans,
  by Tom Fitzmorris
The Eclectic Gourmet Guide to San Diego,
  by Steve Silverman

The Eclectic Gourmet Guide to

San Francisco & the Bay Area

Richard Sterling

MENASHA
RIDGE
PRESS

Menasha Ridge Press, Inc.
P.O. Box 43059
Birmingham, Alabama 35243

Cover and text design by Suzanne H. Holt

Cover art by Michele Natale

ISBN 0-89732-218-5

Library of Congress Catalog Card Number: 96-19467

Manufactured in the United States of America

10 9 8 7 6 5 4 3 2 1

First Edition

CONTENTS

acknowledgments

Special thanks to my research assistant Lois Maclean whose keen eye, good taste, and turn of phrase have made this work the richer. And to my editorial assistant Gina Comaich who made the labor lighter.

The
Eclectic
Gourmet
Guide to
San Francisco
& the Bay Area

About the Author

Richard Sterling is an author of and contributor to numerous cookbooks and guidebooks covering California, Latin America, and Asia. He is well known in the Bay Area for his varied and eclectic achievements. As a contributing editor to *Chile Pepper* magazine he has been a James Beard Foundation nominee for the M.F.K Fisher Distinguished Writing Award, and his book *Dining with Headhunters* is the only cookbook ever to have been banned for sale by the U.S. military post exchange system.

GETTING IT RIGHT

A lot of thought went into this guide. While producing a dining guide may appear to be a straightforward endeavor, I can assure you that it is fraught with peril. I have read dining guides by authors who turn up their noses at anything except four-star French restaurants (of which there are a whole lot fewer than people think). Likewise, I have seen a guide that totally omits Thai and Indian restaurants—among others—because the author did not understand those cuisines. I have read guides absolutely devoid of criticism, written by "experts" unwilling to risk offending the source of their free meals. Finally, I've seen those books that are based on surveys and write-ins from diners whose credentials for evaluating fine dining are mysterious at best and questionable at least.

How, then, do you go about developing a truly excellent dining guide? What is the best way to get it right?

If dining guides are among the most idiosyncratic of reference books, it is primarily because the background, taste, integrity, and personal agenda of each author are problematical. The authors of most dining guides are vocational or avocational restaurant or food critics. Some of these critics are schooled professionals, with palates refined by years of practical experience and culinary study; others are journalists, often with no background in food criticism or cooking, who are arbitrarily assigned the job of reviewing restaurants by their newspaper or magazine publisher. (Although it *is* occasionally possible to find journalists who are also culinary professionals.) The worst cases are the legions of self-proclaimed food critics who mooch their way from restaurant to restaurant, growing fat on free meals in exchange for writing glowing reviews.

Ignorance of ethnic cuisine or old assumptions about what makes for haute cuisine particularly plague authors in cities without much ethnic variety in restaurants, or authors who have been writing for years about the same old white-linen, expense-account tourist traps. Many years ago in Lexington, Kentucky, for example, there was only one Chinese restaurant in town and it was wildly successful—in spite of the fact that it was Chinese in name only. Its specialty dishes, which were essentially American vegetable casseroles smothered in corn starch, were happily gobbled up by loyal patrons who had never been exposed to real Chinese cooking. The food was not bad, but it was not Chinese either. Visitors from out of town, inquiring about a good local Chinese restaurant, were invariably directed to this place. As you would expect, they were routinely horrified by the fare.

And, while you might argue that American diners are more sophisticated and knowledgeable nowadays than at the time of the Lexington pavilion, the evidence suggests otherwise. In Las Vegas, for instance, a good restaurant town with a number of excellent Italian eateries, the local Olive Garden (a chain restaurant) is consistently voted the city's best Italian restaurant in a yearly newspaper poll. There is absolutely nothing wrong with the Las Vegas Olive Garden, but to suggest that it is the best Italian restaurant in the city is ludicrous. In point of fact, the annual survey says much more about the relative sophistication of Las Vegas diners than it does about the quality of local Italian restaurants.

But if you pick up a guide that reflects the views of many survey respondents, a *vox populi* or reader's choice compendium, that is exactly the problem. You are dependent upon the average restaurant-goer's capacity to make sound, qualitative judgments—judgments almost always impaired by extraneous variables. How many times have you had a wonderful experience at a restaurant, only to be disappointed on a subsequent visit? Trying to reconcile the inconsistency, you recall that on your previous visit, you were in the company of someone particularly stimulating, and that perhaps you had enjoyed a couple of drinks before eating. What I am getting at is that our reflections on restaurant experiences are often colored by variables having little or nothing to do with the restaurant itself. And while I am given to the democratic process in theory, I have my doubts about depending entirely on survey forms that reflect such experiences.

There are more pragmatic arguments to be made about such eaters' guides as well. If you cannot control or properly qualify your survey respondents, you cannot assure their independence, knowledge, or critical sensitivity. And, since literally anyone can participate in such surveys, the ratings can be easily slanted by those with vested interests. How many bogus responses would it take to dramatically upgrade a restaurant's rating in a survey-based, big city dining guide? Forty or even fewer. Why? Because the publisher receives patron reports (survey responses, readers' calls) covering more restaurants than can be listed in the book. Thus the "voting" is distributed over such a large number of candidate restaurants that the median number of reports for the vast majority of establishments is 120 or fewer. A cunning restaurant proprietor who is willing to stuff the ballot box, therefore, could easily improve his own rating—or lower that of a competitor.

So my mission in the *Eclectic Gourmet Guides* is to provide you with the most meaningful, useful, and accessible restaurant evaluations possible. Weighing the alternatives, I have elected to work with culinary experts, augmenting their opinions with a carefully qualified survey population of totally independent local diners of demonstrated culinary sophistication. The experts I have sought to author the *Eclectic Gourmet Guides* are knowledgeable, seasoned professionals; they have studied around the world, written cookbooks or columns, and closely follow the development of restaurants in their cities. They are well versed in ethnic dining, many having studied cuisines in their native lands. And they have no prejudice about high or low cuisine. They are as at home in a Tupelo, Mississippi, catfish shack as in an exclusive French restaurant on New York's Upper East Side. Thus the name "Eclectic Gourmet."

Equally important, I have sought experts who make every effort to conduct their reviews anonymously, and who always pay full menu prices for their meals. We are credible not only because we are knowledgeable, but also because we are independent.

You, the reader of this *Eclectic Gourmet Guide,* are the inspiration for and, we hope, the beneficiary of our diligence and methodology. Though we cannot evaluate your credentials as a restaurant critic, your opinion as a consumer—of this guide and the restaurants within—is very important to us. A clip-out survey can be found at the back of the book; please tell us about your dining experiences and let us know whether you agree with our reviews.

Eat well. Be happy.

Bob Sehlinger

dining in san francisco and the bay area

Echoes of the Barbary Coast still ring in the voluptuous pleasures of San Francisco's table. This is a place where people have been writing of memorable dining since Mark Twain sojourned in the city and wrote of its charms in the 1860s.

Now more than ever, people in the Bay Area find restaurants and the culinary arts one of the most important topics of discussion. Both the artists and their patrons concern themselves not only with the end result, but also with the entire process of the craft: from the origins and freshness of the ingredients, through the utensils in which they are cooked and served, to the state of mind of the diners and servers as well. There's a personal quality to gastronomy in the Bay Area. Chefs adapt the lessons learned in European kitchens to the dictates of locally grown foodstuffs and further incorporate the diverse cultural influences of the region.

In San Francisco there's a restaurant to suit any occasion, and you won't have to look long to find a very good, even great, place to dine within walking distance from anywhere you might be in the city. After all, San Francisco is known as "The Walking City." And in the rest of the Bay Area, Marin, Oakland/Berkeley, and Silicon Valley, most everything is easily drivable or BARTable.

A feature perhaps unique to the Bay Area is the possibility of genuinely friendly service. The best San Francisco restaurants are not stuffy or formal and will not treat you with condescension. Most restaurants are happy to be told about unsatisfactory service or a dish that has not been properly prepared. Unlike New York, the Bay Area has few of the imposing, intimidating, ghastly expensive Taj Mahals of gastronomy whose raison d'être has been obscured by interests other than the table. As for Los Angeles—well, San Francisco eats L.A.'s lunch!

This region is the capital of the three-star restaurant. Diners here want the best in food, service, and price—and no snooty waiters. Even the four- and five-star restaurants here are short on pretense, but long on service. The common man is king here. He just happens to have a discriminating palate.

Whence came this egalitarian gastronomy? The Old West is newest here, with its frontier meritocracy, lusty democracy, and demand for good vittles. You still find the legacies of Spanish missionaries and ranchers, Chinese railroad workers, Italian vintners, Japanese, Vietnamese, and Russian émigrés, and nouveau riche gold miners seeking to mirror European splendor. To this melting pot, add the organic and sustainable agricultural movement; local growers' experimentation with artisan crops such as Japanese persimmons, kiwis, and habanero peppers, as well as heirloom varieties of fruits and vegetables; and the blossoming of boutique wineries, cheesemakers, and game farms. Put it all together with a skepticism of highfalutin New York ways and you have the makings of the culinary revolution that began in the 1970s. Creative chefs are drawn to the Bay Area because of the year-round availability of superior produce and the relative sophistication of native palates and tastes, along with their sense of humor and commitment to a casual, unfussy brand of elegance.

In a tightening economic climate of two-income families, it's a toss-up which is the greater luxury: the time to cook at home or the expense of eating out. Even in affluent Marin, expensive dinner houses are giving way to smaller, more personal neighborhood establishments with moderately priced menu options. There's a restaurant to satisfy any mood, budget, or taste, and, with a little research, all three at once. With so many excellent choices available, it's a shame to pay a pocketful for a less than wonderful meal.

There is an array of notable dining establishments in the Bay Area. Marin County, comprised of a long freeway corridor with boulevards spiraling off into shady suburban villages and miles of rolling ranchlands and seacoast to the west, proffers a banquet of epicure's choices. Just north of San Francisco, along the bayside crescent encircling Sausalito, Tiburon, and, a few miles inland, downtown Mill Valley, await restaurants spanning a spectrum from Swedish bakeries, cozy French bistros, chic Italian trattorii, lively Mexican cantinas, dim sum palaces, and, yes, all-American burger and seafood houses. Farther north, in suburban Ross Valley, San Rafael, and Novato, a similar selection flourishes. To the west, on the roads leading over Mount Tamalpais to the beach and on Highway 1 winding its way north to Point Reyes, oyster bars, wild west saloons, and a country inn or two beckon to travelers with promises of hearty sustenance.

In Marin County, as in San Francisco, you need not drive far to enjoy an excellent meal; however, doing so can provide an excursion through lovely countryside with glimpses of surprisingly rural areas near the city. And the county's splendid scenery provides a wide variety of options for al fresco dining, which has enjoyed a recent renaissance. Diners enjoy such settings as heated terraces cantilevered over the Bay, busy sidewalk cafes, protected courtyard gardens, and windswept mountain aeries. In this mecca for lovers of the great outdoors, only a handful of restaurants are so formal as to necessitate a change of clothes after a day at the beach or on the hiking trails; none requires jackets or ties for men.

In the East Bay, in Berkeley and Oakland, **Chez Panisse** and **Bay Wolf** represent the leading lights. The former California and the latter Mediterranean, they command the respect of the industry and the loyalty of their patrons, and both rode the crest of the wave that became the culinary revolution. Today, these two stars are surrounded by many other lights. People come from afar to make a pilgrimage to these places. And locally, the presence of the University of California with its thousands of academics, scientists, and artists has given these restaurants a unique patronage. The famous eateries must cater to some of the sharpest minds and most creative spirits in the world: professors, lecturers, researchers, and Nobel and Pulitzer Prize winners whose demands for excellence extend to all they see and do. Dining is no exception. With such an articulate population, any restaurant that isn't up to snuff will learn of it quickly and in no uncertain terms.

In the South Bay, "Silicon Valley" was, until recently, agricultural land known mainly for its pears and prunes. Now it's an intellectual ferment levened by immigration from Asia and Latin America. It's a young place with a population to match. Consequently, many eateries are also places to drink and dance or to repair after a day of bungee jumping or scuba diving. This area also offers great barbecue—many places are locally famous for their ribs. Being only 30 miles from Gilroy, the "garlic capital of the world," it's no wonder that spicy styles of cookery are especially popular here. Korean, Mexican, and Vietnamese places abound. The variety is such that you could drive across Santa Clara county along El Camino Real and find a representative of nearly every cuisine from Asia and south of the border.

NEW plACES

A restaurant must have some 18 months' seasoning to warrant inclusion in this book, so a number of interesting newcomers failed to get reviewed. The following may well be worth a visit.

◆ Marin

Barnaby's by the Bay
12938 Sir Francis Drake Boulevard
Inverness   (415) 669-1114
Steaks and seafood on Tomales Bay.

Cafe Linguini
9 Ross Common
Ross   (415) 925-9465
Intimate Italian in a charming setting.

Chalet Basque
405 North San Pedro Road
San Rafael   (415) 479-1070
Fifties-style continental cuisine; outdoor patio; full dinners are an especially good value.

Ever Rain
7089 Redwood Boulevard
Novato   (415) 892-6563
Taiwan-style Chinese.

Guernica
2009 Bridgeway
Sausalito   (415) 332-1512
Spanish and Basque specialties; flamenco guitar on weekends.

Hawaiian Chieftain
3020 Bridgeway
Sausalito   (415) 331-3214
1780s replica of a three-masted sailing schooner; lunch, brunch, sunset, and dinner sails.

Marin Brewing Company
1809 Larkspur Landing Circle
Larkspur (415) 461-4677
Microbrewery serving American food; outdoor patio; live music
on weekends.

Scoma's
588 Bridgeway
Sausalito (415) 332-9551
Classic seafood with a bay view.

Tutto Mare
9 Main Street
Tiburon (415) 435-4747
Italian seafood in a historic waterfront building.

◆ San Francisco

Bruno's
2389 Mission Street
San Francisco (415) 550-7455
Acres of red leather booths, reminiscent of Chasen's of Hollywood.
Italian/American cookery with occasional lounge music in the bar.

Gabbiano's
1 Ferry Plaza
San Francisco (415) 391-8403
Italian specialties on Pier 2 with dramatic views of the Bay Bridge and
Treasure Island.

Palomino
345 Spear
San Francisco (415) 512-7400
Euro-American menu as well as a smashing decor and location.

Scala's Bistro
432 Powell Street in Sir Francis Drake Hotel
San Francisco (415) 395-8555
Italian cuisine in luxurious surroundings; excellent service.

Sol Y Luna
475 Sacramento
San Francisco   (415) 296-8696, (415) 296-8191
Tapas, Spanish dishes, and South American cuisine; live music and flamenco dancing as well as late-night dancing.

Taiwan
445 Clement
San Francisco   (415) 387-1789
Great Chinese value in The Avenues.

♦ East Bay

Citron
5484 College Avenue
Oakland   (510) 653-5484
A bit of the continent in the gourmet ghetto.

Omnivore
3015 Shattuck Avenue
Berkeley   (510) 848-4346
Fresh California cuisine.

Piedmont House
3909 Grand Avenue
Oakland   (510) 420-1885
Eclectic American cooking in a beautiful old converted mansion.

Sujatha's Indian Restaurant and Sweets
48 Shattuck Square
Berkeley   (510) 549-1814
Indian food, music, and classical dance.

MORE RECOMMENDATIONS

◆ Bagels

Holey Bagel
308 Strawberry Village, Mill Valley   (415) 381-2600
Marin Bagel Company
1560 Fourth Street, San Rafael   (415) 457-8127
Noah's New York Bagels
Bon Air Center, Greenbrae   (415) 925-9971

◆ Beer Lists

Duke of Edinburgh
10801 North Wolf Road, Cupertino   (408) 446-3853
Mayflower Inne
1533 Fourth Street, San Rafael   (415) 456-1011
Pacific Tap and Grill
812 Fourth Street, San Rafael   (415) 457-9711
The Pelican Inn
10 Pacific Way, Muir Beach   (415) 383-6000
Tommy's Joynt
1101 Geary Street   (415) 775-4216

◆ Bread

Bucci's
6121 Hollis Street, Emeryville   (510) 547-4725
Fontina
1730 Shattuck Avenue, Berkeley   (510) 649-8090
Greens
Building A Fort Mason (Marina Boulevard and Buchannan),
    San Francisco   (415) 771-6222
Il Fornaio
223 Town Center, Corte Madera   (415) 927-4400
Il Fornaio Panetteria
1 Main Street, Tiburon   (415) 435-0777
Marin County Farmer's Market
Marin County Civic Center, San Rafael   (415) 456-3276

Oliveto
5655 College Avenue, Oakland   (510) 547-5356
Whole Foods
414 Miller Avenue, Mill Valley   (415) 381-1200

◆ Burgers

Bubba's
566 San Anselmo Avenue, San Anselmo   (415) 459-6862
The Golden Nugget
2200 Fourth Street, San Rafael   (415) 456-9066
Harpoon Louie's
55 Stevenson Street, San Francisco   (415) 543-3540
Kirk's
1330 Sunnyvale-Saratoga Road, Sunnyvale   (408) 446-2988
Pat O'Shea's Mad Hatter
3848 Geary Boulevard, San Francisco   (415) 752-3148
Perry's
1944 Union Street, San Francisco   (415) 922-9022
Rockridge Cafe
5492 College Avenue, Oakland   (510) 653-1567
Spanky's
1900 Sir Francis Drake Boulevard, Fairfax   (415) 455-9050

◆ Business

Adriana's
999 Anderson Drive, San Rafael   (415) 454-8000
Bizou
598 Fourth Street, San Francisco   (415) 543-2222
California Cafe
The Village Center, Corte Madera   (415) 924-2233
The Carnelian Room
555 California, San Francisco   (415) 433-7500
The Duck Club
100 El Camino Real, Menlo Park   (415) 322-1234
Joe LoCoco's
300 Drakes Landing Road, Greenbrae   (415) 925-0808
Ristorante Dalecio
340 Ignacio Boulevard, Novato   (415) 883-0960

Rue de Main
22622 Main Street, Hayward   (510) 537-0812
Tadich Grill
240 California, San Francisco   (415) 391-2373

◆ Coffee

Brasserie Tomo
745 Columbus Avenue, San Francisco   (415) 296-7668
The Dipsea Cafe
200 Shoreline Highway, Mill Valley   (415) 381-0298
Il Fornaio Panetteria
1 Main Street, Tiburon   (415) 435-0777
Jazzed
816 Fourth Street, San Rafael   (415) 455-8077

◆ Desserts

Campton Place
340 Stockton Street, San Francisco   (415) 781-5555
Masa's
648 Bush Street, San Francisco   (415) 989-7154
Piazza D'Angelo
22 Miller Avenue, Mill Valley   (415) 388-2216

◆ Dining and Dancing

Chez Luis
4170 El Camino Real, Palo Alto   (415) 493-9365
Harry Denton's
169 Steuart Street, San Francisco   (415) 882-1333
Horizons
558 Bridgeway, Sausalito   (415) 331-3232
Jose's Caribbean Restaurant
2275 El Camino Real, Palo Alto   (415) 326-6522
Miss Pearl's Jam House
601 Eddy Street, San Francisco   (415) 775-5267

◆ Entertaining Decor

The Duck Club
100 El Camino Real, Menlo Park   (415) 322-1234
Fleur de Lys
777 Sutter Street, San Francisco   (415) 673-7779
Hamburger Mary's
1582 Folsom Street, San Francisco   (415) 626-5767 or (415) 626-1985
John's Grill
63 Ellis Street, San Francisco   (415) 986-DASH
Menara Moroccan
41 East Gish Road, San Jose   (408) 453-1983
Mikayla at the Casa Madrona
801 Bridgeway, Sausalito   (415) 332-0502
PlumpJack Cafe
3127 Fillmore, San Francisco   (415) 563-4755
Red's Java House
Pier 30, San Francisco   No Phone
Smokey Joe's Cafe
1620 Shattuck Avenue, Berkeley   (510) 548-4616
St. James Infirmary
390 Moffet Boulevard, Mountain View   (415) 969-0806
The Stinking Rose
325 Columbus Avenue, San Francisco   (415) 781-7673
Tommy Toy's
655 Montgomery Street, San Francisco   (415) 379-4888

◆ Family Dining

Anthony's
1701 Powel Street, San Francisco   (415) 391-4488
Art and Larry's
1242 Fourth Street, San Rafael   (415) 457-3354
Avatar's
2656 Bridgeway, Sausalito   (415) 332-8083
The Basque Hotel/Restaurant
15 Romolo Place, San Francisco   (415) 788-9404
Bubba's
566 San Anselmo Avenue, San Anselmo   (415) 459-6862

Cacti
1200 Grant Avenue, Novato   (415) 898-2234
The Cantina
4239 Park Boulevard, Oakland   (510) 482-3663
Casa Aguila
1240 Noriega Street, San Francisco   (415) 661-5593
Chevy's
302 Bon Air Center, Greenbrae   (415) 461-3203
Chez Panisse Cafe
1617 Shattuck Avenue, Berkeley   (510) 548-5525
Chopsticks
508 Third Street, San Rafael   (415) 456-4942
David's Finest Produce & Taqueria
341 Corte Madera Town Center, Corte Madera   (415) 927-6572
The Dipsea Cafe
200 Shoreline Highway, Mill Valley   (415) 381-0298
Gertie's Chesapeake Bay Cafe
1919 Addison Street, Berkeley   (510) 841-2722
Greens
Building A Fort Mason (Marina Boulevard and Buchannan),
   San Francisco   (415) 771-6222
The Half Day Cafe
848 College Avenue, Kentfield   (415) 459-0291
Helmand
430 Broadway, San Francisco   (415) 362-0641
High Tech Burrito
118 Strawberry Village Shopping Center, Mill Valley
   (415) 388-7002
Hong Kong Flower Lounge
5322 Geary Boulevard, San Francisco   (415) 668-8998
Hunan Village
839 Kearny Street, San Francisco   (415) 956-7868
Il Fornaio Panetteria
1 Main Street, Tiburon   (415) 435-0777
Mayflower Inne
1533 Fourth Street, San Rafael   (415) 456-1011
Nakapan
1921 Martin Luther King Way, Berkeley   (510) 548-3050
Noah's New York Bagels
Bon Air Center, Greenbrae   (415) 925-9971

Olema Farm House
Highway 1, Olema   (415) 663-1264
Pacific Tap and Grill
812 Fourth Street, San Rafael   (415) 457-9711
The Station House
Main Street, Point Reyes Station   (415) 663-1515
Zza's
552 Grand Avenue, Oakland   (510) 839-9124

◆ Late Night Dining

Bistro Clovis
1596 Market Street, San Francisco   (415) 864-0231
The Brazen Head
3166 Buchanan at Greenwich, San Francisco   (415) 921-7600
Bucci's
6121 Hollis Street, Emeryville   (510) 547-4725
Cava 555
555 Second Street, San Francisco   (415) 543-2282
Fog City Diner
1300 Battery Street, San Francisco   (415) 982-2000
Frankie Johnnie & Luigi Too
939 West El Camino Real, Mountain View   (415) 967-5384
Hamburger Mary's
1582 Folsom Street, San Francisco
    (415) 626-5767 or (415) 626-1985
Jazzed
816 Fourth Street, San Rafael   (415) 455-8077
Left Bank Cafe
507 Magnolia, Larkspur   (415) 927-3331
Lefty O'Doul's
333 Geary Boulevard, San Francisco   (415) 982-8900
Marin Joe's
1585 Casa Buena Drive, Corte Madera   (415) 924-2081
Mexicali Rose
7th and Clay streets, Oakland   (510) 451-2450
Original Joe's
144 Taylor Street, San Francisco   (415) 775-4877
Perry's
1944 Union Street, San Francisco   (415) 922-9022

Piazza D'Angelo
22 Miller Avenue, Mill Valley   (415) 388-2216
Salute
706 Third Street, San Rafael   (415) 453-7596
Sam Woh
815 Washington Street, San Francisco   (415) 982-0596
Stars
150 Redwood Alley, San Francisco   (415) 861-7827
Yuet Lee
1300 Stockton Street, San Francisco   (415) 982-6020
Zuni Cafe and Grill
1658 Market Street, San Francisco   (415) 552-2522

◆ Lunch Buffets

Asia Palace
885 Fourth Street, San Rafael   (415) 457-9977
India Palace
707 Redwood Highway, Mill Valley   (415) 388-3350
India Village
555 Francisco Boulevard, San Rafael   (415) 456-2411
Villa Romana
901 B Street, San Rafael   (415) 457-7404

◆ Martinis

The Buckeye
17 Shoreline Highway, Mill Valley   (415) 331-2600
Compass Rose
315 Powel Street, St. Francis Hotel, San Francisco   (415) 774-0167
House of Prime Rib
1906 Van Ness, San Francisco   (415) 885-4605
No Name Bar
757 Bridgeway, Sausalito   (415) 332-1392
Stars
150 Redwood Alley, San Francisco   (415) 861-7827

◆ Oyster Bars

LuLu
816 Folsom Street, San Francisco   (415) 495-5775

PJ's Oyster Bed
737 Irving Street, San Francisco   (415) 566-7775
Swan Oyster Depot
1517 Polk Street, San Francisco   (415) 673-1101

◆ Pastry

Il Fornaio Panetteria
1 Main Street, Tiburon   (415) 435-0777
Pasticceria Rulli
464 Magnolia, Larkspur   (415) 924-7478
Sweden House Conditori
35 Main Street, Tiburon   (415) 435-9767

◆ Pizza

Baci Ristorante
247 Shoreline Highway, Mill Valley   (415) 381-2022
Benissimo Ristorante
18 Tamalpais Drive, Corte Madera   (415) 927-2316
Frankie Johnnie & Luigi Too
939 West El Camino Real, Mountain View   (415) 967-5384
LoCoco's Pizzeria
638 San Anselmo Avenue, San Anselmo   (415) 453-1238
31 Del Ganado Road, San Rafael   (415) 472-3236
Milano Pizza
1 Blackfield Drive, Tiburon   (415) 388-9100
Mulberry Street Pizza
101 Smith Ranch Road, San Rafael   (415) 472-7272
Ruby's
489 Third Street, San Francisco   (415) 541-0795
Salute
706 Third Street, San Rafael   (415) 453-7596

◆ Quiet and Romantic Dining

Alain Rondelli
126 Clement Street, San Francisco   (415) 387-0408
Baci Ristorante
247 Shoreline Highway, Mill Valley   (415) 381-2022

17

Baywolf
3853 Piedmont Avenue, Oakland   (510) 655-6004
Bistro Alsacienne
655 Redwood Highway, Mill Valley   (415) 389-0921
The Caprice
2000 Paradise Drive, Tiburon   (415) 435-3400
The Carnelian Room
555 California, San Francisco   (415) 433-7500
Christophe
1919 Bridgeway, Sausalito   (415) 332-9244
Comforts
337 San Anselmo Avenue, San Anselmo   (415) 454-6790
The Dining Room at the Ritz-Carlton
600 Stockton Street, San Francisco   (415) 296-7465
El Paseo
17 Throckmorton Avenue, Mill Valley   (415) 388-0741
The Ganges
775 Frederick Street, San Francisco   (415) 661-7290
Griffin's
23 Ross Common, Ross   (415) 925-9200
The Heights
3235 Sacramento Street, San Francisco   (415) 474-8890
Joe LoCoco's
300 Drakes Landing Road, Greenbrae   (415) 925-0808
Lark Creek Inn
234 Magnolia Avenue, Larkspur   (415) 924-7766
Manka's Inverness Lodge
Calendar Way at Argyle, Inverness   (415) 669-1034
Mikayla at the Casa Madrona
801 Bridgeway, Sausalito   (415) 332-0502
Ristorante Fabrizio
455 Magnolia Avenue, Larkspur   (415) 924-3332
Santa Fe Bar & Grill
1310 University Avenue, Berkeley   (510) 841-4740
Thep Lela
411 Strawberry Village, Mill Valley   (415) 383-3444
Ti Bacio
5912 College Avenue, Oakland   (510) 428-1703
Zarzuela
2000 Hyde Street, San Francisco   (415) 346-0800

◆ Rest Rooms

First and Last Chance Saloon
56 Jack London Square, Oakland   (510) 839-6761
Harry Denton's
169 Steuart Street, San Francisco   (415) 882-1333
Ristorante Dalecio
340 Ignacio Boulevard, Novato   (415) 883-0960

◆ Seafood

The Fish Market
3150 El Camino Real, Palo Alto   (415) 493-9188
Gate Five
305 Harbor Drive, Sausalito   (415) 331-5355
Rooney's
38 Main Street, Tiburon   (415) 435-1911
Sam's Anchor Cafe
27 Main Street, Tiburon   (415) 435-4527
Tadich Grill
240 California, San Francisco   (415) 391-2373

◆ Sunday Brunches

The Buckeye
17 Shoreline Highway, Mill Valley   (415) 331-2600
California Cafe
The Village Center, Corte Madera   (415) 924-2233
Lark Creek Inn
234 Magnolia Avenue, Larkspur   (415) 924-7766
Mikayla at the Casa Madrona
801 Bridgeway, Sausalito   (415) 332-0502
North Sea Village
300 Turney Street, Sausalito   (415) 331-3300
The Station House
Main Street, Point Reyes Station   (415) 663-1515

◆ Sushi Bars

Robata Grill
591 Redwood Highway, Mill Valley   (415) 381-8400

Samurai
2633 Bridgeway, Sausalito   (415) 332-8245
Yoshi's
6030 Claremont Avenue, Oakland   (510) 652-9200

◆ Tapas or Appetizers

The Avenue Grill
44 East Blithedale, Mill Valley   (415) 388-6003
The Buckeye
17 Shoreline Highway, Mill Valley   (415) 331-2600
Cha Cha Cha
1805 Haight Street, San Francisco   (415) 386-7670
Enrico's
504 Broadway, San Francisco   (415) 982-6223
Guaymas
5 Main Street, Tiburon   (415) 435-6300
Stoyanof's
1240 Ninth Avenue, San Francisco   (415) 664-3664
Zarzuela
2000 Hyde Street, San Francisco   (415) 346-0800

◆ Views

The Caprice
2000 Paradise Drive, Tiburon   (415) 435-3400
The Carnelian Room
555 California, San Francisco   (415) 433-7500
Chart House
8150 Cabrillo Highway, Montara Beach   (415) 728-7366
Guaymas
5 Main Street, Tiburon   (415) 435-6300
Joe LoCoco's
300 Drakes Landing Road, Greenbrae   (415) 925-0808
Kincaid's Bayhouse
1 Franklin Street, Jack London Square, Oakland   (510) 835-8600
Mikayla at the Casa Madrona
801 Bridgeway, Sausalito   (415) 332-0502
Moss Beach Distillery
Beach Way and Ocean Boulevard, Moss Beach   (415) 728-5595

The Mountain Home Inn
810 Panoramic Highway, Mill Valley   (415) 381-9000
Oakland Grill
3rd and Franklin streets, Oakland   (510) 835-1176
Sam's Anchor Cafe
27 Main Street, Tiburon   (415) 435-4527

◆ Wee Hours Service

Marin Joe's
1585 Casa Buena Drive, Corte Madera   (415) 924-2081
Max's Opera Cafe
601 Van Ness, San Francisco   (415) 771-7300
Yuet Lee
1300 Stockton Street, San Francisco   (415) 982-6020

◆ Wine Bars

Cava 555
555 Second Street, San Francisco   (415) 543-2282
El Paseo
17 Throckmorton Avenue, Mill Valley   (415) 388-0741
Enoteca Mastro
933 San Pablo Avenue, Albany   (510) 524-4822
Manka's Inverness Lodge
Calendar Way at Argyle, Inverness   (415) 669-1034
The Mountain Home Inn
810 Panoramic Highway, Mill Valley   (415) 381-9000
Rue de Main
22622 Main Street, Hayward   (510) 537-0812

UNDERSTANdiNG THE RATiNGS

We have developed detailed profiles for the best restaurants (in our opinion) in town. Each profile features an easily scanned heading which allows you, in just a second, to check out the restaurant's name, cuisine, star rating, cost, quality rating, and value rating.

Star Rating. The star rating is an overall rating that encompasses the entire dining experience, including style, service, and ambience in addition to the taste, presentation, and quality of the food. Five stars is the highest rating possible and connotes the best of everything. Four-star restaurants are exceptional and three-star restaurants are well above average. Two-star restaurants are good. One star is used to connote an average restaurant that demonstrates an unusual capability in some area of specialization, for example, an otherwise unmemorable place that has great barbecued chicken.

Cost. Below the star rating is an expense description that provides a comparative sense of how much a complete meal will cost. A complete meal for our purposes consists of an entree with vegetable or side dish, and choice of soup or salad. Appetizers, desserts, drinks, and tips are excluded.

Inexpensive	$14 and less per person
Moderate	$15–25 per person
Expensive	$26–40 per person
Very Expensive	Over $40 per person

Quality Rating. Below the cost rating appears a number and a letter. The number is a quality rating based on a scale of 0–100, with 100 being the highest (best) rating attainable. The quality rating is based expressly on the taste, freshness of ingredients, preparation, presentation, and creativity of food served. There is no consideration of price. If you are a person who wants the best food available, and cost is not an issue, you need look no further than the quality ratings.

Value Rating.   If, on the other hand, you are looking for both quality and value, then you should check the value rating, expressed in letters. The value ratings are defined as follows:

A   Exceptional value, a real bargain
B   Good value
C   Fair value, you get exactly what you pay for
D   Somewhat overpriced
F   Significantly overpriced

locating the restaurant

Just below the restaurant name is a designation for geographic zone. This zone description will give you a general idea of where the restaurant described is located. For ease of use, we divide San Francisco into 14 geographic zones.

Zone 1.	Chinatown
Zone 2.	Civic Center
Zone 3.	Union Square
Zone 4.	Financial District
Zone 5.	Marina
Zone 6.	North Beach
Zone 7.	SOMA/Mission
Zone 8.	Richmond/Avenues
Zone 9.	Waterfront Crescent
Zone 10.	Suburban Marin
Zone 11.	Yonder Marin
Zone 12.	Berkeley
Zone 13.	Oakland
Zone 14.	South Bay

If you are in Berkeley and intend to walk or take a cab to dinner, you may want to choose a restaurant from among those locted in Zone 12. If you have a car, you might include restaurants from contiguous zones in your consideration.

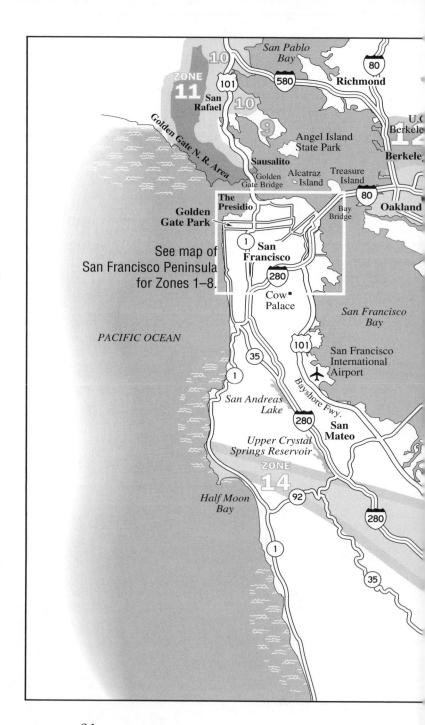

San Pablo Bay

ZONE 11

ZONE 10

ZONE 9

80

580

Richmond

U.C. Berkeley

101

San Rafael

Golden Gate N. R. Area

Angel Island State Park

Berkeley

ZONE 12

Sausalito

Golden Gate Bridge

Alcatraz Island

Treasure Island

80

Oakland

The Presidio

Golden Gate Park

Bay Bridge

See map of
San Francisco Peninsula
for Zones 1–8.

1

San Francisco

280

PACIFIC OCEAN

Cow Palace

San Francisco Bay

101

San Francisco International Airport

35

1

Bayshore Fwy.

San Andreas Lake

280

San Mateo

Upper Crystal Springs Reservoir

ZONE 14

Half Moon Bay

92

280

1

35

24

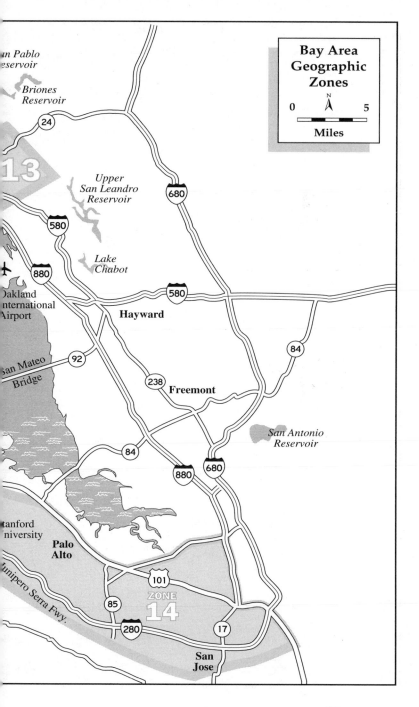

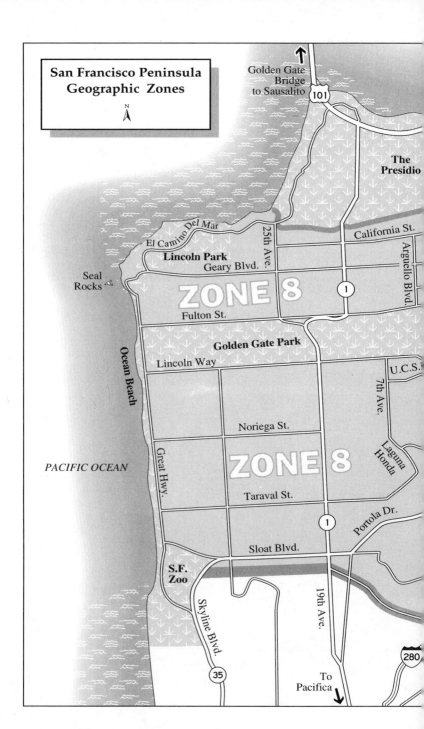

San Francisco Peninsula
Geographic Zones

N

Golden Gate
Bridge
to Sausalito 101

The Presidio

El Camino Del Mar

25th Ave.

California St.

Arguello Blvd.

Lincoln Park

Geary Blvd.

Seal Rocks

ZONE 8

1

Fulton St.

Golden Gate Park

Lincoln Way

U.C.S.F.

Ocean Beach

7th Ave.

Noriega St.

Laguna Honda

PACIFIC OCEAN

Great Hwy.

ZONE 8

Taraval St.

1

Portola Dr.

Sloat Blvd.

S.F. Zoo

19th Ave.

Skyline Blvd.

35

280

To Pacifica

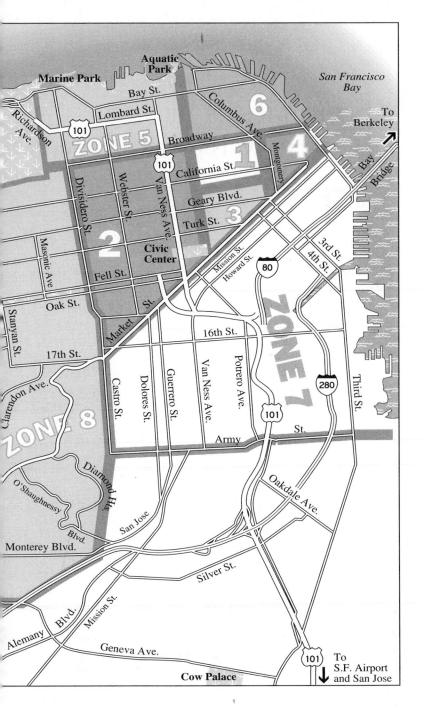

OUR pick of THE bEST SAN fRANCISCO RESTAURANTS

Because restaurants are opening and closing all the time in San Francisco, we have tried to confine our list to establishments—or chefs—with a proven track record over a fairly long period of time. Those newer or changed establishments that demonstrate staying power and consistency will be profiled in subsequent editions.

Also, the list is highly selective. Non-inclusion of a particular place does not necessarily indicate that the restaurant is not good, but only that it was not ranked among the best or most consistent in its genre. Detailed profiles of each restaurant follow in alphabetical order at the end of this chapter.

A NOTE AbOUT spELLiNG

Most diners who enjoy ethnic restaurants have noticed subtle variations in the spelling of certain dishes and preparations from one menu to the next. A noodle dish found on almost all Thai menus, for example, appears in one restaurant as *pad thai,* in another as *Phat Thai,* and in a third as *Phad Thai.*

This and similar inconsistencies arise from attempts to derive a phonetic English spelling from the name of a dish as pronounced in its country of origin. While one particular English spelling might be more frequently used than others, there is usually no definitive correct spelling for the names of many dishes. In this guide, we have elected to use the spelling most commonly found in authoritative ethnic cookbooks and other reference works.

We call this to your attention because the spelling we use in this guide could be different than that which you encounter on the menu in a certain restaurant. We might say, for instance, that the *tabbouleh* is good at the Pillars of Lebanon, while at the restaurant itself the dish is listed on the menu as *tabouli*.

Restaurants by Cuisine

Name	Star Rating	Price	Quality Rating	Value Rating	Zone
Afghani					
Helmand	★★★	Inexp	85	A	6
American					
Campton Place	★★★★★	Exp	99	C	3
Mikayla at the Casa Madrona	★★★★	Mod/Exp	92	B	9
House of Prime Rib	★★★½	Exp	89	B+	2
LuLu	★★★½	Mod	89	B+	7
Cava 555	★★★½	Mod	88	B	7
Griffin's	★★★½	Mod/Exp	86	C+	10
Gate Five	★★★½	Mod	85	C	9
Fog City Diner	★★★	Mod	89	B+	6
Tadich Grill	★★★	Mod	89	A	4
Izzy's Steak and Chop House	★★★	Mod	85	A	5
The Station House	★★★	Mod	85	B	11
The Half Day Cafe	★★★	Inexp	83	B	10
Whole Foods	★★½	Inexp	79	C+	10
Bubba's	★★½	Inexp	78	B	10
Ruth's Chris Steak House	★★½	Mod	78	B	2
Spoons	★★½	Inexp	78	B	14
The Courtyard	★★½	Mod	77	B	5
Garden City	★★½	Mod	77	C+	14
Olema Farm House	★★½	Mod	75	C+	11
First and Last Chance Saloon	★★	Mod	78	A	13
Original Joe's	★★	Inexp	78	B	3
Oakland Grill	★★	Inexp	77	A	13
Mama's Royal Cafe	★★	Inexp	75	B	13
Perry's	★★	Inexp	75	B+	5
Rockridge Cafe	★★	Inexp	75	B	13
Sam's Anchor Cafe	★★	Mod	75	C+	9
Tommy's Joynt	★★	Inexp	75	A	2
Hamburger Mary's	★½	Inexp	69	C	7
Jazzed	★½	Inexp	69	A	10
The Mountain Home Inn	★½	Mod	69	D	10
Waterfront Cafe	★½	Inexp	69	B	9
Kirk's	★½	Inexp	68	B	14
The Dipsea Cafe	★	Inexp	67	D	10

Name	Star Rating	Price	Quality Rating	Value Rating	Zone
Bakery Cafe					
Sweden House Conditori	★★★	Inexp	85	B	9
Bar					
Compass Rose	★★★★	Exp	99	B+	3
No Name Bar	★½	Inexp	69	C	9
Bar and Grill					
Harpoon Louie's	★★	Inexp	77	B	7
St. James Infirmary	★★	Inexp	77	A	14
Pat O'Shea's Mad Hatter	★★	Inexp	75	A	8
Barbecue					
The Cats	★★½	Mod	75	B	14
Henry's World Famous Hi-Life	★★	Inexp	77	A	14
Max's Opera Cafe	★½	Mod	79	B	2
Basque					
The Basque Hotel/Restaurant	★★	Inexp	77	B	6
Bookstore Cafe					
The Depot	★½	Inexp	69	C	10
British Pub					
The Pelican Inn	★★½	Mod	78	C+	11
Mayflower Inne	★½	Inexp	69	C	10
Burmese					
Nan Yang	★★★	Mod	85	A	13
Cafeteria					
Salmagundi	★★	Inexp	75	B	3
California					
Chez Panisse Restaurant	★★★★½	Exp	95	B	12
Moose's	★★★★	Mod	95	A-	6
Chez Panisse Cafe	★★★½	Exp	89	C	12
Cafe Majestic	★★★½	Exp	87	B+	2
The Duck Club	★★★½	Mod	85	B+	14
Square One	★★★	Mod	85	A	4

Name	Star Rating	Price	Quality Rating	Value Rating	Zone
California *(continued)*					
California Culinary Academy	★★½	Inexp	79	A	2
Horizons	★½	Mod	69	C	9
Cambodian					
Cambodiana's	★★★	Mod	89	A	12
Phnom Penh House	★★	Inexp	79	B+	13
Caribbean					
Miss Pearl's Jam House	★★★	Mod	85	B	2
Jose's Caribbean Restaurant	★★½	Inexp	78	C+	14
Chinese					
Tommy Toy's	★★★½	Mod	85	B+	4
China House Bistro	★★★½	Inexp/Mod	84	A	8
Chrysanthemum	★★★	Inexp	85	A	10
Hunan Village	★★★	Inexp	83	B+	1
Feng Nian	★★½	Inexp/Mod	79	B	9
Hong Kong Flower Lounge	★★½	Inexp	79	B	8
Jennie Low's	★★½	Inexp	79	C	10
Yuet Lee	★★½	Inexp/Mod	78	A	1
House of Bamboo	★★½	Mod	76	B	2
North Sea Village	★★½	Mod	75	C+	9
Yank Sing	★★	Inexp	76	B	4
Chopsticks	★½	Inexp	69	A	10
Sam Woh	★½	Inexp	69	B+	1
Continental					
Bizou	★★★½	Mod	89	B	7
Manka's Inverness Lodge	★★★½	Exp	89	D+	11
The Brazen Head	★★★	Mod	80	A	5
Crêperie					
Ti Couz	★★	Inexp	74	B	7
Czech					
Nadine's	★★½	Mod	79	C+	13
Vlasta's	★★½	Inexp	79	A	5

Restaurants by Cuisine (continued)

Name	Star Rating	Price	Quality Rating	Value Rating	Zone
Delicatessen					
Noah's New York Bagels	★★½	Inexp	79	B	10
Let's Eat	★★½	Inexp	77	C	9
Art and Larry's	★★	Inexp	75	C	10
Max's Opera Cafe	★½	Mod	79	B	2
Diner					
Smokey Joe's Cafe	★½	Inexp	65	B	12
Dive					
Red's Java House	★	Inexp/Cheap	65	A	4
Eclectic					
Stars	★★★★½	Exp	95	B	2
Marin County Farmer's Market	★★★	Inexp	85	A	10
Eulipia	★★½	Exp	77	D	14
Avatar's	★★	Inexp	79	B	9
Momi Toby's Revolution Cafe	★★	Inexp	78	C+	2
English					
Duke of Edinburgh	★★½	Mod	75	B	14
French					
Masa's	★★★★★	Exp	99	C	3
Alain Rondelli	★★★★★	Mod/Exp	98	A	8
The Heights	★★★★★	Exp	97	B+	8
Fleur de Lys	★★★★	Exp	95	B+	4
Fringale	★★★★	Mod	95	A	7
El Paseo	★★★★	Mod	92	B	10
Amelio's	★★★★	Exp	90	B+	6
Emile's	★★★½	Exp	89	B+	14
South Park Cafe	★★★½	Mod	87	A	7
Christophe	★★★½	Mod	85	A	9
Bistro M	★★★	Mod	89	B+	7
Brasserie Tomo	★★★	Mod	88	A	6
Bistro Alsacienne	★★★	Mod	85	C	10
Woodward's Gardens	★★★	Mod	83	B	7

Restaurants by Cuisine (continued)

Name	Star Rating	Price	Quality Rating	Value Rating	Zone
French (continued)					
Baker Street Bistro	★★½	Inexp / Mod	79	A	5
Le Trou	★★½	Mod	79	B	7
La Petite Auberge	★★½	Mod	78	C	10
Chez Luis	★★½	Mod	75	B	14
Bistro Clovis	★★	Mod	78	B	2
Rue de Main	★★	Mod	75	C	13
French Bistro					
Left Bank Cafe	★★★★	Mod	91	B	10
German					
Bistro Alsacienne	★★★	Mod	85	C	10
Speckman's	★★	Inexp	75	B	7
Greek					
Stoyanof's	★★★	Inexp / Mod	85	B	8
Hof Brau					
Lefty O'Doul's	★★	Inexp	75	B	3
Indian					
The Ganges	★★★	Inexp	80	A	8
India Palace	★★½	Mod	78	D	10
Indonesian					
The Rice Table	★★★	Mod	83	B	10
Iraqi / Mesopotamian					
YaYa Cuisine	★★★½	Mod	88	B	8
Italian					
Blue Fox	★★★★	Exp	90	B+	4
Joe LoCoco's	★★★½	Mod	89	B	10
Oliveto	★★★½	Mod	89	A–	13
Rossetti	★★★½	Mod	88	B	10
Piazza D'Angelo	★★★½	Mod	87	B	10
Ristorante Fabrizio	★★★½	Mod	87	B	10
Baci Ristorante	★★★½	Mod	85	B	10
Fior d' Italia	★★★½	Mod	85	A	6

Name	Star Rating	Price	Quality Rating	Value Rating	Zone
Ristorante Ecco	★★★½	Mod	85	C	7
Buca Giovanni	★★★	Mod	89	B	6
Italian Colors Ristorante	★★★	Mod	89	B+	13
Milano	★★★	Mod	89	B	13
Nicolino's Garden Cafe	★★★	Mod	89	B+	14
Zuni Cafe and Grill	★★★	Mod	89	B+	2
Enrico's	★★★	Mod	88	B	6
Splendido's	★★★	Mod	88	B+	4
Washington Square Bar and Grill	★★★	Mod	88	B+	6
Adriana's	★★★	Mod	85	B	10
Enoteca Mastro	★★★	Mod	85	A	12
Il Fornaio	★★★	Mod	85	B	10
La Fiammetta	★★★	Mod	85	A	2
Ti Bacio	★★★	Mod	85	B	13
Venezia Cafe & Ristorante	★★★	Mod	85	B	12
Rosmarino	★★★	Mod	84	B-	8
The Stinking Rose	★★★	Mod	80	B	6
Fontina	★★½	Inexp	79	C+	12
Frankie Johnnie & Luigi Too	★★½	Inexp	79	A	14
Ruby's	★★½	Inexp	79	C+	7
Aromi	★★½	Exp	78	B	2
Ristorante Dalecio	★★½	Mod	78	C	10
Salute	★★½	Mod	77	B	10
Marin Joe's	★★½	Inexp/Mod	70	C	10
Bucci's	★★	Inexp	79	B+	13
Zza's	★★	Inexp	75	B	13
Original Joe's	★½	Inexp	67	C-	14

Italian Bakery

Name	Star Rating	Price	Quality Rating	Value Rating	Zone
Pasticceria Rulli	★★★½	Inexp	89	A	10
Il Fornaio Panetteria	★★★	Inexp	85	A	9

Japanese

Name	Star Rating	Price	Quality Rating	Value Rating	Zone
Robata Grill	★★★½	Mod	85	C	10
Samurai	★★½	Mod	79	B	9
Yoshi's	★★½	Mod	78	B	13

Restaurants by Cuisine (continued)

Name	Star Rating	Price	Quality Rating	Value Rating	Zone
Korean					
Sorabol	★★½	Inexp	78	B	13
Latin American					
Cha Cha Cha	★★★½	Inexp/Mod	85	A	8
Cafe de la Paz	★★½	Mod	79	B	12
Mediterranean					
Baywolf	★★★★	Mod	90	A	13
Lalime's	★★★	Exp	89	B	12
PlumpJack Cafe	★★★	Mod	83	B	5
Mexican					
Guaymas	★★★½	Mod	85	C+	9
The Cantina	★★★	Inexp	80	B+	13
Casa Aguila	★★½	Mod	79	B	8
David's Finest Produce & Taqueria	★★½	Inexp	79	B	10
Chevy's	★★½	Inexp	78	A	10
Las Camelias	★★½	Inexp	77	B	10
High Tech Burrito	★★	Inexp	77	A	10
Mexicali Rose	★★	Inexp	75	B	13
Mongolian					
Colonel Lee's Mongolian Barbecue	★★	Inexp	75	B	14
Moroccan					
Menara Moroccan	★★½	Mod	77	B	14
New American					
The Dining Room at the Ritz-Carlton	★★★★★	Exp	97	B	3
The Buckeye	★★★★½	Mod	95	A	10
Lark Creek Inn	★★★★½	Exp	95	B	10
The Carnelian Room	★★★★	Exp	93	B	4
Sheraton Palace Garden Court	★★★★	Exp	92	C-	4
Harry Denton's	★★★★	Mod	90	A	7

Restaurants by Cuisine (continued)

Name	Star Rating	Price	Quality Rating	Value Rating	Zone
California Cafe	★★★½	Mod	89	B	10
The Caprice	★★★½	Mod	89	C	9
The Avenue Grill	★★★½	Mod	88	B	10
Comforts	★★★	Mod	84	C+	10
Town's End Restaurant and Bakery	★★★	Mod	84	B+	7
Clement Street Bar and Grill	★★	Mod	78	C+	8
Rooney's	★½	Mod	69	C+	9
Book Passage Cafe	★½	Inexp	68	B	10
Oyster Bar					
Swan Oyster Depot	★★	Inexp	78	A	2
Pan Asian					
Ginger Island	★★½	Mod	77	C+	12
Puerto Rican					
El Nuevo Fruitlandia	★★	Inexp	76	B+	7
Seafood					
Gertie's Chesapeake Bay Cafe	★★★	Mod	88	B+	12
PJ's Oyster Bed	★★★	Mod	87	B	8
Kincaid's Bayhouse	★★★	Mod	85	A	13
Chart House	★★★	Mod	80	B	14
Moss Beach Distillery	★★★	Mod	80	B+	14
Anthony's	★★½	Mod	78	B	6
The Fish Market	★★½	Mod	78	B	14
Baby Sal's	★★	Mod	78	C-	10
Southwestern					
Santa Fe Bar & Grill	★★★	Mod	88	A-	12
Cacti	★★	Mod	79	C-	10
Spanish					
Zarzuela	★★★½	Mod	83	A	5
Steak					
John's Grill	★★★	Mod	80	A	3

Name	Star Rating	Price	Quality Rating	Value Rating	Zone
Swiss					
Emile's	★★★½	Exp	89	B+	14
Thai					
Orchid	★★★½	Inexp	89	B	10
Thep Lela	★★★½	Inexp	88	B	10
Dusit	★★½	Inexp	79	B+	7
Royal Thai	★★½	Inexp	76	B	10
Nakapan	★★½	Inexp	75	B+	12
Bangkok Spoon	★★	Inexp	75	C+	14
Vegetarian					
Greens	★★★★	Mod	99	A	5
The Ganges	★★★	Inexp	80	A	8
Vietnamese					
Thanh Long	★★★	Inexp/Mod	86	B	8
Pho An Dao	★★	Inexp	77	B+	13
Hung Yen	★½	Inexp	69	B+	7
Tu Lan	★½	Inexp	69	A	7

Restaurants by Star Rating

Name	Cuisine	Price	Quality Rating	Value Rating	Zone
Five-Star Restaurants					
Campton Place	American	Exp	99	C	3
Masa's	French	Exp	99	C	3
Alain Rondelli	French	Mod/Exp	98	A	8
The Dining Room at the Ritz-Carlton	New American	Exp	97	B	3
The Heights	French	Exp	97	B+	8
Four-and-a-Half Star Restaurants					
The Buckeye	New American	Mod	95	A	10
Chez Panisse Restaurant	California	Exp	95	B	12
Lark Creek Inn	New American	Exp	95	B	10
Stars	Eclectic	Exp	95	B	2
Four-Star Restaurants					
Compass Rose	Bar	Exp	99	B+	3
Greens	Vegetarian	Mod	99	A	5
Fleur de Lys	French	Exp	95	B+	4
Fringale	French	Mod	95	A	7
Moose's	California	Mod	95	A-	6
The Carnelian Room	New American	Exp	93	B	4
El Paseo	French	Mod	92	B	10
Mikayla at the Casa Madrona	American	Mod/Exp	92	B	9
Sheraton Palace Garden Court	New American	Exp	92	C-	4
Left Bank Cafe	French Bistro	Mod	91	B	10
Amelio's	French	Exp	90	B+	6
Baywolf	Mediterranean	Mod	90	A	13
Blue Fox	Italian	Exp	90	B+	4
Harry Denton's	New American	Mod	90	A	7
Three-and-a-Half Star Restaurants					
Bizou	Continental	Mod	89	B	7
California Cafe	New American	Mod	89	B	10

Restaurants by Star Rating *(continued)*

Name	Cuisine	Price	Quality Rating	Value Rating	Zone
Three-and-a-Half Star Restaurants *(continued)*					
The Caprice	New American	Mod	89	C	9
Chez Panisse Cafe	California	Exp	89	C	12
Emile's	French/Swiss	Exp	89	B+	14
House of Prime Rib	American	Exp	89	B+	2
Joe LoCoco's	Italian	Mod	89	B	10
LuLu	American	Mod	89	B+	7
Manka's Inverness Lodge	Continental	Exp	89	D+	11
Oliveto	Italian	Mod	89	A–	13
Orchid	Thai	Inexp	89	B	10
Pasticceria Rulli	Italian Bakery	Inexp	89	A	10
The Avenue Grill	New American	Mod	88	B	10
Cava 555	American	Mod	88	B	7
Rossetti	Italian	Mod	88	B	10
Thep Lela	Thai	Inexp	88	B	10
YaYa Cuisine	Iraqi/ Mesopotamian	Mod	88	B	8
Cafe Majestic	California	Exp	87	B+	2
Piazza D'Angelo	Italian	Mod	87	B	10
Ristorante Fabrizio	Italian	Mod	87	B	10
South Park Cafe	French	Mod	87	A	7
Griffin's	American	Mod/Exp	86	C+	10
Baci Ristorante	Italian	Mod	85	B	10
Cha Cha Cha	Latin American	Inexp/Mod	85	A	8
Christophe	French	Mod	85	A	9
The Duck Club	California	Mod	85	B+	14
Fior d' Italia	Italian	Mod	85	A	6
Gate Five	American	Mod	85	C	9
Guaymas	Mexican	Mod	85	C+	9
Ristorante Ecco	Italian	Mod	85	C	7
Robata Grill	Japanese	Mod	85	C	10
Tommy Toy's	Chinese	Mod	85	B+	4
China House Bistro	Chinese	Inexp/Mod	84	A	8
Zarzuela	Spanish	Mod	83	A	5

Name	Cuisine	Price	Quality Rating	Value Rating	Zone
Three-Star Restaurants					
Bistro M	French	Mod	89	B+	7
Buca Giovanni	Italian	Mod	89	B	6
Cambodiana's	Cambodian	Mod	89	A	12
Fog City Diner	American	Mod	89	B+	6
Italian Colors Ristorante	Italian	Mod	89	B+	13
Lalime's	Mediterranean	Exp	89	B	12
Milano	Italian	Mod	89	B	13
Nicolino's Garden Cafe	Italian	Mod	89	B+	14
Tadich Grill	American	Mod	89	A	4
Zuni Cafe and Grill	Italian	Mod	89	B+	2
Brasserie Tomo	French	Mod	88	A	6
Enrico's	Italian	Mod	88	B	6
Gertie's Chesapeake Bay Cafe	Seafood	Mod	88	B+	12
Santa Fe Bar & Grill	Southwestern	Mod	88	A–	12
Splendido's	Italian	Mod	88	B+	4
Washington Square Bar and Grill	Italian	Mod	88	B+	6
PJ's Oyster Bed	Seafood	Mod	87	B	8
Thanh Long	Vietnamese	Inexp/Mod	86	B	8
Adriana's	Italian	Mod	85	B	10
Bistro Alsacienne	French/German	Mod	85	C	10
Chrysanthemum	Chinese	Inexp	85	A	10
Enoteca Mastro	Italian	Mod	85	A	12
Helmand	Afghani	Inexp	85	A	6
Il Fornaio	Italian	Mod	85	B	10
Il Fornaio Panetteria	Italian Bakery	Inexp	85	A	9
Izzy's Steak and Chop House	American	Mod	85	A	5
Kincaid's Bayhouse	Seafood	Mod	85	A	13
La Fiammetta	Italian	Mod	85	A	2
Marin County Farmer's Market	Eclectic	Inexp	85	A	10

Name	Cuisine	Price	Quality Rating	Value Rating	Zone
Three-Star Restaurants *(continued)*					
Miss Pearl's Jam House	Caribbean	Mod	85	B	2
Nan Yang	Burmese	Mod	85	A	13
Square One	California	Mod	85	A	4
The Station House	American	Mod	85	B	11
Stoyanof's	Greek	Inexp/Mod	85	B	8
Sweden House Conditori	Bakery Cafe	Inexp	85	B	9
Ti Bacio	Italian	Mod	85	B	13
Venezia Cafe & Ristorante	Italian	Mod	85	B	12
Comforts	New American	Mod	84	C+	10
Rosmarino	Italian	Mod	84	B-	8
Town's End Restaurant and Bakery	New American	Mod	84	B+	7
The Half Day Cafe	American	Inexp	83	B	10
Hunan Village	Chinese	Inexp	83	B+	1
PlumpJack Cafe	Mediterranean	Mod	83	B	5
The Rice Table	Indonesian	Mod	83	B	10
Woodward's Gardens	French	Mod	83	B	7
The Brazen Head	Continental	Mod	80	A	5
The Cantina	Mexican	Inexp	80	B+	13
Chart House	Seafood	Mod	80	B	14
The Ganges	Vegetarian Indian	Inexp	80	A	8
John's Grill	Steak	Mod	80	A	3
Moss Beach Distillery	Seafood	Mod	80	B+	14
The Stinking Rose	Italian	Mod	80	B	6
Two-and-a-Half Star Restaurants					
Baker Street Bistro	French	Inexp/Mod	79	A	5
Cafe de la Paz	Latin American	Mod	79	B	12
California Culinary Academy	California	Inexp	79	A	2
Casa Aguila	Mexican	Mod	79	B	8
David's Finest Produce & Taqueria	Mexican	Inexp	79	B	10

Name	Cuisine	Price	Quality Rating	Value Rating	Zone
Dusit	Thai	Inexp	79	B+	7
Feng Nian	Chinese	Inexp/Mod	79	B	9
Fontina	Italian	Inexp	79	C+	12
Frankie Johnnie & Luigi Too	Italian	Inexp	79	A	14
Hong Kong Flower Lounge	Chinese	Inexp	79	B	8
Jennie Low's	Chinese	Inexp	79	C	10
Le Trou	French	Mod	79	B	7
Nadine's	Czech	Mod	79	C+	13
Noah's New York Bagels	Delicatessen	Inexp	79	B	10
Ruby's	Italian	Inexp	79	C+	7
Samurai	Japanese	Mod	79	B	9
Vlasta's	Czech	Inexp	79	A	5
Whole Foods	American	Inexp	79	C+	10
Anthony's	Seafood	Mod	78	B	6
Aromi	Italian	Exp	78	B	2
Bubba's	American	Inexp	78	B	10
Chevy's	Mexican	Inexp	78	A	10
The Fish Market	Seafood	Mod	78	B	14
India Palace	Indian	Mod	78	D	10
Jose's Caribbean Restaurant	Caribbean	Inexp	78	C+	14
La Petite Auberge	French	Mod	78	C	10
The Pelican Inn	British Pub	Mod	78	C+	11
Ristorante Dalecio	Italian	Mod	78	C	10
Ruth's Chris Steak House	American	Mod	78	B	2
Sorabol	Korean	Inexp	78	B	13
Spoons	American	Inexp	78	B	14
Yoshi's	Japanese	Mod	78	B	13
Yuet Lee	Chinese	Inexp/Mod	78	A	1
The Courtyard	American	Mod	77	B	5
Eulipia	Eclectic	Exp	77	D	14
Garden City	American	Mod	77	C+	14

Name	Cuisine	Price	Quality Rating	Value Rating	Zone
Two-and-a-Half Star Restaurants *(continued)*					
Ginger Island	Pan Asian	Mod	77	C+	12
Las Camelias	Mexican	Inexp	77	B	10
Let's Eat	Delicatessen	Inexp	77	C	9
Menara Moroccan	Moroccan	Mod	77	B	14
Salute	Italian	Mod	77	B	10
House of Bamboo	Chinese	Mod	76	B	2
Royal Thai	Thai	Inexp	76	B	10
The Cats	Barbecue	Mod	75	B	14
Chez Luis	French	Mod	75	B	14
Duke of Edinburgh	English	Mod	75	B	14
Nakapan	Thai	Inexp	75	B+	12
North Sea Village	Chinese	Mod	75	C+	9
Olema Farm House	American	Mod	75	C+	11
Marin Joe's	Italian	Inexp/Mod	70	C	10
Two-Star Restaurants					
Avatar's	Eclectic	Inexp	79	B	9
Bucci's	Italian	Inexp	79	B+	13
Cacti	Southwestern	Mod	79	C-	10
Phnom Penh House	Cambodian	Inexp	79	B+	13
Baby Sal's	Seafood	Mod	78	C-	10
Bistro Clovis	French	Mod	78	B	2
Clement Street Bar and Grill	New American	Mod	78	C+	8
First and Last Chance Saloon	American	Mod	78	A	13
Momi Toby's Revolution Cafe	Eclectic	Inexp	78	C+	2
Original Joe's	American	Inexp	78	B	3
Swan Oyster Depot	Oyster Bar	Inexp	78	A	2
The Basque Hotel/ Restaurant	Basque	Inexp	77	B	6
Harpoon Louie's	Bar and Grill	Inexp	77	B	7
Henry's World Famous Hi-Life	Barbecue	Inexp	77	A	14

Name	Cuisine	Price	Quality Rating	Value Rating	Zone
High Tech Burrito	Mexican	Inexp	77	A	10
Oakland Grill	American	Inexp	77	A	13
Pho An Dao	Vietnamese	Inexp	77	B+	13
St. James Infirmary	Bar and Grill	Inexp	77	A	14
El Nuevo Fruitlandia	Puerto Rican	Inexp	76	B+	7
Yank Sing	Chinese	Inexp	76	B	4
Art and Larry's	Delicatessen	Inexp	75	C	10
Bangkok Spoon	Thai	Inexp	75	C+	14
Colonel Lee's Mongolian Barbecue	Mongolian	Inexp	75	B	14
Lefty O'Doul's	Hof Brau	Inexp	75	B	3
Mama's Royal Cafe	American	Inexp	75	B	13
Mexicali Rose	Mexican	Inexp	75	B	13
Pat O'Shea's Mad Hatter	Bar and Grill	Inexp	75	A	8
Perry's	American	Inexp	75	B+	5
Rockridge Cafe	American	Inexp	75	B	13
Rue de Main	French	Mod	75	C	13
Salmagundi	Cafeteria	Inexp	75	B	3
Sam's Anchor Cafe	American	Mod	75	C+	9
Speckman's	German	Inexp	75	B	7
Tommy's Joynt	American	Inexp	75	A	2
Zza's	Italian	Inexp	75	B	13
Ti Couz	Crêperie	Inexp	74	B	7

One-and-a-Half Star Restaurants

Name	Cuisine	Price	Quality Rating	Value Rating	Zone
Max's Opera Cafe	Deli/Barbecue	Mod	79	B	2
Chopsticks	Chinese	Inexp	69	A	10
The Depot	Bookstore cafe	Inexp	69	C	10
Hamburger Mary's	American	Inexp	69	C	7
Horizons	California	Mod	69	C	9
Hung Yen	Vietnamese	Inexp	69	B+	7
Jazzed	American	Inexp	69	A	10
Mayflower Inne	British Pub	Inexp	69	C	10
The Mountain Home Inn	American	Mod	69	D	10

Name	Cuisine	Price	Quality Rating	Value Rating	Zone
One-and-a-Half Star Restaurants *(continued)*					
No Name Bar	Bar	Inexp	69	C	9
Rooney's	New American	Mod	69	C+	9
Sam Woh	Chinese	Inexp	69	B+	1
Tu Lan	Vietnamese	Inexp	69	A	7
Waterfront Cafe	American	Inexp	69	B	9
Book Passage Cafe	New American	Inexp	68	B	10
Kirk's	American	Inexp	68	B	14
Original Joe's	Italian	Inexp	67	C-	14
Smokey Joe's Cafe	Diner	Inexp	65	B	12
One-Star Restaurants					
The Dipsea Cafe	American	Inexp	67	D	10
Red's Java House	Dive	Inexp/Cheap	65	A	4

Restaurants by Zone

Name	Star Rating	Price	Quality Rating	Value Rating
Zone 1—China Town				
◆ *Chinese*				
Hunan Village	★★★	Inexp	83	B+
Yuet Lee	★★½	Inexp/Mod	78	A
Sam Woh	★½	Inexp	69	B+
Zone 2—Civic Center				
◆ *American*				
House of Prime Rib	★★★½	Exp	89	B+
Ruth's Chris Steak House	★★½	Mod	78	B
Tommy's Joynt	★★	Inexp	75	A
◆ *California*				
Cafe Majestic	★★★½	Exp	87	B+
California Culinary Academy	★★½	Inexp	79	A
◆ *Caribbean*				
Miss Pearl's Jam House	★★★	Mod	85	B
◆ *Chinese*				
House of Bamboo	★★½	Mod	76	B
◆ *Deli/Barbecue*				
Max's Opera Cafe	★½	Mod	79	B
◆ *Eclectic*				
Stars	★★★★½	Exp	95	B
Momi Toby's Revolution Cafe	★★	Inexp	78	C+
◆ *French*				
Bistro Clovis	★★	Mod	78	B
◆ *Italian*				
Zuni Cafe and Grill	★★★	Mod	89	B+
La Fiammetta	★★★	Mod	85	A
Aromi	★★½	Exp	78	B
◆ *Oyster Bar*				
Swan Oyster Depot	★★	Inexp	78	A

Name	Star Rating	Price	Quality Rating	Value Rating
Zone 3—Union Square				
◆ *American*				
Campton Place	★★★★★	Exp	99	C
Original Joe's	★★	Inexp	78	B
◆ *Bar*				
Compass Rose	★★★★	Exp	99	B+
◆ *Cafeteria*				
Salmagundi	★★	Inexp	75	B
◆ *French*				
Masa's	★★★★★	Exp	99	C
◆ *Hof Brau*				
Lefty O'Doul's	★★	Inexp	75	B
◆ *New American*				
The Dining Room at the Ritz-Carlton	★★★★★	Exp	97	B
◆ *Steak*				
John's Grill	★★★	Mod	80	A
Zone 4—Financial District				
◆ *American*				
Tadich Grill	★★★	Mod	89	A
◆ *California*				
Square One	★★★	Mod	85	A
◆ *Chinese*				
Tommy Toy's	★★★½	Mod	85	B+
Yank Sing	★★	Inexp	76	B
◆ *Dive*				
Red's Java House	★	Inexp/Cheap	65	A
◆ *French*				
Fleur de Lys	★★★★	Exp	95	B+

Restaurants by Zone (continued)

Name	Star Rating	Price	Quality Rating	Value Rating
◆ Italian				
Blue Fox	★★★★	Exp	90	B+
Splendido's	★★★	Mod	88	B+
◆ New American				
The Carnelian Room	★★★★	Exp	93	B
Sheraton Palace Garden Court	★★★★	Exp	92	C-
Zone 5—Marina				
◆ American				
Izzy's Steak and Chop House	★★★	Mod	85	A
The Courtyard	★★½	Mod	77	B
Perry's	★★	Inexp	75	B+
◆ Continental				
The Brazen Head	★★★	Mod	80	A
◆ Czech				
Vlasta's	★★½	Inexp	79	A
◆ French				
Baker Street Bistro	★★½	Inexp/Mod	79	A
◆ Mediterranean				
PlumpJack Cafe	★★★	Mod	83	B
◆ Spanish				
Zarzuela	★★★½	Mod	83	A
◆ Vegetarian				
Greens	★★★★	Mod	99	A
Zone 6—North Beach				
◆ Afghani				
Helmand	★★★	Inexp	85	A
◆ American				
Fog City Diner	★★★	Mod	89	B+
◆ Basque				
The Basque Hotel/Restaurant	★★	Inexp	77	B

Name	Star Rating	Price	Quality Rating	Value Rating
◆ *California*				
Moose's	★★★★	Mod	95	A–
◆ *French*				
Amelio's	★★★★	Exp	90	B+
Brasserie Tomo	★★★	Mod	88	A
◆ *Italian*				
Fior d' Italia	★★★½	Mod	85	A
Buca Giovanni	★★★	Mod	89	B
Enrico's	★★★	Mod	88	B
Washington Square Bar and Grill	★★★	Mod	88	B+
The Stinking Rose	★★★	Mod	80	B
◆ *Seafood*				
Anthony's	★★½	Mod	78	B
Zone 7—SOMA/Mission				
◆ *American*				
LuLu	★★★½	Mod	89	B+
Cava 555	★★★½	Mod	88	B
Hamburger Mary's	★½	Inexp	69	C
◆ *Bar and Grill*				
Harpoon Louie's	★★	Inexp	77	B
◆ *Continental*				
Bizou	★★★½	Mod	89	B
◆ *Crêperie*				
Ti Couz	★★	Inexp	74	B
◆ *French*				
Fringale	★★★★	Mod	95	A
South Park Cafe	★★★½	Mod	87	A
Bistro M	★★★	Mod	89	B+
Woodward's Gardens	★★★	Mod	83	B
Le Trou	★★½	Mod	79	B

Restaurants by Zone (continued)

Name	Star Rating	Price	Quality Rating	Value Rating
◆ *German*				
Speckman's	★★	Inexp	75	B
◆ *Italian*				
Ristorante Ecco	★★★½	Mod	85	C
Ruby's	★★½	Inexp	79	C+
◆ *New American*				
Harry Denton's	★★★★	Mod	90	A
Town's End Restaurant and Bakery	★★★	Mod	84	B+
◆ *Puerto Rican*				
El Nuevo Fruitlandia	★★	Inexp	76	B+
◆ *Thai*				
Dusit	★★½	Inexp	79	B+
◆ *Vietnamese*				
Hung Yen	★½	Inexp	69	B+
Tu Lan	★½	Inexp	69	A
Zone 8—Richmond/Avenues				
◆ *Bar and Grill*				
Pat O'Shea's Mad Hatter	★★	Inexp	75	A
◆ *Chinese*				
China House Bistro	★★★½	Inexp/Mod	84	A
Hong Kong Flower Lounge	★★½	Inexp	79	B
◆ *French*				
Alain Rondelli	★★★★★	Mod/Exp	98	A
The Heights	★★★★★	Exp	97	B+
◆ *Greek*				
Stoyanof's	★★★	Inexp/Mod	85	B
◆ *Iraqi/Mesopotamian*				
YaYa Cuisine	★★★½	Mod	88	B

Name	Star Rating	Price	Quality Rating	Value Rating
◆ *Italian*				
Rosmarino	★★★	Mod	84	B–
◆ *Latin American*				
Cha Cha Cha	★★★½	Inexp/Mod	85	A
◆ *Mexican*				
Casa Aguila	★★½	Mod	79	B
◆ *New American*				
Clement Street Bar and Grill	★★	Mod	78	C+
◆ *Seafood*				
PJ's Oyster Bed	★★★	Mod	87	B
◆ *Vegetarian Indian*				
The Ganges	★★★	Inexp	80	A
◆ *Vietnamese*				
Thanh Long	★★★	Inexp/Mod	86	B
Zone 9—Waterfront Crescent				
◆ *American*				
Mikayla at the Casa Madrona	★★★★	Mod/Exp	92	B
Gate Five	★★★½	Mod	85	C
Sam's Anchor Cafe	★★	Mod	75	C+
Waterfront Cafe	★½	Inexp	69	B
◆ *Bakery Cafe*				
Sweden House Conditori	★★★	Inexp	85	B
◆ *Bar*				
No Name Bar	★½	Inexp	69	C
◆ *California*				
Horizons	★½	Mod	69	C
◆ *Chinese*				
Feng Nian	★★½	Inexp/Mod	79	B
North Sea Village	★★½	Mod	75	C+

Name	Star Rating	Price	Quality Rating	Value Rating
◆ Delicatessen				
Let's Eat	★★½	Inexp	77	C
◆ Eclectic				
Avatar's	★★	Inexp	79	B
◆ French				
Christophe	★★★½	Mod	85	A
◆ Italian Bakery				
Il Fornaio Panetteria	★★★	Inexp	85	A
◆ Japanese				
Samurai	★★½	Mod	79	B
◆ Mexican				
Guaymas	★★★½	Mod	85	C+
◆ New American				
The Caprice	★★★½	Mod	89	C
Rooney's	★½	Mod	69	C+
Zone 10—Suburban Marin				
◆ American				
Griffin's	★★★½	Mod/Exp	86	C+
The Half Day Cafe	★★★	Inexp	83	B
Whole Foods	★★½	Inexp	79	C+
Bubba's	★★½	Inexp	78	B
Jazzed	★½	Inexp	69	A
The Mountain Home Inn	★½	Mod	69	D
The Dipsea Cafe	★	Inexp	67	D
◆ Bookstore Cafe				
The Depot	★½	Inexp	69	C
◆ British Pub				
Mayflower Inne	★½	Inexp	69	C
◆ Chinese				
Chrysanthemum	★★★	Inexp	85	A

Restaurants by Zone (continued)

Name	Star Rating	Price	Quality Rating	Value Rating
◆ Chinese (continued)				
Jennie Low's	★★½	Inexp	79	C
Chopsticks	★½	Inexp	69	A
◆ Delicatessen				
Noah's New York Bagels	★★½	Inexp	79	B
Art and Larry's	★★	Inexp	75	C
◆ Eclectic				
Marin County Farmer's Market	★★★	Inexp	85	A
◆ French				
El Paseo	★★★★	Mod	92	B
La Petite Auberge	★★½	Mod	78	C
◆ French Bistro				
Left Bank Cafe	★★★★	Mod	91	B
◆ French / German				
Bistro Alsacienne	★★★	Mod	85	C
◆ Indian				
India Palace	★★½	Mod	78	D
◆ Indonesian				
The Rice Table	★★★	Mod	83	B
◆ Italian				
Joe LoCoco's	★★★½	Mod	89	B
Rossetti	★★★½	Mod	88	B
Piazza D'Angelo	★★★½	Mod	87	B
Ristorante Fabrizio	★★★½	Mod	87	B
Baci Ristorante	★★★½	Mod	85	B
Adriana's	★★★	Mod	85	B
Il Fornaio	★★★	Mod	85	B
Ristorante Dalecio	★★½	Mod	78	C
Salute	★★½	Mod	77	B
Marin Joe's	★★½	Inexp/Mod	70	C

Name	Star Rating	Price	Quality Rating	Value Rating
◆ *Italian Bakery*				
Pasticceria Rulli	★★★½	Inexp	89	A
◆ *Japanese*				
Robata Grill	★★★½	Mod	85	C
◆ *Mexican*				
David's Finest Produce & Taqueria	★★½	Inexp	79	B
Chevy's	★★½	Inexp	78	A
Las Camelias	★★½	Inexp	77	B
High Tech Burrito	★★	Inexp	77	A
◆ *New American*				
The Buckeye	★★★★½	Mod	95	A
Lark Creek Inn	★★★★½	Exp	95	B
California Cafe	★★★½	Mod	89	B
The Avenue Grill	★★★½	Mod	88	B
Comforts	★★★	Mod	84	C+
Book Passage Cafe	★½	Inexp	68	B
◆ *Seafood*				
Baby Sal's	★★	Mod	78	C−
◆ *Southwestern*				
Cacti	★★	Mod	79	C−
◆ *Thai*				
Orchid	★★★½	Inexp	89	B
Thep Lela	★★★½	Inexp	88	B
Royal Thai	★★½	Inexp	76	B
Zone 11—Yonder Marin				
◆ *American*				
The Station House	★★★	Mod	85	B
Olema Farm House	★★½	Mod	75	C+
◆ *British Pub*				
The Pelican Inn	★★½	Mod	78	C+

Name	Star Rating	Price	Quality Rating	Value Rating
◆ *Continental*				
Manka's Inverness Lodge	★★★½	Exp	89	D+
Zone 12—Berkeley				
◆ *California*				
Chez Panisse Restaurant	★★★★½	Exp	95	B
Chez Panisse Cafe	★★★½	Exp	89	C
◆ *Cambodian*				
Cambodiana's	★★★	Mod	89	A
◆ *Diner*				
Smokey Joe's Cafe	★½	Inexp	65	B
◆ *Italian*				
Enoteca Mastro	★★★	Mod	85	A
Venezia Cafe & Ristorante	★★★	Mod	85	B
Fontina	★★½	Inexp	79	C+
◆ *Latin American*				
Cafe de la Paz	★★½	Mod	79	B
◆ *Mediterranean*				
Lalime's	★★★	Exp	89	B
◆ *Pan Asian*				
Ginger Island	★★½	Mod	77	C+
◆ *Seafood*				
Gertie's Chesapeake Bay Cafe	★★★	Mod	88	B+
◆ *Southwestern*				
Santa Fe Bar & Grill	★★★	Mod	88	A-
◆ *Thai*				
Nakapan	★★½	Inexp	75	B+
Zone 13—Oakland				
◆ *American*				
First and Last Chance Saloon	★★	Mod	78	A
Oakland Grill	★★	Inexp	77	A

Restaurants by Zone (continued)

Name	Star Rating	Price	Quality Rating	Value Rating
Mama's Royal Cafe	★★	Inexp	75	B
Rockridge Cafe	★★	Inexp	75	B
◆ *Burmese*				
Nan Yang	★★★	Mod	85	A
◆ *Cambodian*				
Phnom Penh House	★★	Inexp	79	B+
◆ *Czech*				
Nadine's	★★½	Mod	79	C+
◆ *French*				
Rue de Main	★★	Mod	75	C
◆ *Italian*				
Oliveto	★★★½	Mod	89	A–
Italian Colors Ristorante	★★★	Mod	89	B+
Milano	★★★	Mod	89	B
Ti Bacio	★★★	Mod	85	B
Bucci's	★★	Inexp	79	B+
Zza's	★★	Inexp	75	B
◆ *Japanese*				
Yoshi's	★★½	Mod	78	B
◆ *Korean*				
Sorabol	★★½	Inexp	78	B
◆ *Mediterranean*				
Baywolf	★★★★	Mod	90	A
◆ *Mexican*				
The Cantina	★★★	Inexp	80	B+
Mexicali Rose	★★	Inexp	75	B
◆ *Seafood*				
Kincaid's Bayhouse	★★★	Mod	85	A
◆ *Vietnamese*				
Pho An Dao	★★	Inexp	77	B+

Restaurants by Zone (continued)

Name	Star Rating	Price	Quality Rating	Value Rating
Zone 14—South Bay				
◆ *American*				
Spoons	★★½	Inexp	78	B
Garden City	★★½	Mod	77	C+
Kirk's	★½	Inexp	68	B
◆ *Bar and Grill*				
St. James Infirmary	★★	Inexp	77	A
◆ *Barbecue*				
The Cats	★★½	Mod	75	B
Henry's World Famous Hi-Life	★★	Inexp	77	A
◆ *California*				
The Duck Club	★★★½	Mod	85	B+
◆ *Caribbean*				
Jose's Caribbean Restaurant	★★½	Inexp	78	C+
◆ *Eclectic*				
Eulipia	★★½	Exp	77	D
◆ *English*				
Duke of Edinburgh	★★½	Mod	75	B
◆ *French*				
Chez Luis	★★½	Mod	75	B
◆ *French / Swiss*				
Emile's	★★★½	Exp	89	B+
◆ *Italian*				
Nicolino's Garden Cafe	★★★	Mod	89	B+
Frankie Johnnie & Luigi Too	★★½	Inexp	79	A
Original Joe's	★½	Inexp	67	C-
◆ *Mongolian*				
Colonel Lee's Mongolian Barbecue	★★	Inexp	75	B

Restaurants by Zone (continued)

Name	Star Rating	Price	Quality Rating	Value Rating
◆ *Moroccan*				
Menara Moroccan	★★½	Mod	77	B
◆ *Seafood*				
Chart House	★★★	Mod	88	B
Moss Beach Distillery	★★★	Mod	80	B+
The Fish Market	★★½	Mod	78	B
◆ *Thai*				
Bangkok Spoon	★★	Inexp	75	C+

RESTAURANT profiles

Adriana's

	Italian
Zone 10 Suburban Marin	★★★
999 Anderson Drive, San Rafael	Moderate
(415) 454-8000	
	Quality 85 Value B

Reservations:	Recommended for weekend dinner
When to go:	Any time
Entree range:	$10.50–14.95
Payment:	AMEX, MC, VISA
Service rating:	★★★
Friendliness rating:	★★★
Parking:	Free lot
Bar:	Beer, wine
Wine selection:	Good
Dress:	Informal
Disabled access:	Good
Customers:	Local, business
Lunch:	Monday–Friday, 11:30 A.M.–2:30 P.M.
Dinner:	Monday–Saturday, 5–10 P.M.

Atmosphere / setting: The curious location in an industrial area of San Rafael would seem a handicap, but it has not deterred the success of Adriana Giramonte's ten-year-old establishment. Appointed in restrained high-tech style, with a stainless steel grid ceiling and an open kitchen with luxuriant gusts of garlic billowing through the entrance, Adriana's has an urban, businesslike flavor quite different from the current vogue for vine-covered Tuscan villas with stucco walls and tile floors.

House specialties: Steamed clams or mussels marinara; prosciutto with sliced pears and cheese; fettucini alla carbonara; chicken livers sautéed with mushrooms and white wine; veal with prosciutto and sage; scampi with garlic and lemon. Daily specials include lasagna, cannelloni, and seafood linguine.

Other recommendations: Veal scallopini with mushrooms; roasted chicken with olives, rosemary, and garlic; pasta with sausage, eggplant, and peppers.

Summary & comments: Adriana's traditional, no-nonsense approach to Italian cooking has ardent afficionados, and deservedly so. Mamma Giramonte just keeps whipping up a redolent storm, oblivious to the recent plethora of trendy and more fashionably located Italian eateries. Adriana's is best likened to a well-made suit: durable, serviceable, dresses up or down, always there to fall back on.

Honors / awards: KQED's Great Chefs of San Francisco.

Bocuse 1800

Alain Rondelli

	French
	★★★★★
Zone 8 Richmond/Avenues	Moderate/Expensive
126 Clement Street	
(415) 387-0408	Quality 98 Value A

Reservations:	Required
When to go:	Sundays and weeknights
Entree range:	$16–19; 6-course tasting menu, $55
Payment:	AMEX, MC, VISA
Service rating:	★★★★
Friendliness rating:	★★★★★
Parking:	Street
Bar:	Full service
Wine selection:	Limited but good
Dress:	Informal, dressy
Disabled access:	Good
Customers:	Local, business, tourist
Dinner:	Wednesday–Sunday, 5:30–10 P.M.

Atmosphere/setting: Understated elegance in an area of Clement Street that gains cachet as the sun sets: padded banquettes, pale beamed ceilings, cream walls with glowing sconces, a few flowers and candles. A mirrored copper bar reflects scattered impressionist paintings and servers in bright domino waistcoats; slow, cool jazz on the sound system casts a seductive, dreamy reverie.

House specialties: Stylish and original French menu, changing seasonally, but often including a creamy artichoke and oyster soup strewn with cunning pastry-wrapped oysters, artichoke hearts, and crisp sage; fresh herb salads; onion brioche tart with rosemary; lamb pot au feu with oregano, lemon, and horseradish; tripe Provençal; rabbit cooked in three styles with orange glazed carrots, green olives, and basil.

Other recommendations: Six-, nine-, or twelve-course tasting menus.

Summary & comments: Among the abundantly gifted chefs in San Francisco, Alain Rondelli's genius is unique. His menus read like the offhand musings of a master. But there's nothing casual about his art. Foodstuffs pass through his hands to reveal their humble, miraculous origins in nature; their colors, scents, and textures; their essential vitality. Give yourself over to Rondelli's wizardry and you surrender to a poem of the season, celebrate its most dramatic elements, contemplate its subtlest intimations. The interval between courses can be a bit long. Slow down. Singular art is worth savoring.

Honors/awards: *Esquire* Best New Restaurants 1994; *Bon Appetit* Best New Restaurants 1994.

Amelio's

Zone 6   North Beach
1630 Powel Street
(415) 397-4339

French	
★★★★	
Expensive	
Quality 90	Value B+

Reservations:	Accepted
When to go:	Any time
Entree range:	$14–28
Payment:	Major credit cards
Service rating:	★★★★
Friendliness rating:	★★★
Parking:	Street
Bar:	Full service
Wine selection:	Very good
Dress:	Dressy
Disabled access:	Yes
Customers:	Local, business, tourist
Dinner:	Tuesday–Saturday, 5:30–10:30 P.M.

Atmosphere / setting: In business since 1926, this is one of the oldest places in the city. The handsome decor belongs to an older era when formal was normal. Gilt frames and oil paintings, elegant china sitting on starched napery, and understated floral arrangements all suggest that you've just gone through a time tunnel.

House specialties: The cuisine is as new as the decor is old. Though it is a French kitchen, there is a great deal of improvisation based on what the chef has found on a given day to delight his diners. Ingredients are exceedingly fresh, flavors are very pronounced, and all is done with a light touch and creative presentation: Chicken with red and white wine; sea urchin and pastry; foie gras sautéed with raspberry vinegar; filet of veal stuffed with herbs; caviar with blini ring and potato cake; amaretto custard.

Other recommendations: The butter served at the table is from Normandy.

Summary & comments: Amelio's had a down period in the late '70s and early '80s, but a fiercely loyal clientele kept it going until a new partnership revived it by maintaining the wonderful decor and traditional, attentive service, and breathing new life into the menu. A few of the old favorites have been retained, but it's mainly very modern. Come here when you have time to linger and enjoy the ritual that dinner used to be.

Anthony's

Zone 6 North Beach	Seafood
1701 Powel Street	★★½
(415) 391-4488	Moderate
	Quality 78 Value B

Reservations:	Accepted
When to go:	Any time
Entree range:	$6.95–18.95
Payment:	Major credit cards
Service rating:	★★½
Friendliness rating:	★★★★
Parking:	Street, validation
Bar:	Full service
Wine selection:	Excellent
Dress:	Casual
Disabled access:	Yes
Customers:	Local, tourist
Dinner:	Sunday–Thursday, 5–10 P.M.;
	Friday and Saturday, 5–11 P.M.

Atmosphere / setting: Rather spare decor. Its "wall of fame" and padded dining benches belie the excellent fare to be had here. The general mood is festive and happy, and the owner is a most amiable host.

House specialties: Lobster, lobster, lobster. Very well-priced at $11.95 per pound and served with a bib, steamed veggies, and potatoes. Go ahead and make a mess.

Other recommendations: "The City's Biggest" shrimp cocktail. Good for two or even three. Steak, pasta, pizza, and seafood combos.

Summary & comments: This place can be packed at times. Even with a firm reservation you may have to wait. It's worth it, though. It's not just good food. It's the good and friendly atmosphere that is one of the best aids to happy digestion. Validated parking is available for $3 at 1645 Powel Street.

AROMI

Zone 2   Civic Center
1507 Polk Street
(415) 775-5977

Italian	
★★½	
Expensive	
Quality 78	Value B

Reservations:	Accepted
When to go:	Any time
Entree range:	$7.50–16.50
Payment:	VISA, MC, AMEX
Service rating:	★★
Friendliness rating:	★★
Parking:	Street
Bar:	Full service
Wine selection:	Fair and expensive
Dress:	Business
Disabled access:	Yes
Customers:	Local
Dinner:	Sunday–Thursday, 5–10 P.M.;
	Friday and Saturday, 5–10:30 P.M.

Atmosphere / setting: Located in a rather cacophonous part of town, Aromi is a little island of relative serenity. The wooden bar occupies a marble floor. In the dining room the floor is a superbly crafted wood laid diagonally. The kitchen is set apart by a flower-bedecked counter. Small tables make for an intimate European setting.

House specialties: Osso buco in an aromatic broth with white beans and greens; chicken livers in balsamic vinegar sauce; grilled salmon with pesto; roast pork with sun-dried tomatoes and red wine sauce; shellfish in a tomato and fennel sauce.

Other recommendations: A peppery pasta called penne alla vodka; house-made sausage in red wine and cream.

Summary & comments: A really pleasant little place with a cook who originally majored in chemistry. The menu changes seasonally, and hopefully the wine list will too; it's expensive beyond its worth. But don't stay away. Pay the $8 corkage fee and bring your own. You'll be glad you did.

Art and Larry's

<table>
<tr><td>Zone 10   Suburban Marin</td><td>Delicatessen</td></tr>
<tr><td>1242 Fourth Street, San Rafael</td><td>★★</td></tr>
<tr><td>(415) 457-3354</td><td>Inexpensive</td></tr>
<tr><td></td><td>Quality 75   Value C</td></tr>
</table>

Reservations:	Not necessary
When to go:	Any time
Entree range:	$6.50–14.95
Payment:	AMEX, MC, VISA
Service rating:	★★½
Friendliness rating:	★★½
Parking:	Street, public lots
Bar:	Beer, wine
Wine selection:	House
Dress:	Casual
Disabled access:	Good
Customers:	Local, business
Breakfast:	All day
Brunch:	Saturday and Sunday, 10 A.M.–5 P.M.
Lunch/Dinner:	Tuesday–Friday, 11 A.M.–9 P.M.;
	Saturday, 10 A.M.–9 P.M.;
	Sunday, 10 A.M.–8:30 P.M.

Atmosphere / setting: Art and Larry's offers a basic deli setting: wood-trimmed formica tables, cream walls with green trim, few frills or furbelows. The takeout is at the back of the dining room, as is the cash register; when one enters at crowded times, it's a little confusing whether to sit down, walk to the rear, or wait to be seated.

House specialties: New York Jewish delicatessen: chopped liver; gefilte fish; knishes and kishka; cheese blintzes and potato pancakes; matzo-ball soup or borscht; huge deli sandwiches of pastrami, corned beef, beef brisket, and combinations. Beef brisket plates; meat loaf; knockwurst with sauerkraut and baked beans. Chocolate or vanilla egg creams, New York cheesecake; malted milkshakes.

Other recommendations: Breakfast egg dishes, including lox, eggs and onions, salami and eggs, matzo brie; challah French toast.

Summary & comments: Art and Larry's portions range from the huge to outlandish, but the prices are hefty as well. Ordering more than one item is out of the question for a single diner with a less than gargantuan appetite, so it's best to go with a group or family to share the bounty. Starting at 5 P.M., Art and Larry's offers nightly dinner specials which are regular menu items priced a dollar or two below the usual price. Art and Larry's bills itself as a real New York Deli, but it's the rare New Yorker who admits such a beast exists outside New York.

Avatar's

		Eclectic
Zone 9 Waterfront Crescent		★★
2656 Bridgeway, Sausalito		Inexpensive
(415) 332-8083		Quality 79 Value B

Reservations:	Accepted
When to go:	Any time
Entree range:	$3.95–13.95
Payment:	MC, VISA
Service rating:	★★★★
Friendliness rating:	★★★★
Parking:	Free lot
Bar:	Beer, wine
Wine selection:	House
Dress:	Casual
Disabled access:	Limited
Customers:	Local, business
Lunch/Dinner:	Monday–Saturday, 11 A.M.–9:30 P.M.

Atmosphere / setting: Avatar's is small and simple, distinguished mainly by the stunning black-and-white photographs of scenes of Indian life on the walls. This is a friendly, neighborhood mom, pop, 'n' brother-in-law establishment, and the atmosphere is exceedingly casual.

House specialties: Marindian cuisine: self-described by chefs Avatar, Kala, and Michael as "ethnic confusion," Avatar's blends Indian, Jamaican, Mexican, and California cuisine with surprisingly delicious results. Specialties include vegetarian samosas served with homemade chutneys and tamarind sauce; Punjabi tostadas, whole-wheat parathas topped with a choice of curried lamb, chicken, beef, vegetables, eggplant, seafood, or Jamaican-style chicken, and yogurt, tamarind sauce, Punjabi salsa, and carrot pickles.

Other recommendations: Spinach ravioli; curried rice plates; pasta with curried prawns; rock shrimp in basil, mint, cilantro, garlic, and ginger sauce.

Summary & comments: Avatar's is a sort of enlightened greasy spoon that reggaed off in its own direction, serving truly original dishes in a tiny hole-in-the-wall whose major amenities are the cheerful attitudes of the proprietors and their homemade sauces and chutneys. Imported beers complement the complex flavors of the cookery; the family atmosphere makes up for the sometimes hectic pace in the kitchen. Avatar's isn't a special occasion restaurant, but the food is nonetheless a special experience.

The Avenue Grill

New American
★★★½
Moderate

Quality 88   Value B

Zone 10   Suburban Marin
44 East Blithedale, Mill Valley
(415) 388-6003

Reservations:	Recommended
When to go:	Early weekend evenings; weekdays
Entree range:	$11–14.50
Payment:	MC, VISA
Service rating:	★★★
Friendliness rating:	★★★
Parking:	Free lot, street
Bar:	Full service
Wine selection:	Good
Dress:	Casual, informal
Disabled access:	Good
Customers:	Local, business
Dinner:	Monday–Saturday, 5:30–10 P.M.; Sunday, 5–10 P.M.

Atmosphere / setting: An early, well-executed gas station conversion, Avenue Grill strikes a pleasant note somewhere between a neighborhood hangout and a fancy diner. There are a lot of hard surfaces though, so with an open kitchen, counter service, and a small bar near the front, the din can be overwhelming on busy nights: don't go to the Avenue for a quiet, romantic evening.

House specialties: Regional American and international themes creatively interpreted in a menu that changes daily, although some classics stay the same: house-cured gravlax pizza with pepper cress and horseradish cream; Tuscan toast with roasted garlic and anchovy-basil butter; salmon and rock shrimp croquettes with roasted pepper aioli; meat loaf with gravy and garlic mashed potatoes; grilled mahimahi with warm green bean salad, golden beets, balsamic onions, and roasted potatoes; grilled steaks, chops.

Summary & comments: The Avenue's popularity at the vanguard of the casual/chic Mill Valley restaurant scene has shifted somewhat with the opening of three new venues around the square. For diners, this may be a plus, since the always inspired cookery suffered from such a clamorous pace. Avenue was among the first to design weekly and monthly menus around regional themes, seasonal produce or fish, international holidays and festivals, or whimsy: they once offered dinners showcasing the recipes from *Like Water For Chocolate,* including the infamous quail with rose petal sauce, and from *Babette's Feast* as well. The portions are ample here, and the service, while a little offhand, is usually competent and responsive.

Baby Sal's

	Seafood
	★★
	Moderate
	Quality 78 Value C-

Zone 10   Suburban Marin
60 Corte Madera Avenue,
   Corte Madera
(415) 927-0149

Reservations:	Recommended on weekends
When to go:	Any time
Entree range:	$10.95–14.95
Payment:	MC, VISA
Service rating:	★★★½
Friendliness rating:	★★★½
Parking:	Street
Bar:	Beer, wine
Wine selection:	House
Dress:	Casual
Disabled access:	Good
Customers:	Local
Dinner:	Monday–Saturday, 5–9:30 P.M.

Atmosphere / setting: Reminiscent of a fishhouse in a small seacoast town, Baby Sal's occupies one modest room, decorated in blue and white, on the main road from Corte Madera to Larkspur.

House specialties: Fried calamari with ginger sauce or sautéed with cream sauce and mushrooms; fried seafood sampler with tartar sauce; broiled lobster tails with drawn butter; linguine with clams; bouillabaisse; New York steak.

Other recommendations: Vegetarian or children's platters.

Summary & comments: Baby Sal's is an old-fashioned seafood house with Louis salads, fried-fish platters, and a few Italian dishes thrown in. It's quiet, and the small staff is friendly; the seafood is well prepared, but with a few exceptions, notably the ginger fried calamari, frankly traditional. Dinners include side dishes and soup or salad.

BACI RISTORANTE

Zone 10 Suburban Marin	Italian
247 Shoreline Highway, Mill Valley	★★★½
(415) 381-2022	Moderate
	Quality 85 Value B

Reservations:	Recommended at peak hours
When to go:	Any time
Entree range:	$7.95–15.50
Payment:	AMEX, MC, VISA
Service rating:	★★½
Friendliness rating:	★★★½
Parking:	Free lot
Bar:	Full service
Wine selection:	Good
Dress:	Informal
Disabled access:	Good
Customers:	Local, business
Dinner:	Sunday–Thursday, 5–10 P.M.;
	Friday and Saturday, 5–11 P.M.

Atmosphere / setting: Renovated in early 1995, this formerly appealing restaurant is now quite stunning. From its oddball location on the only seedy street in affluent Mill Valley, the peach and copper interior's high-ceilinged elegance casts an inviting glow. The mouthwatering antipasto display near the entrance and a glossy granite bar give way to a warm and comfortable dining area with a wood-burning oven and an open kitchen.

House specialties: Southern Italian cookery: changing nightly antipasto selection; carpaccio, thinly sliced raw beef with Parmesan, capers, and Dijon; polenta with wild mushrooms; marinated ahi tuna with capers and lemon. Minestrone; salad of lettuce, baked goat cheese, and roasted hazelnuts. Wood-fired pizzas: try the four cheese, or the prawn, scallop, garlic, and basil. Daily risotto and pasta specialties. Almond-wood roasted chicken with rosemary potatoes. Veal saltimbocca with prosciutto and mozzarella.

Other recommendations: Spidini, grilled prawns, and sea scallops with lemon; daily fresh fish selection.

Summary & comments: Another sleek Italian restaurant in Marin? Yes, and this one, which has been around for a while, keeps getting better. The new decor seems to have inspired the kitchen and the service, which in the past was competent, but not exciting. The antipasto dishes have a new verve, and the staff seems happier, too. If Baci were more strategically located, it might be one of the most popular restaurants in the county.

BAKER STREET BISTRO

Zone 5   Marina
2953 Baker Street
(415) 931-1475

French	
★★½	
Inexpensive / Moderate	
Quality 79	Value A

Reservations: Required on weekends; generally recommended
When to go: Weekdays and nights
Entree range: Lunch, $3.50–6.25; Dinner, $8–13;
                        Prix fixe, $14.50
Payment: AMEX, MC, VISA
Service rating: ★★
Friendliness rating: ★★★
Parking: Street
Bar: Beer, wine
Wine selection: Limited but good
Dress: Casual, informal
Disabled access: Good but cramped
Customers: Local, business, tourist
Breakfast: Monday–Saturday, 6:30 A.M.– noon
Lunch: Sunday, Tuesday–Saturday, 11 A.M.–3 P.M.
Dinner: Tuesday–Thursday, 5–9 P.M.;
                        Friday and Saturday, 5–10:30 P.M.

Atmosphere / setting: Bewitchingly minuscule French cafe and bistro occupying two small rooms with yellow walls and an open kitchen, on a quiet, tree-lined street.

House specialties: Duck liver pâté; escargots forestière; mousseline of scallops; lamb stew printanier; blanquette de veau; rabbit in mustard sauce.

Other recommendations: Nightly specials; for lunch, salade Niçoise; baguette sandwiches with cornichons.

Summary & comments: Baker Street Bistro would not be extraordinary on the boulevards of Paris, but it is in San Francisco, primarily for its rock-bottom pricing sauced with generous dollops of Gallic charm. The kitchen is tiny, which makes for slow service, and the food is not of a quality impressive enough to write France about, but it is tasty and attractively served, and the portions are adequate. The daytime cafe is très gentil for coffee and breakfast pastry, or a sandwich or salad lunch.

Bangkok Spoon

Thai
★★
Inexpensive

Quality 75   Value C+

Zone 14   South Bay
702 Villa Street, Mountain View
(415) 968-2038

Reservations:	Yes
When to go:	Lunch
Entree range:	$5.95–15.95
Payment:	MC, VISA, DC
Service rating:	★★½
Friendliness rating:	★★
Parking:	Street
Bar:	Beer, wine
Wine selection:	House
Dress:	Casual
Disabled access:	No
Customers:	Local, business
Lunch:	Monday–Friday, 11 A.M.–2 P.M.
Dinner:	Monday–Saturday, 5–9:30 P.M.

Atmosphere / setting: A simple room pleasantly decorated with Thai hangings and posters. Nothing remarkable, just comfortable. A family affair with a family feeling. A nice, respectable hole-in-the-wall.

House specialties: The usual Thai table. The seafood clay pot is especially good; also, chicken soup with coconut, and red and green Thai curries. Noodle dishes are inconsistent.

Summary & comments: Come in off the shopping circuit for lunch, meet your business associate, or just come in out of the weather for a cold Thai beer. It's a nice little stopping place where the staff will give you a decent meal and then stay out of your way. With 15 years at the same location in downtown Mountain View, they're doing something good.

The Basque Hotel/Restaurant

	Basque
	★★
	Inexpensive
	Quality 77 Value B

Zone 6   North Beach
15 Romolo Place
(415) 788-9404

Reservations:	Accepted
When to go:	Any time
Entree range:	$9–12.50
Payment:	VISA, MC
Service rating:	★★
Friendliness rating:	★★★
Parking:	Street
Bar:	Full service
Wine selection:	Limited but good
Dress:	Casual
Disabled access:	No
Customers:	Business, families, groups
Dinner:	Tuesday–Saturday, 5–9:30 P.M.

Atmosphere / setting: Old, simple, and Mediterranean. Checkered table-cloths, wooden floors, a feeling that you've just walked into a place where the local peasants come when they really want to feed well and abundantly.

House specialties: Basque country kitchen fare including duck confit; sweet breads; braised lamb shanks; beef tongue; oxtail stew.

Other recommendations: Steak; prawns; roast chicken.

Summary & comments: It's a fixed-price menu at the Basque, and all dinners include delicious soup, substantial bread, tossed salad, dessert, and coffee. Nobody in the history of San Francisco has ever left the Basque unsatisfied. Most people have to stagger from the table, as is the Basque custom. The food is simple and unadorned, but lovingly prepared, wholesome, and delicious. The Basque is especially suited to families and large parties.

Baywolf

Zone 13   Oakland
3853 Piedmont Avenue
(510) 655-6004

Mediterranean	
★★★★	
Moderate	
Quality 90	Value A

Reservations:	Recommended
When to go:	Any time
Entree range:	$12.25–17.50
Payment:	VISA, MC
Service rating:	★★★
Friendliness rating:	★★★
Parking:	Street
Bar:	Beer, wine
Wine selection:	Excellent
Dress:	Business
Disabled access:	Fair
Customers:	Local, business, tourist
Lunch:	Monday–Friday, 11:30 A.M.–2 P.M.
Dinner:	Monday–Friday, 6–9 P.M.;
	Saturday and Sunday, 5:30–9 P.M.

Atmosphere / setting: Two relatively small dining rooms and some nooks and alcoves give the place the intimate feeling of a lovely country inn decorated in the earlier part of this century. The sedate interior is contrasted by a more casual atmosphere on the front deck, where an almost seaside feeling prevails.

House specialties: The menu changes every two weeks. Fortnightly offerings usually feature a particular region of the Mediterranean: Spain, South of France, Italy, etc. Occasionally the menu will migrate to New Orleans or the American Southeast, but it always returns to its roots on the Middle Sea. Past offerings at dinner have included crayfish bisque with corn and chervil; buckwheat crêpes with smoked trout; sautéed soft-shell crabs; grilled duck with peach chutney; and horseradish mashed potatoes.

Other recommendations: Lunch has featured zucchini soup with pesto cream; veal and spinach salad with chickpeas; and grilled swordfish with couscous, cilantro, cucumber, and curry vinaigrette.

Summary & comments: Ask for parking secrets before arriving. In its 20 years of operation the Bay Wolf has earned a very loyal following of local people and regular passers-through. Many local businesspeople come here four times a week for lunch. The owners began life in literature and academe, but their devotion to the culinary arts led them along the same path as their contemporary, Alice Waters of Chez Panisse. You can still see the exactitude of the academic and the passion and imagination of the man of letters in their work, though.

BISTRO ALSACIENNE

French / German	
★ ★ ★	
Moderate	
Quality 85	Value C

Zone 10   Suburban Marin
655 Redwood Highway,
    Mill Valley
(415) 389-0921

Reservations:	Recommended on weekends
When to go:	Any time
Entree range:	$11–14.75
Payment:	MC, VISA
Service rating:	★ ★ ★ ½
Friendliness rating:	★ ★ ★ ½
Parking:	Free lot
Bar:	Beer, wine
Wine selection:	Limited but good
Dress:	Informal
Disabled access:	Good
Customers:	Local, business
Dinner:	Tuesday–Sunday, 5–10 P.M.

Atmosphere / setting: With one windowed wall overlooking Shelter Bay, Bistro Alsacienne has the feel of a Swiss or German guest house or country inn. Friendly and welcoming, but not stylish or chic, the atmosphere is as calm and reassuring as the twinkling lights across the little bay. Located just off Highway 101, this is nevertheless a very peaceful spot.

House specialties: Zweibelkuchen; an Alsatian onion tart appetizer; Matjes herring with sour cream and apples; choucroute with champagne; confit of Petaluma duck; boeuf bourguignonne; peach Melba; baked raspberry mousse with vanilla sauce.

Other recommendations: Creamy rutabaga soup, if available; Viennese pork cutlet; cassoulet.

Summary & comments: Bistro Alsacienne's cookery is a fine representation of the sturdy aromas and flavors of the Alsatian countryside: tenderly braised meats; delicately prepared cabbage, beans, onions, and potatoes; butter and cream used in judicious proportion—all the precision of the region. Portions are frugal, particularly with the side dishes and sauces. The service is highly personal; chef/owners Fritz Frankel and Martin Wendel double as host and server on quiet weeknights. Desserts are especially delicate and beautifully presented.

Bistro Clovis

Zone 2   Civic Center
1596 Market Street
(415) 864-0231

	French
	★★
	Moderate
Quality 78	Value B

Reservations:	Accepted
When to go:	Any time
Entree range:	$7.50–12.95
Payment:	MC, VISA
Service rating:	★★★
Friendliness rating:	★★★
Parking:	Street
Bar:	Beer, wine
Wine selection:	Good
Dress:	Casual, business
Disabled access:	Yes
Customers:	Local, business
Dinner:	Monday–Thursday, 11:30 A.M.–11 P.M.; Friday, 5 P.M.–midnight

Atmosphere / setting: Very small, nice, and simple with wood floors. Chairs and tables are restored classics, and tables are set with fresh flowers. Numerous old photos on the walls and high ceilings give the feeling of another time.

House specialties: A very large blackboard displays a wide variety of daily bistro fare. Hot potato salad with herring; lamb salad with sun-dried tomatoes; smoked salmon in white wine sauce; jumbo prawns with avocado; and whatever is fresh in the market that day.

Other recommendations: Beef bourguignonne, veal stew, and a delightful range of appetizers and desserts.

Summary & comments: Traditional and simply prepared, well-presented French bistro food. Come here for dinner after work—it's easily reachable from much of the city. Relax, enjoy a glass of good wine, and dine in peace.

BISTRO M

Zone 7   SOMA / Mission
55 Fifth Street
(415) 543-5554

	French
	★ ★ ★
	Moderate
	Quality 89 Value B+

Reservations:	Accepted
When to go:	Any time
Entree range:	$15–26
Payment:	Major credit cards
Service rating:	★ ★ ★
Friendliness rating:	★ ★ ½
Parking:	Street
Bar:	Full service
Wine selection:	Good
Dress:	Casual
Disabled access:	Yes
Customers:	Local, tourist, business
Breakfast:	Monday–Saturday, 6:30–10:30 A.M.
Brunch / Lunch:	Sunday, Monday–Saturday, 11:30 A.M.–2:30 P.M.
Dinner:	Every day, 5:30–10:30 P.M.

Atmosphere / setting: This contemporary dining room seating 140 is surrounded by a 125-foot mural of the city. Palladian windows stretching from floor to ceiling give the long two-story room a classic air.

House specialties: Roast lamb chops served with white bean sauce; yellowtail carpaccio with a mild ginger dressing; crisply seared Great Lakes whitefish fillets with lobster sauce and pearl-shaped pasta.

Other recommendations: Oxtail in ziti terrine for something different. Don't pass on dessert. Crunchy Napoleon with layers of phyllo dough and crème brûlée are a must.

Summary & comments: The cheese display features 16 different varieties accompanied by rustic breads arranged in baskets. This is one of the city's most stylish restaurants. The intriguing mural affords you a delightful game of "Now what part of the city is that?" while you wait for dinner.

Bizou

Zone 7   SOMA / Mission
598 Fourth Street
(415) 543-2222

	Continental
	★★★½
	Moderate
	Quality 89 Value B

Reservations:	Recommended
When to go:	Any time
Entree range:	Lunch, $7–11; dinner, $10.50–17.50
Payment:	AMEX, MC, VISA
Service rating:	★★★★
Friendliness rating:	★★★★
Parking:	Street
Bar:	Full service
Wine selection:	Limited but good
Dress:	Informal
Disabled access:	Good
Customers:	Local, business, tourist
Lunch:	Monday–Friday, 11:30 A.M.–2:30 P.M.
Dinner:	Monday–Saturday, 5:30–10:30 P.M.

Atmosphere / setting: Simple, rustic, but warm and inviting small bistro with quiet, friendly, and efficient service.

House specialties: Crisp Italian flatbreads and pizzas; baked brandade of local cod; buckwheat ravioli with butternut squash; braised beef cheeks with watercress and horseradish; rosemary-braised lamb shank with creamy polenta; curried vegetable tagine, tomatoes with fresh anchovies in a sherry vinaigrette; Catalan sizzling shrimp.

Other recommendations: Delightfully presented traditional desserts, varying with seasons: summer berry pudding; bittersweet chocolate Vacherin in crème anglaise.

Summary & comments: Jewel-box bistros have sprung up like wildflowers in this formerly industrial area of San Francisco. Attentive, efficient service sets this one apart, along with a quiet atmosphere and some rock-solid creativity and know-how in the kitchen. Bizou's chef Loretta Keller provides a panoply of sturdy, unaffected cuisine from the provinces of France, Italy, and Spain.

BLUE FOX

Zone 4   Financial District
659 Merchant Street
(415) 981-1177

Italian
★★★★
Expensive
Quality 90   Value B+

Reservations:	Recommended
When to go:	Dinner only
Entree range:	$15–35
Payment:	Major credit cards
Service rating:	★★★★★
Friendliness rating:	★★★½
Parking:	Street
Bar:	Full service
Wine selection:	Very good
Dress:	Dressy
Disabled access:	Yes
Customers:	Local, tourist, business
Dinner:	Monday–Saturday, 6–10 P.M.

Atmosphere / setting: Could be intimidating upon entering if you're not used to wearing a necktie or paying for a meal that could provide foreign aid for a small nation. Add wine to the meal only after consulting with your banker. But do consult. Everybody should come here once, which is what most of us could afford anyway. Even if you arrive wearing a clip-on tie, the highly trained and willing staff will see that you are made comfortable and welcome and that you will go home and tell your friends about it for years to come.

House specialties: Seafood and Italian dishes superbly cooked, beautifully presented, and served by some of the best restaurant staff in the city. Carpaccio is good to start; the pasta dishes are especially colorful and flavorful; lobster with red onion coulis is spectacular.

Other recommendations: Menu del Giorno is always a good first dinner at Blue Fox: a well-balanced and delightful meal costing somewhat less (it's all relative) than a la carte selections. Desserts are always super, especially gelato and tiramisu.

Summary & comments: This is a very old restaurant that has had its ups and downs. It is currently up and rising and on the way to being one of the best Italian eateries anywhere. It's extremely formal and pricey; and it's definitely worth the splurge if you're not sending the kids to college anytime soon.

Book Passage Cafe

Zone 10 Suburban Marin	New American
51 Tamal Vista Boulevard,	★½
Corte Madera	Inexpensive
(415) 927-1503	Quality 68 Value B

Reservations:	Not needed
When to go:	Any time
Entree range:	$3.50–6.50
Payment:	AMEX, DISC, MC, VISA
Service rating:	★★★
Friendliness rating:	★★★
Parking:	Shopping center lot
Bar:	Beer, wine
Wine selection:	House
Dress:	Casual
Disabled access:	Good
Customers:	Local, student
Open:	Monday–Thursday, 7 A.M.–10 P.M.;
	Friday, 7 A.M.–11 P.M.;
	Saturday, 9 A.M.–11 P.M.;
	Sunday, 9 A.M.–10 P.M.

Atmosphere / setting: A cozy corner in a destination bookstore which specializes in travel literature. Book Passage offers numerous literary events, classes, and workshops, and is the sponsor of the annual Book Passage Travel Writer's conference. The cafe provides indoor tables, wicker settees and easy chairs, outdoor courtyard seating at umbrellaed tables, and all the reading material anyone could possibly wish for.

House specialties: Coffee drinks and Italian sodas; sandwiches, soups, and quiches. Try the hummus and tabbouleh; the pad thai salad; or the grilled chicken with couscous salad.

Other recommendations: Bagels, muffins, and pastries; beer and wine by the glass.

Summary & comments: There are three other bookstore cafes in Marin, but Book Passage allows the best window into the writer's world. The many classes and events attract the literati of the area; writer's groups meet at the cafe tables and share their trials and travails; the staff is pleasant and helpful; and there's an easy flow from the main bookstore out to the patio, and on to the annex, which houses used books and mysteries. The food is tasty, although not memorable. This is a comfortable place to while away an hour or a rainy afternoon.

BRASSERIE TOMO

French	
★★★	
Moderate	
Quality 88	Value A

Zone 6   North Beach
745 Columbus Avenue
(415) 296-7668

Reservations:	Accepted
When to go:	Any time
Entree range:	$9.95–17
Payment:	AMEX, VISA, MC
Service rating:	★★★
Friendliness rating:	★★★
Parking:	Street
Bar:	Beer, wine
Wine selection:	Very good
Dress:	Business
Disabled access:	Yes
Customers:	Local, business
Dinner:	Monday–Friday, 6–10 P.M.

Atmosphere / setting: Small, intimate, French style; well-set tables covered with linen matching the decor, plentiful silver, and monogrammed plates.

House specialties: There is an old Persian saying to the effect that if you can make a good soup, you can do anything well. They make a good soup here. Despite the Marx Brothers connotations, the duck soup is worth the trip. Absolutely fresh greens and salads; sauced dishes such as sweetbreads; excellent foie gras; desserts relying on fresh fruits and cream.

Other recommendations: An eight-course set menu.

Summary & comments: Chef Tomo Okuda, a French-trained Japanese practitioner, strives for perfection, not only in the kitchen but in every facet of the restaurant's operation and the patrons' experience. Perhaps that's why the place is so small: attention to detail is easier. Chicago calls itself the city that works. This is a restaurant that does the same.

The Brazen Head

Zone 5   Marina
3166 Buchanan at Greenwich
(415) 921-7600

Continental	
★★★	
Moderate	
Quality 80	Value A

Reservations:	Not accepted
When to go:	Before 8 P.M. and after 10 P.M.
Entree range:	$10.95–14.95
Payment:	ATM cards, no credit cards
Service rating:	★★
Friendliness rating:	★★★
Parking:	Street
Bar:	Full service
Wine selection:	Good
Dress:	Casual
Disabled access:	None
Customers:	Locals, other restaurant workers, writers
Dinner:	Every day, 5:30 P.M.–1 A.M.

Atmosphere / setting: Except for the lack of trophy heads, this place has the look and feel of a rich, cozy European hunting lodge. All is polished hardwood, brass trim, deep and dark. Antique etchings and photographs cover the walls. A loyal patronage returns here regularly and one sometimes gets the feeling of being in the television bar "Cheers." No credit cards or checks are accepted, but there is an ATM at the bar.

House specialties: Meat! (and fish) as befits the hunting lodge atmosphere. Grills and roasts of lamb, beef, and pork. Also pan-fried trout, sautéed prawns, chicken, and a daily pasta dish. Burgers. All entrees include vegetable of the day and potato or rice.

Other recommendations: A good selection of salads and appetizers such as crab cakes, oysters, and roasted garlic; mixed greens, shrimp, and Caesar salads.

Summary & comments: Situated on a street corner not far from the Golden Gate Bridge, the cheery lights of this place beckon through the San Francisco fog like a warm cabin in a cold woods. There is often a wait for a table, but you can join the locals and regulars at the bar for a very convivial drink.

Bubba's

Zone 10 Suburban Marin	American
566 San Anselmo Avenue, San Anselmo	★★½
(415) 459-6862	Inexpensive
	Quality 78 Value B

Reservations:	Accepted for parties of 6 or more
When to go:	Avoid peak lunch and dinner hours
Entree range:	$5–11
Payment:	MC, VISA
Service rating:	★★½
Friendliness rating:	★★★½
Parking:	Street, public lots
Bar:	Beer, wine
Wine selection:	House
Dress:	Casual
Disabled access:	Limited
Customers:	Local, business
Breakfast:	Wednesday–Monday, 8 A.M.–2 P.M.
Lunch:	Wednesday–Monday, 11:30 A.M.–2 P.M.
Dinner:	Wednesday–Monday, 5:30–9 P.M.; closed Tuesday

Atmosphere / setting: Bubba's is your basic diner: streetcar narrow with counter service or booth seating; chrome and formica; leatherette and linoleum. It's loud and crowded and boisterous during peak hours, so go for the quiet moments, when little details emerge: cakes and pies and jars of home-canned pickles and preserves on display, bright baskets of fruit, and happy smiles.

House specialties: Cinnamon raisin French toast; whole-wheat flapjacks; fried green tomatoes; biscuits and gravy for breakfast. Lunch sandwiches: portobello mushroom, homemade meat loaf, fried egg, ground chuckburger. Poached salmon salad, shredded chicken Caesar salad. For supper, try the chicken-fried steak or the daily blue plate special, which might be barbecued ribs, fried chicken, liver and onions, pot roast, or fish and chips. Chocolate cake, tapioca pudding, or hot fudge sundae for dessert.

Other recommendations: Black-eyed pea chili; chicken pot pie.

Summary & comments: Simple and hearty chow, nothing terribly fancy, seasoned with a dash of nostalgia for, yes, believe it or not, the best of the elementary school cafeteria. Vegetarians, take heart: along with the meat loaf and chicken-fried steak, there are specials such as grits with chanterelles and mustard greens, or a barbecued vegetable burger. Bubba's blue plate specials are not great bargains, and they're not served on blue plates, but they're reasonable. Bubba's is tiny; expect a long wait on weekends and during the lunch and dinner rush.

Buca Giovanni

Zone 6   North Beach
800 Greenwich Avenue
(415) 776-7766

Italian	
★★★	
Moderate	
Quality 89	Value B

Reservations:	Accepted
When to go:	Any time
Entree range:	$8.50–14.95
Payment:	AMEX, VISA, MC
Service rating:	★★★
Friendliness rating:	★★★
Parking:	Street
Bar:	Full service
Wine selection:	Good
Dress:	Casual
Disabled access:	Yes
Customers:	Local, tourist
Dinner:	Monday–Thursday, 5:30–10:30 P.M.;
	Friday and Saturday, 5:30–11 P.M.

Atmosphere / setting: The main restaurant is in the basement, where the walls are lined with wine racks and the small bar awaits the thirsty diner. Here you will find friendly comfort and lots of elbow room. The basement puts you at a distance from the street and gives the place a more intimate, almost conspiratorial feeling. There is also dining space at street level for those who like to watch the city go by.

House specialties: Many kinds of flavorful antipasti; rich pasta dishes; game such as venison in ravioli with mushrooms; rabbit cooked in a style similar to that of the ancient Romans, with honey and vinegar. Excellent seafood, veal dishes, and lamb.

Other recommendations: Smoked salmon with herbs and sour cream; mezzaluna; cappelletti; and salsa rosa, a spread of sun–dried tomatoes and spices.

Summary & comments: People of all walks of life come here, which should be no surprise, given its location in the heart of North Beach where people from all walks of life pass through. But here they like to stop, slow down, and eat. The extensive menu itself is reason enough to slow down and enjoy. Nothing to intimidate–everything says "come hither."

Bucci's

		Italian
		★★
Zone 13 Oakland		Inexpensive
6121 Hollis Street, Emeryville		
(510) 547-4725		Quality 79 Value B+

Reservations:	Not accepted
When to go:	Mondays
Entree range:	$6.75–15
Payment:	Cash
Service rating:	★★★
Friendliness rating:	★★
Parking:	Lot
Bar:	Beer, wine
Wine selection:	Good
Dress:	Casual
Disabled access:	Yes
Customers:	Local, food professional
Lunch:	Monday–Friday, 11:30 A.M.–2:30 P.M.
Dinner:	Monday–Saturday, 5:30–9:30 P.M.

Atmosphere / setting: Almost discolike, but not unpleasant. Very informal and friendly. A generally youngish crowd who knows food and where to find it.

House specialties: The basic menu is very short, with pizza, salads, and some Italian staples such as antipasti that should not be missed. The main attractions are on the board on the wall. They change constantly depending on available ingredients and may include gnocchi, lamb, pork, and polenta. The salads are particularly good, as are the desserts.

Other recommendations: Late-night pizza is served Monday–Saturday, 9:30–10:30 P.M.

Summary & comments: This is mainly unpretentious traditional Italian cooking expertly prepared. It's one of the few restaurants you'll find doing its best business on a Monday night. The fact that it's located in a light industrial area makes it the more remarkable that it can still draw crowds of regulars.

The Buckeye

	New American
Zone 10 Suburban Marin	★★★★½
17 Shoreline Highway, Mill Valley	Moderate
(415) 331-2600	Quality 95 Value A

Reservations:	Required
When to go:	Weeknights, lunch, Sunday brunch
Entree range:	$6–15
Payment:	All major credit cards
Service rating:	★★★★
Friendliness rating:	★★★★
Parking:	Free lot
Bar:	Full service
Wine selection:	Extensive
Dress:	Informal
Disabled access:	Good
Customers:	Local, tourist, business
Brunch:	Sunday, 10:30 A.M.–3 P.M.
Lunch/Dinner:	Every day, 11 A.M.–10 P.M.

Atmosphere / setting: The Buckeye calls itself a roadhouse, but the interior, with its massive river stone fireplace, towering beamed ceiling, dark wood paneling, and flower-strewn green carpet, is more reminiscent of a Bavarian hunting lodge, and a very welcoming one indeed.

House specialties: Crisp clouds of feathery onion rings with homemade ketchup; oysters on the half shell; warm spinach salad with olives, feta, and applewood-smoked bacon; meats, fish, and poultry cured in the brick backyard smoker; Dungeness crab cakes; smoked pheasant hunter's pie. Brunch favorites include a sinfully rich cheese grits soufflé; oysters Bingo, broiled with spinach and aïoli; smoked Atlantic salmon; corned-beef hash with poached eggs. Baked lemon pudding; butterscotch brûlée; and chocolate pecan cake à la mode.

Other recommendations: New Orleans gumbo; braised lamb shank with shallots, mint, and fennel; grilled beer sausages with sweet-and-sour cabbage.

Summary & comments: The Buckeye elevates restaurant dining to a plane of pure pleasure. Owner Cindy Pawclin, of Fog City Diner fame, aims true again with her fairy-tale country roadhouse: the wanderer welcomed to a blazing baronial fireside, with some highly sophisticated elves working their magic in the kitchen. The jocular, moderately priced menu is so loaded with scrumptious comfort food, it's hard to get enough in just one visit: might as well just move in. Only trouble is, The Buckeye's excellence is no secret. Call at least a week and a half in advance for reservations for a weekend dinner. Do go for Sunday brunch, the coziest in the county on a foggy day.

Cacti

1200 Grant Avenue, Novato
(415) 898-2234

Southwestern
★★
Moderate
Quality 79   Value C-

Reservations:	Recommended
When to go:	Any time
Entree range:	$6.95–18.75
Payment:	All major credit cards
Service rating:	★★★
Friendliness rating:	★★½
Parking:	Free lot, street
Bar:	Full service
Wine selection:	Fair
Dress:	Informal
Disabled access:	Good
Customers:	Local, business, tourist
Lunch:	Every day, 11:30 A.M.–2 P.M.
Dinner:	Sunday–Thursday, 5–9 P.M.;
	Friday and Saturday, 5–10 P.M.

Atmosphere / setting: In a converted church with adobe-style walls, arched doorways, a high open-beamed ceiling, and a belfry, Cacti's yucca-lined entrance leads the way to old California. The interior is cool, with a selection of canciones on the sound system, and there's a walled patio as well.

House specialties: Crab cakes with roasted red pepper sauce; grilled tuna with tequila-lime butter; BBQ baby-back ribs. Mexican specialties: tamales, tostadas, chile rellenos; rib eye with adobo sauce.

Other recommendations: Chicken lime tortilla soup; sirloin burger; grilled mixed vegetable platter; chicken tostada; pecan pie.

Summary & comments: Cacti's cuisine is more Baja than haute, and perhaps a bit overpriced. But it is a delightful place to hang out on a warm evening, especially on the patio, and the more moderately priced menu items, including the burgers, Mexican dishes, and vegetarian plates are decently prepared in satisfying portions.

Cafe de la Paz

Zone 12   Berkeley
1600 Shattuck Avenue
(510) 843-0662

	Latin American
	★★½
	Moderate
	Quality 79 Value B

Reservations:	Accepted
When to go:	Any time
Entree range:	$6.95–12.75
Payment:	DC, MC
Service rating:	★★
Friendliness rating:	★★½
Parking:	Street
Bar:	Beer, wine
Wine selection:	Limited but good
Dress:	Casual
Disabled access:	Yes
Customers:	Local
Dinner:	Tuesday–Saturday, 5:30–10 P.M.;
	Sunday and Monday, 5–9 P.M.

Atmosphere / setting: This space originally housed a Japanese restaurant, and its light wood and small fountain recall that. The tables and other decor are accordingly simple. A few posters and textile hangings calmly announce that the theme now is south of the border–far south, i.e., southern Mexico and South America. The kitchen is separated from the dining area by a picture window, and the view is excellent.

House specialties: Seafood, poultry, and vegetarian dishes. Enchiladas of sautéed vegetables, roasted corn, and almond pieces with red ranchero sauce; mushroom stew with sun-dried tomatoes and a Venezuelan corn cake; Brazilian seafood stew with coconut milk and incendiary habanero peppers; Ecuadorian potato-onion cake stuffed with cheeses and covered in red sauce.

Other recommendations: Cafe cornbread made with whole kernels and buttermilk.

Summary & comments: The theme of the menu may seem a bit diffuse, drawing as it does on a wide range of styles. But it draws on those things that are common to the region between Yucatan and the Amazon: corn, chilies, beans, dairy products, and seafood; and the grill and the sauté pan. The vegetarian selections are particularly satisfying, especially considering that it's hard to find this style of cookery without meat.

Cafe Majestic

Zone 2   Civic Center
1500 Sutter Street
(415) 776-6400

California
★★★½
Expensive

Quality 87   Value B+

Reservations:	Recommended
When to go:	Any time
Entree range:	$14–25
Payment:	AMEX, MC, VISA
Service rating:	★★★★
Friendliness rating:	★★★
Parking:	Valet
Bar:	Full service
Wine selection:	Limited but very good
Dress:	Business
Disabled access:	Yes
Customers:	Local, tourist, business
Breakfast:	Tuesday–Friday, 7–11 A.M.
Brunch:	Saturday and Sunday, 8 A.M.–2 P.M.
Lunch:	Tuesday–Friday, 11:30 A.M.–2 P.M.
Dinner:	Every day, 6–10 P.M.

Atmosphere / setting: Evokes an older, more elegant San Francisco, when long black Cadillacs pulled up to the awning at the entrance and disgorged their tuxedoed and begowned passengers.

House specialties: Ravioli stuffed with salmon and a lemon-thyme sauce; lamb-stuffed egg rolls; pork medallions with apples, calvados, and cream.

Other recommendations: The appetizer menu, which is in constant flux.

Summary & comments: Located in the hotel of the same name, this place counts as a landmark. The menu reflects the diversity of California culture and cuisine: cooking techniques and equipment are traditional western, and seasonings and many ingredients take advantage of Asian contributions. Ginger, pepper, and sesame are a common baseline in the culinary tune.

California Cafe

Zone 10   Suburban Marin
The Village Center, Corte Madera
(415) 924-2233

New American	
★★★½	
Moderate	
Quality 89	Value B

Reservations:	Recommended on weekends
When to go:	Any time
Entree range:	Brunch or lunch, $7.95–10.95; dinner, $8.95–18.95
Payment:	AMEX, MC, VISA
Service rating:	★★★½
Friendliness rating:	★★★½
Parking:	Free lot
Bar:	Full service
Wine selection:	Good
Dress:	Casual, informal
Disabled access:	Good
Customers:	Local, business, tourist,
Brunch:	Sunday, 11 A.M.–3 P.M.
Lunch:	Every day, 11 A.M.–5 P.M.
Dinner:	Every day, 5–9 P.M.

Atmosphere / setting: With its airy, plant-filled atrium, buttoned-down Mediterranean interior, and tinkling baby grand, California Cafe presents a soothing haven for shopped-out matrons, harried business folk, and cruising tourists. The Village Center is perhaps Marin County's poshest shopping area.

House specialties: Roasted garlic with melted Cambozola cheese and tomato chutney; Maryland crab cakes; scallion noodles with spicy Thai curried duck; roast western veal loin with apple butter and parsnip fritters; steamed mahimahi with baby bok choy, carrots, broccoli, and dipping sauces; house-smoked baby-back ribs.

Other recommendations: Black-bean burger on a cilantro roll for vegetarians; savory bread pudding with Roquefort cheese and walnuts; pot roast in cabernet with horseradish and vegetables.

Summary & comments: California cuisine (you should pardon the expression) ably interpreted by chef Maureen Hayes. The California Cafe is a reliable standby for eclectic, creatively prepared dishes utilizing fresh, local ingredients and catering to a variety of tastes. No longer unique, but it's still hard to go wrong here. Desserts are especially delicious.

California Culinary Academy

Zone 2   Civic Center
625 Polk Street
(415) 771-1655

California
★★½
Inexpensive

Quality 79   Value A

Reservations:	Accepted
When to go:	Any time
Entree range:	$7.50–12
Payment:	Major credit cards
Service rating:	★★★
Friendliness rating:	★★★
Parking:	Street
Bar:	Full service
Wine selection:	Good
Dress:	Casual to business
Disabled access:	Yes
Customers:	Everybody
Lunch:	Monday–Friday, 11:30 A.M.–2 P.M.
Dinner:	Monday–Friday, 5:30–9 P.M.

Atmosphere / setting: Respectable without being ponderous. Bright and airy with a happy feeling.

House specialties: California cuisine prepared under the direction of European masters. Mesquite grill dishes; monster steaks; pastas in creamy sauces; freshest of fresh vegetable dishes.

Other recommendations: Chile con carne; corn bread and other grain dishes. Light menu items low on cream, butter, and salt.

Summary & comments: The cooks and waiters are all students, and the food they prepare and serve is their class work. Because they are students, we get a real deal on the price. It's one of the best bargains in town. They operate three different dining rooms, each with its own menu. In the main room the fixed-price menu offers five courses for about $27.

Cambodiana's

Zone 12   Berkeley
2156 University Avenue
(510) 843-4630

	Cambodian
	★★★
	Moderate
	Quality 89 Value A

Reservations:	Accepted
When to go:	Any time
Entree range:	$6.25–12
Payment:	Major credit cards
Service rating:	★★★
Friendliness rating:	★★
Parking:	Street
Bar:	Beer, wine
Wine selection:	Limited but good
Dress:	Casual, business
Disabled access:	Fair
Customers:	Local, ethnic
Lunch:	Monday–Friday, 11:30 A.M.–3 P.M.
Dinner:	Monday–Thursday, 5–10 P.M.;
	Friday and Saturday, 5–10:30 P.M.;
	Sunday, 5–9:30 P.M.

Atmosphere / setting: Small, deep, narrow, and intimate. The decor recalls Angkor Wat, but in a subdued way. It tells you you're in a Southeast Asian restaurant, but it doesn't scream it at you.

House specialties: Traditional Cambodian dishes with a strong French influence. The menu is arranged by sauce type, and the chef uses butter and wine in addition to Asian ingredients. Lamb Chops Cambodiana is the signature dish of the house. Marinated in lemongrass, sugar, lime leaves, garlic, turmeric, and galanga, and then grilled to a glaze. Served drizzled with shallot butter, parsley, and fresh red jalapeño minced so fine that its flavor is delivered in little sparkles of heat that dance on the tongue and never quite burn.

Other recommendations: Smokey eggplant country style. A charred and peeled eggplant, chopped and served dressed with a spicy mixture of stir-fried pork. Steaks and snails and pork-stuffed quails.

Summary & comments: Located at the top of University Avenue among so many other Asian restaurants, it would seem to be a bit of Far Eastern overkill. But this place is unique. Owner Sidney Ke is a highly educated man with one foot in the East and one foot in the West and his palate in the middle. The result in the kitchen is a cookery in which the whole is greater than the sum of its parts.

Campton Place

Zone 3 Union Square	American
340 Stockton Street	★★★★★
(415) 781-5555	Expensive
	Quality 99 Value C

Reservations:	Recommended
When to go:	Always
Entree range:	$24–28
Payment:	All credit cards
Service rating:	★★★★★
Friendliness rating:	★★★★
Parking:	Valet
Bar:	Full service
Wine selection:	Excellent
Dress:	Wear a tie
Disabled access:	Yes
Customers:	Business, tourist, demanding
Breakfast:	Monday–Friday, 7–11 A.M.; Saturday, 8–11 A.M.
Brunch:	Sunday, 8 A.M.–2:30 P.M.
Lunch:	Monday–Friday, 11:30 A.M.–2:30 P.M.
Dinner:	Sunday–Thursday, 5:30–10 P.M.;
	Friday and Saturday, 5:30–10:30 P.M.

Atmosphere / setting: Formal but friendly. Tieless men won't be turned away, but they will feel more comfortable with them. Decor is modern, clean, and spare compared to most luxurious establishments. Lots of flowers. An elegant setting for a breakfast of corned beef hash and poached eggs.

House specialties: Breakfast is famous here. All the traditional favorites, including corn muffins light as a cloud. For dinner: duck ravioli with a summer vegetable; lobster Napoleon with crisp potatoes; roasted meats well seasoned and juicy; variety of terrines; veal rack with pasta.

Other recommendations: Desserts. Especially the fig tart.

Summary & comments: In the hotel of the same name. This is a temple to the muse of American cooking in a city famous for its foreign culinary deities. Excellent American fare prepared to the most rigorous European standards but without the emphasis on fancy sauces. Mark Twain would have dined here and written glowingly of it, had it existed in his time. It's very expensive, right down to the drinks in the bar. But there is nothing here that's overpriced. Quality is king and you get what you pay for.

THE CANTINA

Zone 13   Oakland
4239 Park Boulevard
(510) 482-3663

Mexican
★★★
Inexpensive

Quality 80   Value B+

Reservations:	Recommended for weekend nights
When to go:	Any time
Entree range:	$6.99–13.99
Payment:	VISA, MC, AMEX
Service rating:	★★★
Friendliness rating:	★★★★
Parking:	Free lot
Bar:	Full service
Wine selection:	House
Dress:	Casual
Disabled access:	Good
Customers:	Local
Brunch:	Sunday, 10 A.M.–noon
Lunch/Dinner:	Monday–Thursday, 11:30 A.M.–9 P.M.;
	Friday and Saturday, 11:30 A.M.–10 P.M.

Atmosphere / setting: A large and spacious dining room, a place for happy crowds. A Norte Americano Mexican decor with overtones of sports bardom. Includes a screened veranda for semi-alfresco dining. Heat lamps make it usable year-round.

House specialties: The "Outrageous Combo," an enormous plate of well-prepared Mexican usuals. It easily feeds two people, and couples can sometimes be seen eating it together from the one huge plate. Also, the tortilla soup is wonderful. Fish tacos, common in Mexico but rarely seen north of the border. A great variety of fajitas.

Other recommendations: All the Mexican standards.

Entertainment & amenities: A mariachi trio strolls throughout the place on Thursday and Saturday nights. The guitarist is father to Carlos Santana. The bar features "Taco Tuesday" every week, offering dinner tacos for $.25 from 3–8 P.M.

Summary & comments: Come here a second time and you're bound to see faces from your first visit. In the bar the staff will either remember your name or address you as "Captain." Some of the many regulars call this place the Bodega, after Hemmingway's hangout in Havana. Dining in the bar is especially pleasant here, as is drinking pitchers of margaritas and watching the game, or just hanging out.

THE CAPRICE

Zone 9   Waterfront Crescent
2000 Paradise Drive, Tiburon
(415) 435-3400

New American	
★★★½	
Moderate	
Quality 89	Value C

Reservations:	Accepted
When to go:	Dinner
Entree range:	$13.50–22.50
Payment:	MC, VISA
Service rating:	★★★
Friendliness rating:	★★★
Parking:	Free lot
Bar:	Beer, wine
Wine selection:	Excellent
Dress:	Informal
Disabled access:	Good
Customers:	Local, tourist, business
Brunch:	Seasonal, call
Lunch:	Seasonal, call
Dinner:	Every day, 5:30–9:30 P.M.

Atmosphere / setting: The Caprice, cantilevered over Tiburon Bay, enjoys breathtaking views of Angel Island, San Francisco, and the Golden Gate. The dining rooms are snug and cozy with low-beamed ceilings. Quiet, romantic, a bit old-fashioned; a fire flickers in the entry hall, and the windows reflect the glow from cut-glass candleholders on each table. No al fresco dining available here, which can be a drawback on summer evenings.

House specialties: Seasonal changing menu: pasta with braised beef, wild mushrooms, and vegetables; sesame-crusted salmon; rack of lamb with artichoke hearts, olives, tomatoes, and grilled polenta. Chocolate bread pudding; pear and ginger clafouti; cranberry and roasted chestnut crème brûlée.

Other recommendations: Smoked prawn and tomatillo bisque in a cornbread tureen; braised duck and potato cakes; warm wild mushroom terrine.

Summary & comments: The Caprice is an anomaly: wildly dramatic setting, slightly fusty, antiquated decor, and chef Kirke Byer's bold, imaginative menu. The total effect is a little bewildering, like watching a movie that can't decide if it's a thriller, a romance, or a comedy. Still, watching the ferries and party boats twinkle across the choppy straits from the warmth of Caprice's tiny dining room; savoring a goblet of red wine and a complex cassoulet and melting crème brûlée; who cares if the furniture lacks panache? There's also a heady stroll along the waterfront providing an opportunity to walk off the rich cuisine.

The Carnelian Room

New American

★★★★

Expensive

Quality 93   Value B

Zone 4   Financial District
555 California
(415) 433-7500

Reservations:	Recommended
When to go:	Sunset, brunch, or any time
Entree range:	Sunday champagne brunch, $22.50; prix-fixe dinner, $31; entrees, $19–29
Payment:	All major credit cards
Service rating:	★★★½
Friendliness rating:	★★½
Parking:	Pay lots and garages, street
Bar:	Full service
Wine selection:	Excellent
Dress:	Informal, dressy
Disabled access:	Good
Customers:	Tourist, business, local
Brunch:	Sunday, 10 A.M.–2 P.M.
Dinner:	Every day, 5:30–10 P.M.

Atmosphere / setting: High above the city on the 52nd floor of the Bank of America Building, the Carnelian Room is a private banker's club by day, and it looks it, with high, dark wood paneling, soft carpet, and upholstered chairs. But the main set decoration is the breathtaking wrap-around views of San Francisco, the bay, the fog, and the hills beyond. The main dining room is the most formal; there's a lounge with equally stunning views and limited food service.

House specialties: Pâté of Sonoma foie gras; Dungeness crab cake with French green bean salad; fresh dill-cured salmon; escargots in phyllo; tableside Caesar salad; twice-roasted duck breast; roasted rack of lamb gremolata; braised sea scallops with Swiss chard; live Maine lobster.

Other recommendations: Prix-fixe three-course dinner; Grand Marnier soufflé with crème anglaise.

Summary & comments: Restaurant trends may come and go, but nothing quite equals the glamour of an expensive dinner high in the sky. The Bank of America's high speed elevator has an unnerving rumble as it zooms to the top of the world, but in the bar and dining room, luxury and peace prevail. Service is impeccable, if a bit stiff, and the food is fine, though not wildly adventuresome. Appetizers and drinks, or coffee and desserts in the more intimate lounge, are an excellent way to enjoy the amenities for less money, and the three-course Sunday brunch, with unlimited champagne, is a decent value.

Honors / awards: *Wine Spectator* Grand Award since 1982.

Casa Aguila

Zone 8   Richmond/Avenues
1240 Noriega Street
(415) 661-5593

Mexican	
★★½	
Moderate	
Quality 79	Value B

Reservations:	Not accepted
When to go:	Any time
Entree range:	$8.50–14.50
Payment:	AMEX, VISA, MC
Service rating:	★★
Friendliness rating:	★★★
Parking:	Street
Bar:	Beer, wine
Wine selection:	House
Dress:	Casual
Disabled access:	Yes
Customers:	Local
Lunch:	Every day, 11:30 A.M.–3:30 P.M.
Dinner:	Every day, 4:30–10 P.M.

Atmosphere / setting: Bright and colorful, a fiesta of color. Neat and orderly and well kept. Numerous paper fruits, vegetables, and cacti hanging from the walls.

House specialties: All the usual suspects in a Mexican restaurant: tacos, burritos, enchiladas, but much more as well. Moles sweetened with raisins and dates; ceviche with crisp veggies in it; carne erlinda; puerco adobado marinated in citrus and garlic and broiled, served with vegetable and rice; roast beef.

Other recommendations: Very serious seafood, mostly grilled and basted with citrus and cilantro.

Summary & comments: One of the most memorable things about Casa Aguila is the presentation. Dishes are sculpted rather than simply arranged on a hot plate and set on the table as in most Mexican restaurants. The shapes, colors, and textures of food are presented to bring out their most pleasing qualities. A great attention to detail is paid to everything here.

The Cats

Zone 14   South Bay
17533 Highway 17, Los Gatos
(408) 354-4020

Barbecue	
★★½	
Moderate	
Quality 75	Value B

Reservations:	Not accepted
When to go:	Any time
Entree range:	$8.95–14.95
Payment:	VISA, MC
Service rating:	★★
Friendliness rating:	★★★
Parking:	Lot
Bar:	Full service
Wine selection:	Fair
Dress:	Casual
Disabled access:	Yes
Customers:	Local
Dinner:	Tuesday–Sunday, 5:30–10:30 P.M.

Atmosphere / setting: An old highway roadhouse. Warm and dark, with exposed beams and that feeling for the traveler that "here there is succor." Just off the bar is a lounge where a fire burns when it's cold outside. In the dining room you sit in view of the brick barbecue pit. Tables are wood with simple check cloths, almost a picnic setting, as befits a barbecue place.

House specialties: Barbecue, baked potatoes, and salad. You only have to choose what meat you want. Beef, pork, chicken, or sausage.

Entertainment & amenities: In the lounge sits a baby grand piano, a somewhat incongruous instrument for the rustic setting. But the local folk are a sophisticated lot, and on weekends some pretty good music of any variety might be played.

Summary & comments: It's very easy to miss this place. It's on the west side of Highway 17 just as you leave Los Gatos heading south. It's on a bend in the road and if you blink you'll miss it. Call and ask directions first. Because of its coziness and feeling of rustic isolation, this is an especially good place to go in bad weather. Snuggle next to the fire, sip a hot buttered rum, and pretend the world is far away.

CAVA 555

Zone 7   SOMA / Mission
555 Second Street
(415) 543-2282

American	
★★★½	
Moderate	
Quality 88	Value B

Reservations:	Recommended
When to go:	Any time
Entree range:	Lunch, $5.55; dinner, $13.25–22
Payment:	AMEX, VISA, MC
Service rating:	★★★
Friendliness rating:	★★★
Parking:	Street
Bar:	Full service
Wine selection:	Excellent
Dress:	Casual, informal
Disabled access:	Good
Customers:	Local, business, tourist
Lunch:	Tuesday–Friday, 11:30 A.M.–2:30 P.M.
Dinner:	Monday–Friday, 5–10:30 P.M.;
	Saturday, 6–10:30 P.M.

Atmosphere / setting: Black, red, and burnished steel with starlight chandeliers and two walls of wine racks, this intimate urban jazz and supper club vibrates with chromium and champagne style. Nightly live jazz, with a $5 cover charge only on the weekends. Take note: smoking is allowed in this narrow little space, but happily the high ceiling wafts away most of the fumes.

House specialties: Roast eggplant soup with sage cream; buckwheat blinis with caviar, gravlax, and vodka crème fraiche; grilled rare tuna with braised leeks and gremolata; roast stuffed chicken with garlic mashed potatoes and pear eau de vie.

Other recommendations: Small, luscious seasonal desserts: warm strawberry rhubarb crisp with vanilla bean gelato; chocolate torte with Grand Marnier.

Summary & comments: After a surfeit of Mediterranean bistros, brasseries, and trattorii, this frankly postmodern club would be a breath of fresh air were it not for the smoking at the bar. Still, the small menu is enticing and admirably executed, and the jazz is wonderful. Late-night desserts and appetizers are served on weekends.

Cha Cha Cha

<table>
<tr><td></td><td>Latin American</td></tr>
<tr><td>Zone 8   Richmond/Avenues</td><td>★★★½</td></tr>
<tr><td>1805 Haight Street</td><td>Inexpensive/Moderate</td></tr>
<tr><td>(415) 386-7670</td><td>Quality 85   Value A</td></tr>
</table>

Reservations:	Not accepted
When to go:	Lunch or early weekday dinner
Entree range:	Tapas, $4.50–7.75; Entrees, $10.50–12.50
Payment:	Cash only
Service rating:	★★★
Friendliness rating:	★★½
Parking:	Street
Bar:	Beer, wine
Wine selection:	House
Dress:	Casual
Disabled access:	Limited
Customers:	Local, tourist
Brunch:	Saturday and Sunday, 10 A.M.–4 P.M.
Lunch:	Monday–Friday, 11:30 A.M.–3 P.M.
Dinner:	Sunday–Thursday, 5–11 P.M.;
	Friday and Saturday, 5–11:30 P.M.

Atmosphere / setting: Astonishingly noisy and crowded, with a funky location, nightmare parking, punk decor, and totally awesome local color.

House specialties: Sangria by the glass or pitcher; tapas plates—really medium-sized entree portions—which include the regular menu and daily specials: warm spinach salad; Cajun sautéed shrimp; saffron steamed mussels with garlic, tomatoes, and onions; BBQ pork quesadilla; Jamaican jerk chicken over rice; fried calamari with lemon-garlic aïoli; flatiron steak with mashed potatoes, ancho garlic gravy, and warm roasted corn and squash salad; ceviche; fried chili pepper snapper with salsa and rice. .

Summary & comments: Haight Street in the 90s is not for the faint of heart. Neither is Cha Cha Cha, where you're practically frisked at the door, the noise level approaches the ballistic, and the wait at the counter is sometimes three deep. But, pierced body parts and all, the pandemonium is engaging, the service surprisingly efficient, and the tapas superb, served with lots of warm French bread to soak up the piquant and savory sauces. Cha Cha Cha is for a night when you're feeling young and ready for adventure; go with a group to share the substantial portions.

CHART HOUSE

Seafood	
★★★	
Moderate	
Quality 80	Value B

Zone 14   South Bay
8150 Cabrillo Highway, Montara Beach
(415) 728-7366

Reservations:	Accepted
When to go:	Sunset
Entree range:	$12.95–36.95
Payment:	Major credit cards
Service rating:	★★½
Friendliness rating:	★★½
Parking:	Lot
Bar:	Full service
Wine selection:	Good
Dress:	Casual
Disabled access:	Yes
Customers:	Local, tourist
Lunch:	Only for groups of 20 or more
Dinner:	Monday–Friday, 5–9 P.M.;
	Saturday and Sunday, 4–9 P.M.

Atmosphere / setting: A big, attractive building sitting right on the beach and facing the sea with high windows. A lot of heavy, padded lounge furniture makes it a good place to relax and watch the sun go down.

House specialties: Seafood, steak, prime rib, etc. All dinners include rice or potato and all-you-can-eat salad bar. The menu is good, featuring the usual stuff, but not terribly innovative.

Summary & comments: No one could ever complain about the menu. It's good, solid, honest, fresh-from-the-sea fish and shellfish, top quality meats, and crisp vegetables and salads. But anyone could do it. What you come here for is the setting. It's a long drive from anywhere and it's worth it. The beach house architecture and decor, the gentile air of the place, and the sound of the surf are all tonic for care.

Chevy's

Zone 10 Suburban Marin	Mexican
302 Bon Air Center, Greenbrae	★★½
(415) 461-3203	Inexpensive
	Quality 78 Value A

Reservations:	Accepted for parties of 5 or more
When to go:	Any time
Entree range:	$6.95–13.95
Payment:	AMEX, MC, VISA
Service rating:	★★★★
Friendliness rating:	★★★★
Parking:	Free shopping center lot
Bar:	Full service
Wine selection:	House
Dress:	Casual
Disabled access:	Good
Customers:	Locals, families, parties
Lunch/Dinner:	Sunday–Thursday, 11:30 A.M.–10 P.M.;
	Friday and Saturday, 11:30 A.M.–11 P.M.

Atmosphere / setting: Chevy's is arguably one of the best of the new breed of chain restaurants which began to emerge in the '80s: amusing, casual settings with economically priced menus. The decor mirrors any other restaurant in the chain: droll Mexican, with painted concrete floors, faux adobe textured walls, neon desert scenes and murals; colorful oilcloth table covers; stacks of beer cases, and the centerpiece tortilla machine. The cheerful din is ideal for family dining and group celebrations. Off-street patio seating is available in good weather.

House specialties: Homemade chips and roasted tomato salsa; homemade flour tortillas; chicken, pork, beef, or vegetable fajitas; carne asada; mesquite-grilled quail; fresh fish.

Other recommendations: Mexican combination plates; chile rellenos; whole-wheat chicken quesadillas; Mexican coffee with Kahlua and whipped cream.

Summary & comments: With the hum of the tortilla machine, the effervescent burble of salsa music, and the swiftly moving young staff, Chevy's is definitely not the place for a quiet evening. But the chain claims to use only the freshest ingredients; a new batch of salsa is made every 20 minutes. The platters are generous, the flavors hearty, and the service friendly and upbeat. Chevy's is crowded on weekend evenings, but large enough that the wait is seldom long. Since reservations are available for groups of five or more, for families, or economy-minded group parties, lunch or dinner at Chevy's is satisfying, reasonable, and generally a lot of fun.

Chez Luis

Zone 14   South Bay
4170 El Camino Real, Palo Alto
(415) 493-9365

French	
★★½	
Moderate	
Quality 75	Value B

Reservations:	Accepted
When to go:	Wednesdays and Thursdays
Entree range:	$15–23.95
Payment:	Major credit cards
Service rating:	★★★
Friendliness rating:	★★½
Parking:	Free lot
Bar:	Full service
Wine selection:	Excellent
Dress:	Business
Disabled access:	Yes
Customers:	Local, regulars
Lunch:	Monday–Friday, 11:30 A.M.–2 P.M.
Dinner:	Monday–Saturday, 5:30–10:30 P.M.

Atmosphere / setting: French country cottage. Blue collar with Gallic flair. The usual French table settings and wall hangings juxtaposed to shag carpet and exposed ceilings, and a cigarette vending machine in the foyer. A definite pattina of age.

House specialties: Magret of duck, milk-fed veal (nothing PC here), rack of lamb, and the usual entrees that we expect with a French menu. No surprises.

Other recommendations: Housemade vinegars for sale.

Entertainment & amenities: Dance floor.

Summary & comments: Behind the main dining room is the bistro, a room that can only be described as a Gallic bar and grill with a dance floor and wide-screen TV. A good selection of sandwiches and light entrees are to be had here. Major sporting events draw a crowd of TV regulars, and on Wednesday and Thursday evenings a two-drink minimum will get you free ballroom dance lessons. The bartender is quite friendly and her Scottish burr is charming. If this place sounds hard to define, it's only because it is. But a restaurant doesn't last for decades without good reason.

Chez Panisse Cafe

<table>
<tr><td></td><td>California</td></tr>
<tr><td>Zone 12   Berkeley</td><td>★★★½</td></tr>
<tr><td>1617 Shattuck Avenue</td><td>Expensive</td></tr>
<tr><td>(510) 548-5525</td><td>Quality 89   Value C</td></tr>
</table>

Reservations:	Monday–Thursday only
When to go:	Early or late
Entree range:	$14–16.50
Payment:	VISA, MC, AMEX, DC
Service rating:	★★★
Friendliness rating:	★★★
Parking:	Street
Bar:	Beer, wine
Wine selection:	Good
Dress:	Casual
Disabled access:	Good
Customers:	Local, regular
Lunch:	Monday–Thursday, 11:30 A.M.–3 P.M.; Friday and Saturday, 11:30 A.M.–4 P.M.
Dinner:	Monday–Saturday, 5–11 P.M.

Atmosphere / setting: Upstairs at Chez Panisse. Seating just under a hundred, it's twice the size of the restaurant downstairs. A much less formal atmosphere with wood floors and walls. It looks a bit like a large deck, but it's indoors. The open kitchen sits in the center of the long, narrow room, and watching the cooks at work is a lesson in superior craftsmanship. It's a good place to bring the kids, and it's a lot cheaper (relative term) than some of the other choices in the area.

House specialties: The menu changes constantly with what is available and up to the exacting standards the place is famous for. There is usually a grill dish such as leg of lamb with white bean salad; seafood is normal, such as baked chili pepper cod; fowl includes duck braised in red wine with grilled polenta; pastas are a favorite with such choices as hand-cut noodles with capers and ricotta salad.

Other recommendations: Pizzetta, rocket salad, black figs with prosciutto, and fruit tarts with ice cream.

Summary & comments: All the standards that apply to the restaurant apply to the cafe. But things here are simpler, less formal, and less expensive, though still not cheap. You get what you pay for. Nobody leaves here thinking they were overcharged. It's a popular place for a rendezvous, or to bring the kids, or simply to relax over an aperitif at the end of the day.

Chez Panisse Restaurant

Zone 12 Berkeley	California
1517 Shattuck Avenue	★★★★½
(510) 548-5525	Expensive
	Quality 95 Value B

Reservations:	Recommended
When to go:	Any time
Entree range:	Fixed-price menu only
Payment:	VISA, MC, AMEX, DC
Service rating:	★★★
Friendliness rating:	★★★
Parking:	Street
Bar:	Beer, wine
Wine selection:	Excellent
Dress:	Business
Disabled access:	Good
Customers:	Local, tourist
Dinner:	Monday–Saturday, first sitting 6 P.M., second sitting 8:30 P.M.

Atmosphere / setting: The restaurant is surprisingly small and, while rather formal, unpretentious considering its international reputation. The decor is soft, comfortable, trimmed in redwood, and deeply carpeted. Walls, fixtures, settings, etc., are all attractive but rather muted. Nothing to distract you from your dinner.

House specialties: The menu is set. Everybody gets the same dinner for the same price, differing only in your wine selection. A recent menu included grilled quail salad with pancetta crostini, summer savory, and pickled cherries; white corn soup with roasted chilies; Northern halibut with new potatoes, Chino ranch beans, tomatoes, and wild fennel; summer pudding.

Other recommendations: Whatever is for dinner the following night.

Summary & comments: This is where Alice Waters birthed California cuisine. It's hard to think of a restaurant, or any other human enterprise, where standards are higher or more rigorously adhered to. Only the freshest ingredients possible are used here. Over the years Chef Waters has developed her own sources of supply, which are often named in the menu. The single menu idea gives the kitchen staff the opportunity to concentrate their efforts and ensure that everything is perfect.

CHINA HOUSE BISTRO

Zone 8 Richmond/Avenues	Chinese
501 Balboa at Sixth Street	★★★½
(415) 752-2802	Inexpensive/Moderate
	Quality 84 Value A

Reservations:	Recommended on weekends
When to go:	Any time
Entree range:	$6.50–32
Payment:	All major credit cards
Service rating:	★★★★
Friendliness rating:	★★★★
Parking:	Street
Bar:	Full service
Wine selection:	Fair
Dress:	Informal
Disabled access:	Good
Customers:	Local, business, tourist
Dinner:	Every day, 5:30–10:30 P.M.

Atmosphere / setting: 1930s Shanghai-style cafe, with muted, provocative color scheme and lighting, ceiling fans, and schoolhouse lamps; antique wood bar and bentwood chairs; white tablecloths and a mural of old Shanghai.

House specialties: Shanghai cooking, including exceptional vegetarian or pork pot stickers; sautéed pea sprouts with prawns; silver sprouts; jumping hot fish; sea bass in seaweed; Shanghai smoked pomfret; warm celery and shrimp salad; Peking spare ribs; Lion's Head, huge, tender pork meatballs with gravy; hot chili fried prawns oriental; Beijing tossed noodles with minced pork or mushrooms; Shanghai crispy duck.

Other recommendations: Eight treasure rice pudding for dessert; or Yang Chow crêpes.

Summary & comments: In a setting reminiscent of the cultured cafe society of Shanghai in the 1930s, owners Joseph and Cecilia Chung have created a timeless showcase for their memorable dishes. This is a Chinese cafe with something extra: a subtle glimpse into another era, complete with welcoming host and hostess, who happily expound on the particulars of their cookery and the Shanghai experience. And the food is distinctive, unlike Cantonese or Szechuan styles, with a smoky, almost tropical quality all its own.

Chopsticks

Zone 10   Suburban Marin
508 Third Street, San Rafael
(415) 456-4942

	Chinese
	★½
	Inexpensive
	Quality 69 Value A

Reservations:	Not necessary
When to go:	Any time
Entree range:	$3.79–6.29
Payment:	Cash
Service rating:	★★★½
Friendliness rating:	★★★½
Parking:	Free lot
Bar:	Beer, wine
Wine selection:	House
Dress:	Casual
Disabled access:	Limited
Customers:	Local, business
Lunch:	Monday–Saturday, 11 A.M.–3 P.M.
Dinner:	Monday–Saturday, 11 A.M.–9:30 P.M.

Atmosphere / setting: Your basic, no frills, workingman's Chinese. The atmosphere is notable for its anonymity; this is not the place to go for ambiance. However, the proprietor keeps a stack of newspapers handy, so if you like to bury your nose in the news over a hot, cheap meal, Chopsticks is your place.

House specialties: Salt and pepper prawns; seasonal greens with barbecued pork; crispy Hong Kong–style chow mein; vegetable chow fun; and curried Sing Chew rice noodles with pork, shrimp, and eggs.

Other recommendations: Lunch special plates including soup, fried wontons, fried rice, chow mein, and choice of entree; also the special dishes handwritten on the wall nearest the door.

Summary & comments: Most Marin County Chinese restaurants spiff up their decor to appeal to affluent diners, raising their prices to match. Not Chopsticks, which specializes in large portions, low prices, and basic amenities. The place has passionate devotees, possibly because of the cheapest Chinese food in the county, but also because the staff is very kind, and the chef woks up a few unusual items hard to find outside of Chinatown. The wontons, served in a tasty broth with some bok choy and carrot and a pot of chili paste on request, hold their own with the best. The Sing Chew rice noodles are an adventure all by themselves. The Hong Kong–style chow mein is a gargantuan pancake of noodles fried crisp on the outside, gooey on the inside, topped with lots of sauce and smoky greens and your choice of meat.

Christophe

	French
Zone 9 Waterfront Crescent	★★★½
1919 Bridgeway, Sausalito	Moderate
(415) 332-9244	Quality 85 Value A

Reservations:	Recommended on weekends
When to go:	Any time, but especially before 6:30 P.M. on weekdays, and 6 P.M. on weekends
Entree range:	Early bird dinner, $12.75; prix fixe, $20; a la carte, $12.75–16.50
Payment:	MC, VISA
Service rating:	★★★½
Friendliness rating:	★★★½
Parking:	Street
Bar:	Beer, wine
Wine selection:	Good
Dress:	Informal
Disabled access:	Limited
Customers:	Local, business, tourist
Dinner:	Tuesday–Sunday, 5:30–9:30 P.M.

Atmosphere / setting: Tiny and très charmant, Christophe is a French doll's dinner house, complete with Moulin Rouge stained glass, stylized Parisian ladies etched on the china, and Edith Piaf on the sound system. If you tend to feel claustrophobic in small places, Christophe may not be for you. Go early on a weekday for maximum space.

House specialties: Seasonal changing menu, which may include phyllo-wrapped brie in a roasted pepper sauce; duck confit; homemade duck liver pâté; spring lamb stew with white wine and seasonal vegetables; braised beef roast with mushroom cabernet sauce; chicken breast filled with spinach, cream cheese, and hazelnuts, baked in pastry.

Other recommendations: Cassoulet; brochette of pork with mustard and honey; veal medallions sautéed in vermouth and sage.

Summary & comments: Christophe has been around since 1978, long enough to go out of style and come back in a couple of times. One can only be glad for owner Gerald Maurange and his faithful clientele, since not only the four-course early bird dinners, served before 6:30 on weeknights and before 6 on weekends, but the regular prix-fixe menu as well may be the best values in Marin County. Christophe's cuisine is brilliant for its frugality, which is no small compliment in an era of growing austerity. To offer a four-course French dinner for $20 is an accomplishment; for $12.75 it is a grand coup.

CHRYSANTHEMUM

Zone 10   Suburban Marin
2214 Fourth Street, San Rafael
(415) 456-6926

	Chinese
	★★★
	Inexpensive
	Quality 85 Value A

Reservations:	Recommended on weekends
When to go:	Any time
Entree range:	Lunch plates, $4.95–5.95; dinner, $6.48–10.98
Payment:	MC, VISA
Service rating:	★★★½
Friendliness rating:	★★★
Parking:	Street, free lot
Bar:	Beer, wine
Wine selection:	House
Dress:	Casual, informal
Disabled access:	Good
Customers:	Local, business
Lunch:	Monday–Friday, 11:30 A.M.–2:30 P.M.; Sunday, noon–9:30 P.M.
Dinner:	Monday–Saturday, 4:30–10 P.M.; Sunday, noon–9:30 P.M.

Atmosphere / setting: Restful white, pink, green, and teak decor; several small dining rooms with cushioned chairs, brush painted prints, and soft classical music.

House specialties: Green onion pancake; cilantro beef soup; Mongolian beef or lamb; dry fried pepper pork chops; red braised whole rock cod; sizzling iron plates; Singapore-style curry rice noodles; prawn chow fun.

Summary & comments: On a night when a noisy table at a busy restaurant sounds like more trouble than it's worth, try tasteful little Chrysanthemum. The menu incorporates many styles of Chinese cooking, and all are executed with color and precision. Service is cordial, and the china and glassware are chosen with an eye to aesthetics unusual to a neighborhood Chinese place. Chrysanthemum is a rarity: inexpensive, unpretentious, yet obviously managed with care and attention to detail.

Clement Street
Bar and Grill

<table>
<tr><td>New American</td></tr>
<tr><td>★★</td></tr>
<tr><td>Moderate</td></tr>
</table>

Zone 8   Richmond/Avenues
708 Clement Street
(415) 386-2200

Quality 78   Value C+

Reservations:	Recommended on weekends
When to go:	Any time
Entree range:	Brunch, $4.95–9.50; lunch, $4.95–7.50; dinner, $8.95–14.95
Payment:	All major credit cards
Service rating:	★★★
Friendliness rating:	★★★½
Parking:	Street, metered during day
Bar:	Full service
Wine selection:	Fair
Dress:	Casual
Disabled access:	Good
Customers:	Local, business
Brunch:	Saturday and Sunday, 10:30 A.M.–3 P.M.
Lunch:	Tuesday–Friday, 11:30 A.M.–3 P.M.
Dinner:	Tuesday–Saturday, 5:30–10:30 P.M.; Sunday, 4:30–9:30 P.M.

Atmosphere / setting: From the entrance, Clement Street Bar and Grill seems dim, narrow, and dominated by the bar, but there's a roomy rear dining area with a sort of ship's cabin atmosphere and an impressive brick fireplace. It's simply furnished, but the cut-glass candles and white tablecloths add a touch of ceremony; coat hooks at the entry lend a genial, neighborhood mood. No smoking is allowed, despite the barroom atmosphere.

House specialties: Daily specials, which may include roasted garlic with crostini; roasted red pepper filled with three cheeses, herbs, and pine nuts over spinach salad; grilled fish specials; veal scallopini with wild mushrooms. Vegetarian offerings: grilled portobella mushroom with warm spinach and hazelnuts; grilled and roasted vegetables; wild mushroom tortellini.

Other recommendations: Salads, sandwiches, and burgers.

Summary & comments: Clement Street Bar and Grill is a sociable place, the sort of neighborhood restaurant one might head for when friends drop by unexpectedly. The service combines admirable professionalism with a nice absence of pretense. The regular menu offers standards, but there are daily special appetizers and entrees which are more interesting, generally decent, and often quite good.

Colonel Lee's Mongolian Barbecue

Mongolian	
★★	
Inexpensive	
Quality 75	Value B

Zone 14   South Bay
304 Castro Street, Mountain View
(415) 968-0381

Reservations:	Accepted
When to go:	Lunch
Entree range:	$7.55
Payment:	MC, VISA
Service rating:	★★
Friendliness rating:	★★
Parking:	Street
Bar:	Beer, wine
Wine selection:	House
Dress:	Casual
Disabled access:	Yes
Customers:	Local, business
Lunch:	Monday–Friday, 11 A.M.–2 P.M.
Dinner:	Every day, 5–9:30 P.M.

Atmosphere / setting: A big open space with tables and not-too-overt Far Eastern decor.

House specialties: There's only one thing here. You pick up a large bowl and walk by a long counter laden with meats and vegetables and pile on whatever strikes your gustatory fancy. Hand it off to one of the cooks at the equally long grill, and with great aplomb he dumps it onto the hot surface where he adds unusual blends of spices and sauces, tosses and pokes at it, and then launches it back into your bowl. Bon appétit Mongolian style.

Summary & comments: Every working day at lunchtime this place teems with hungry office workers. When the cooks are really hitting their rhythm, the service can be twice as fast as fast food and three times as good. Discounts for kids under 12.

Comforts

Zone 10 Suburban Marin	New American
337 San Anselmo Avenue, San Anselmo	★★★
(415) 454-6790	Moderate
	Quality 84 Value C+

Reservations:	Recommended .
When to go:	Any time
Entree range:	Breakfast, $3.95–7.50; lunch, $5.95–9.95; dinner, $6.95–16.95
Payment:	AMEX, MC, DC, VISA
Service rating:	★★½
Friendliness rating:	★★★
Parking:	Street, public lot
Bar:	Beer, wine
Wine selection:	Moderate
Dress:	Informal
Disabled access:	Limited but good
Customers:	Local, business
Breakfast:	Tuesday–Saturday, 9 A.M.–noon
Brunch:	Saturday and Sunday, 9 A.M.–3 P.M.
Lunch:	Tuesday–Saturday, 11:30 A.M.–3 P.M.
Dinner:	Wednesday–Sunday, 5:30–9:30 P.M.

Atmosphere / setting: Tucked away in San Anselmo, Comforts emits a careful, genteel charm. The small dining room is decorated in cream and green, trimmed with gilt and a few grapevines. The lighting is subdued, as is the noise level. There's a green marble counter for quick bites. San Anselmo Avenue's bookstores, antique shops, jewelers, and vintage clothing stores provide pleasant strolling and window shopping.

House specialties: For lunch, Chinese chicken salad; Thai lemon-lime chicken soup; roasted eggplant sandwich; seafood wonton soup; fresh mahimahi salad; pork satay sandwich. Dinners include starters of potato pancakes with smoked black pepper salmon; grilled polenta with prosciutto and red onions. Entree specialties are rack of lamb in mint, apricot jam, ginger, and brandy, and sautéed fillet of fresh sea bass with mango, sweet pepper, and red onion salsa.

Other recommendations: Eggplant lasagna; fresh scallops, prawns, and mussels with cappelini; Thai yellow curry beef. Housemade pies and chocolate cakes; teas.

Summary & comments: Comforts' blend of East-West cooking styles reflects its name: contemporary approaches to familiar dishes; no surprises, but reliably attractive and tasteful fare. Comforts also operates a gourmet deli, Comforts Too, next door, with a few tables for casual lunches or suppers and extensive takeout offerings.

Compass Rose

Zone 3   Union Square
315 Powel Street
   in the St. Francis Hotel
(415) 774-0167

	Bar
	★★★★
	Expensive
Quality 99	Value B+

Reservations:	Not accepted
When to go:	Tea time
Entree range:	$9–20
Payment:	Major credit cards
Service rating:	★★★
Friendliness rating:	★★★
Parking:	Street, garage
Bar:	Full service
Wine selection:	Limited but good
Dress:	Business
Disabled access:	No
Customers:	Businesspeople, travelers, correspondents, and spies
Lunch:	Every day, 11:30 A.M.–2:30 P.M.; high tea, 3–5 P.M.

Atmosphere / setting: Art deco. Large, spacious lounge, comfortably appointed with couches and easy chairs arranged around decorative coffee tables. Long polished bar set immediately adjacent to the lobby of the hotel.

House specialties: This is basically a bar, one that offers expensive finger foods: caviar; smoked salmon; finger sandwiches; all served with elegance and aplomb.

Other recommendations: High tea in the afternoon.

Summary & comments: Step in and enter the decade of the 30s. Meet and talk discreetly with private eyes, mysterious ladies, and intriguing gentlemen while the trio plays Gershwin. Indulge your fantasies. This place is rich; it's better if you are, too.

The Courtyard

Zone 5   Marina
2436 Clement Street
(415) 387-7616

American
★★½
Moderate
Quality 77   Value B

Reservations: Accepted
When to go: Any time
Entree range: $6.95–16.95
Payment: Major credit cards
Service rating: ★★★
Friendliness rating: ★★★
Parking: Street
Bar: Full service
Wine selection: Very good
Dress: Business
Disabled access: Yes
Customers: Local and yuppie
Lunch: Every day, 11:30 A.M.–2:30 P.M.
Dinner: Sunday–Thursday, 5–9:30 P.M.;
                     Friday and Saturday, 5–10 P.M.

Atmosphere / setting: Lots and lots of wood. Modern without being cold or impersonal. The wood keeps it warm. Full of yuppie types, but they don't bite or overbear. All are welcome to this convivial and pleasant place.

House specialties: Steak. It's the one thing to come here for. There are a lot of other things on the menu, and none of them are bad, but it's the steak that makes this place worth the trip. Top quality beef is cooked to your specifications and served with mushroom and red wine sauce. Carnivores come hither.

Other recommendations: Excellent bar.

Summary & comments: This is a great restaurant for drinking. The wine list is one of the best in town, and reasonably priced, too. The bar has a wide selection of single malt scotches, cognacs, and international beers. People come here for a good time as well as food and drink.

David's Finest
Produce & Taqueria

Zone 10   Suburban Marin
341 Corte Madera Town Center,
    Corte Madera
(415) 927-6572

Mexican	
★★½	
Inexpensive	
Quality 79	Value B

Reservations:	Not necessary
When to go:	Any time
Entree range:	$3.50–6.99
Payment:	Cash
Service rating:	★★
Friendliness rating:	★★★
Parking:	Free lot
Bar:	None
Wine selection:	None
Dress:	Casual
Disabled access:	Good
Customers:	Local
Open:	Monday–Saturday, 10:30 A.M.–9 P.M.;
	Sunday, 10:30 A.M.–8 P.M.

Atmosphere / setting: David's is a produce shop extraordinaire in a newly renovated shopping center, with a highly authentic Mexican taqueria attached. In front it's sandwiched between a Taco Bell and McDonald's, whose tables line the front entrance, so the best choices for seating are the wrought iron tables in the landscaped interior courtyard, complete with fountain and piped-in classical music.

House specialties: Soft rolled tacos, tamales, burritos, and barbecued chicken. Four choices of salsas, including one made with fresh fruit and chilies for the chicken. Excellent guacamole. Fresh-squeezed fruit juices and smoothies. The produce store carries breads, pastries, and other snacks and condiments.

Summary & comments: David's started out as a produce truck, specializing in the best tasting fruits available. To justify his high prices, he offered tastes of everything; this custom prevails today in his large and well-stocked store. You can graze the produce while you wait for your order, then add a few goodies from the shop to round out your meal. The Mexican specialties are all authentic, well seasoned, and satisfying, and they are priced much more reasonably than the fruit and vegetables inside.

THE DEPOT

Zone 10   Suburban Marin
87 Throckmorton Avenue, Mill Valley
(415) 383-2665

Bookstore cafe	
★½	
Inexpensive	
Quality 69	Value C

Reservations: Not accepted
When to go: Any time
Entree range: Breakfast, $2.40–4.55;
                       lunch or dinner, $2.95–6.25
Payment: Cash
Service rating: ★
Friendliness rating: ★★
Parking: Street, metered lots
Bar: Beer, wine
Wine selection: House
Dress: Casual
Disabled access: Limited
Customers: Local, tourist, business
Breakfast/Brunch: Every day, 7 A.M.–11 A.M.
Lunch/Dinner: Every day, 11 A.M.–10 P.M.

Atmosphere / setting: A crowded little cafe sharing the historic rail station and bus terminal with an equally cramped local bookstore. The good news is that the building fronts the pleasant town plaza, with outdoor tables and tree-shaded benches; locals, tourists, and teenaged hackysack players gather there during the day and on warm evenings. Mill Valley is a coffee drinker's paradise, with two take-out coffee purveyors, a bistro, and an Italian cafe all within a stone's throw of the square, so if the line at the Depot is just too long, there are several options nearby.

House specialties: Coffee and pastries; breakfast hot cereal; lunch and dinner sandwiches, soups, and salads. Great gooey fruit muffins and pecan squares; daily salad specials displayed where orders are taken.

Summary & comments: The Depot is a local favorite in a town with more street life than many in Marin. Mill Valley residents love their little hamlet, and tend to patronize its shops, cafes, and restaurants, so the Depot stays pretty busy. But since the menu is simple, the wait at the counter is usually not very long, and the turnover rate usually produces a table just when you need one. This is a place you can bring your dog, run into a few people you know, sip coffee, read the paper, eat a bowl of soup, write in your journal.

The Dining Room at the Ritz-Carlton

New American
★★★★★
Expensive

Quality 97   Value B

Zone 3   Union Square
600 Stockton Street
(415) 296-7465

Reservations:	Recommended
When to go:	Any time
Entree range:	Prix-fixe dinners, $43, $50, and $57
Payment:	All major credit cards
Service rating:	★★★★★
Friendliness rating:	★★★★★
Parking:	Valet, street
Bar:	Full service
Wine selection:	Excellent
Dress:	Informal, dressy, formal
Disabled access:	Good
Customers:	Tourist, local, business
Dinner:	Tuesday–Saturday, 6–10 P.M.

Atmosphere / setting: Genteel and decorous, the Dining Room's cushioned chairs and couches, antique china collections, and 19th-century paintings echo an older, stodgier San Francisco. But the tone is refreshingly down to earth and contemporary. Soft strains of a classical harp waft through the rarefied air.

House specialties: Seasonal changing menu: seared foie gras with caramelized onions and Fuji apples; warm quail salad with wild mushrooms, goat cheese, and pear-ginger chutney; glazed oysters with zucchini pearls and caviar; striped bass with artichoke, Meyer lemon, and fennel oil; sautéed veal medallion with chestnuts, apples, and wild mushrooms.

Other recommendations: Astonishing selection of cheeses presented at table; caramelized pears with gingerbread and nutmeg ice cream; baked noncholesterol Grand Marnier soufflé with raspberry sauce; trio of crème brûlées.

Summary & comments: The Ritz-Carlton's unerring taste and elegance aside, what makes it the Ritz is the genuine cordiality of the service. The gracious staff treat awestruck oglers and haughty billionaires with the same friendly willingness to help. This lack of pretension is confidence inspiring: most people feel better about spending a large amount of money when they are made to feel at ease. The food in the Dining Room is simply fabulous; chef Gary Danko seamlessly combines his passion for local and seasonal provender with trained international awareness and a highly evolved sense of color, texture, and flavor. A dinner in the Dining Room is a truly wonderful, memorable experience.

The Dipsea Cafe

Zone 10   Suburban Marin
200 Shoreline Highway,
   Mill Valley
(415) 381-0298

American	
★	
Inexpensive	
Quality 67	Value D

Reservations:	Recommended for parties of 4 or more
When to go:	Weekdays
Entree range:	$4.95–7.95
Payment:	AMEX, DC, MC, VISA
Service rating:	★
Friendliness rating:	★
Parking:	Free lot
Bar:	No
Wine selection:	House
Dress:	Casual
Disabled access:	Good
Customers:	Local, tourist, business
Breakfast:	Every day, from 7 A.M. on
Brunch:	Saturday, Sunday, and holidays, 8 A.M.–3 P.M.
Lunch:	Every day, 11 A.M.–4 P.M.

Atmosphere / setting: The Dipsea's spacious, airy room presents an especially inviting atmosphere for breakfast. This is a storybook farmhouse kitchen, with white scrolled woodwork; blue checked tablecloths; murals of cows; and idealized barnyard scenes. Everything has a fresh-washed quality, and the views through the high windows, complete with footbridge, ducks, and egrets, can be stunning. The location at the crossroads to several popular hiking areas is also ideal.

House specialties: Big farm-style breakfasts with biscuits, home fries, and sausages; pancakes, scones, and muffins; homemade granola, fresh juices and fruit smoothies. Hamburgers and grilled sandwiches; Niçoise salad with grilled ahi; braised lamb shank with rigatoni; Caesar salad. Children's menu for both breakfast and lunch.

Summary & comments: The locally popular Dipsea Cafe is so pretty and so evocative of childhood fantasies of farm life that one trusts the food to fulfill a promise of lighter-than-air biscuits and pancakes, savory sausages, crisp potatoes, and mouthwatering omelets stuffed with homegrown vegetables and home-cured cheeses. Alas. The breakfasts often arrive tasting as though the kitchen was in a great hurry, and the service has a sort of can't-you-see-I'm-very-busy quality. The coffee's good, and it's served in satisfyingly oversized white mugs. And children seem to receive attentive service, which is a plus for families.

120

The Duck Club

	California
Zone 14 South Bay	★★★½
100 El Camino Real, Menlo Park	Moderate
(415) 322-1234	Quality 85 Value B+

Reservations:	Accepted
When to go:	Any time
Entree range:	$8.95–19.50
Payment:	Major credit cards
Service rating:	★★★
Friendliness rating:	★★★
Parking:	Free lot
Bar:	Full service
Wine selection:	Good
Dress:	Business
Disabled access:	Yes
Customers:	Locals, hotel guests
Breakfast:	Every day, 6:45–11 A.M.
Brunch:	Sunday, 10:30 A.M.–2 P.M.
Lunch:	Monday–Saturday, 11:30 A.M.–2 P.M.
Dinner:	Every day, 5:30–10 P.M.

Atmosphere / setting: A Great Lakes country lodge accented with lots of deep colored wood and rose print curtains. Murals display ducks of all kinds: in flight, swimming, at rest in the rushes. Duck sculptures and floral arrangements decorate the shelves and other surfaces. The L-shaped dining room is large and roomy, yet maintains an intimate, cozy feel. Patrons can sometimes be exhuberant, but the many soft surfaces absorb sound. The result is conviviality as well as quiet.

House specialties: Duck! Roasted crispy with ginger sauce and candied orange; smoked and served with sour cherries and corn cakes; as sausage in a quesadilla with a blue corn tortilla. Also roast chicken; pork tenderloin with chutney; rack of lamb; and beef steak.

Other recommendations: Pasta; a good, if limited, selection of seafood; dinner salads; starters including a sampler for two; crab and shrimp sandwich; seafood chowder; prawn strudel. Do not miss the fresh apple tart à la mode!

Summary & comments: Aside from a few salads, there is little here for the vegetarian. Come here to eat meat, fish, and fowl—especially fowl. The duck is the best available and is prepared with a deft hand and a sure touch of inspiration. Chef Michael Martin-Vegue knows his onions when it comes to duck. Located in the Stanford Court Hotel, the place attracts a lot of business travelers, but many locals make it a regular stop as well. One seldom can recommend a hotel dining room as an outstanding culinary achievement, but this is a happy exception.

Duke of Edinburgh

Zone 14   South Bay
10801 North Wolf Road, Cupertino
(408) 446-3853

English	
★★½	
Moderate	
Quality 75	Value B

Reservations:	Yes
When to go:	Any time
Entree range:	$5.50–20
Payment:	Major credit cards
Service rating:	★★★
Friendliness rating:	★★★
Parking:	Lot
Bar:	Full service
Wine selection:	Good
Dress:	Casual, business
Disabled access:	Yes
Customers:	Local, business
Lunch:	Every day, 11:30 A.M.–2 P.M.
Dinner:	Every day, 5:30–10 P.M.

Atmosphere / setting: Deep pile English club. So much red velvet and rich wood it looks like it was imported as a kit from the Victorian age. A lot of nooks and booths add to the sense of entering into a different time. Leaving here after an hour or so, one is always taken a little aback at returning to the present.

House specialties: "English Fayre." Such a term might put a lot of people off, but give it a chance. It doesn't have the heavy, oily, dull taste that might be common in the mother country. Fish and chips; bangers and mash; ploughman's lunch; steak or roast beef and Yorkshire pudding. Don't come here looking for veggie fayre.

Other recommendations: A pretty good complimentary spread during happy hour, 5–7 P.M. Its composition depends on what's available but can include sausages, ham, assorted breads, and cheeses.

Summary & comments: The Duke is also a bar (or pub if you must) and is open continuously from 11 A.M.–2 A.M.; bar menu is available. It has eight different suds on tap. There is a separate room for darts, and a lot of regulars play. In fair weather patrons take their drinks out onto the front patio and pretend they aren't looking into the depths of the adjacent shopping mall.

Dusit

Zone 7   SOMA / Mission
3221 Mission Street
(415) 826-4639

	Thai
	★★½
	Inexpensive
	Quality 79 Value B+

Reservations:	Accepted
When to go:	Any time
Entree range:	$5.95–9.95
Payment:	Major credit cards
Service rating:	★★½
Friendliness rating:	★★
Parking:	Street
Bar:	Beer, wine
Wine selection:	House
Dress:	Casual
Disabled access:	No
Customers:	Local
Lunch:	Monday–Friday, 11:30 A.M.–2:30 P.M.
Dinner:	Every day, 5–10 P.M.

Atmosphere / setting: A small place in an ordinary neighborhood. Nothing remarkable to look at, though it's clean, well lighted, and even has just a touch of class. But this is a temple of Thai cuisine and the votaries of this muse are happily at work, pleasing anyone who walks in.

House specialties: Most of the items you would expect on a Thai menu, but done so much better than most, especially considering the price: orchid duck boned and sautéed with ginger, mushrooms, tomatoes, pineapple, and onions; garlic prawn with black pepper and veggies; sautéed squid with bamboo, chili, and basil; chicken salad with sweet spicy dressing.

Other recommendations: Good fried noodles. Vegetarian dinners.

Summary & comments: At lunchtime prices are somewhat lower, for unknown reasons. The food is just as good and plentiful. But even at dinner it's still downright cheap. For quality and quantity versus money, this place is at the top of the list. It's worth a trip across town to dine well at such low prices in a pleasant, undemanding environment.

El Nuevo Fruitlandia

Zone 7   SOMA / Mission
3077 24th Street
(415) 648-2958

Puerto Rican
★★
Inexpensive
Quality 76   Value B+

Reservations:	Not accepted
When to go:	Any time
Entree range:	$.50–8.50
Payment:	Cash
Service rating:	★★★
Friendliness rating:	★★★
Parking:	Street
Bar:	Beer, wine
Wine selection:	House
Dress:	Casual
Disabled access:	Yes
Customers:	Local
Open:	Every day, 11:30 A.M.–9:15 P.M.

Atmosphere / setting: Unadorned, uncomplicated, unpretentious, and small. But it's friendly and comfortable, and the staff will treat you well.

House specialties: Roast pork with rice and yucca; a variety of plantains; chicken in green sauce; shredded beef with peppers; Puerto Rican dumplings; shrimp in garlic sauce.

Other recommendations: Batidos de frutas: thick fruit shakes or smoothies.

Summary & comments: This a good place for a lunch that will stay with you for the rest of the day and into the evening. If you're planning nocturnal activities and won't be able to sit down to a leisurely dinner, you may want to fortify yourself here first. Que rico!

El Paseo

	French
	★★★★
Zone 10 Suburban Marin	Moderate
17 Throckmorton Avenue, Mill Valley	
(415) 388-0741	Quality 92 Value B

Reservations:	Recommended on weekends
When to go:	Any time
Entree range:	$11.75–17.25
Payment:	All major credit cards
Service rating:	★★★½
Friendliness rating:	★★★
Parking:	Street, public lots
Bar:	Beer, wine
Wine selection:	Excellent
Dress:	Informal, dressy
Disabled access:	Good
Customers:	Local, business, tourist
Dinner:	Every day, 5:30–10 P.M.

Atmosphere / setting: Coveyed in several snug dining rooms and a wine bar meandering along a brick-lined, vine-strewn passageway; El Paseo truly qualifies as a hidden gem. Red and white, copper and candlelight produce an allure impervious to fad or furor.

House specialties: Seasonal changing menu: potato blini with smoked salmon, golden caviar, and sour cream; smoked duck with green cabbage and mango; green lentil salad with ginger and cucumber; filet mignon with brandy, green peppercorns, and ginger; crispy roasted salmon with lobster sauce; steak tartare.

Other recommendations: Steamed and sautéed vegetables with couscous; frozen mousse with cherries and Armagnac.

Summary & comments: A few steps into El Paseo's winding walkway the weary traveler is transported into a more gracious world. Although El Paseo updates its menu seasonally, effortlessly staying current with the food fashions blowing across the bay from San Francisco, the service is of the old school: hushed, courtly, even a little formal. Perhaps because of this, El Paseo is a better choice for special, intimate dinners or quiet business entertainment than for lively group parties. The separate wine bar is a delightful, tranquil stop for a glass of wine and appetizer. The wine list has been judged by the *Wine Spectator* as one of the best in the world, but the desserts do not quite live up to the rest of the menu.

Honors / awards: *Wine Spectator* Grand Award.

125

Emile's

Zone 14   South Bay
545 South Second Street, San Jose
(408) 289-1960

	French / Swiss
	★★★½
	Expensive
Quality 89	Value B+

Reservations:	Accepted
When to go:	Any time
Entree range:	$15–28
Payment:	Major credit cards
Service rating:	★★★
Friendliness rating:	★★★
Parking:	Valet
Bar:	Full service
Wine selection:	Very good
Dress:	Dressy
Disabled access:	Yes
Customers:	Local, business
Dinner:	Tuesday–Saturday, 6–9 P.M.

Atmosphere / setting: Understated elegance with beautiful floral arrangements and sculpted leaves across the ceiling, dominated by the regular presence of its dapper and exacting owner, Emile. The neighborhood is a bit lowbrow, but here is an island of civilized refinement and good taste.

House specialties: A menu with few surprises, but everything is done with a sure hand and an eye for excellence. Grilled swordfish with seafood risotto; osso buco; rack of lamb with herb crust; desserts.

Other recommendations: Grand Marnier soufflé.

Summary & comments: Emile's has been the bright star in the gastronomic firmament of San Jose for nearly two decades. Many places have come and gone in that time, and trends have trended in and trended out. But Emile's is always there, relying on the classics, adjusted just so to fit the personality and demands of the owner.

ENOTECA MASTRO

Zone 12   Berkeley
933 San Pablo Avenue, Albany
(510) 524-4822

	Italian
	★★★
	Moderate
	Quality 85 Value A

Reservations:	Recommended
When to go:	Any time
Entree range:	$10.50–15
Payment:	VISA, MC
Service rating:	★★★
Friendliness rating:	★★★
Parking:	Street
Bar:	Beer, wine
Wine selection:	Excellent
Dress:	Casual
Disabled access:	Yes
Customers:	Local
Dinner:	Tuesday–Saturday, 6–10 P.M.

Atmosphere / setting: San Pablo Avenue in Albany is not noted for ambiance, charm, high architectural standards, or much else other than being the local main drag. Curiously, a number of pretty good restaurants have located here, and Enoteca is far and away the best of the lot. The exterior is of a type popular in the Berkeley area: you can't tell if it's going up or coming down. The first room you enter is an unprepossessing wine shop and tasting room. Behind that is one of the best dining rooms in the East Bay.

House specialties: Rustic Italian fare done to perfection, the result of love and attention to detail and the competence of a master of the craft. The menu is short, changes almost daily, and may include chicken, garbanzo, and vegetable soup; carpaccio; grilled mushrooms with polenta; grilled salmon; duck breast sautéed in extra virgin olive oil.

Other recommendations: Superior pastas and gnocchi with freshly made sauces.

Summary & comments: The wine list has one of the best selections of California and Italian wines to be found in the Bay Area—fitting, as this place is the product of a well-known local chef and a well-known local wine expert. The wine shop and its tasting bar are open Tuesday–Saturday, 11 A.M.–9 P.M. The decor is plain, though pleasant enough. But you don't come here to look at the wall hangings; you come here for some of the best food at the best prices in town.

ENRICO'S

Zone 6   North Beach
504 Broadway
(415) 982-6223

Italian	
★★★	
Moderate	
Quality 88	Value B

Reservations:	Accepted
When to go:	Any time
Entree range:	$9.25–16.95
Payment:	Major credit cards
Service rating:	★★★
Friendliness rating:	★★
Parking:	Street
Bar:	Full service
Wine selection:	Very good
Dress:	Casual, business
Disabled access:	Yes
Customers:	Eclectic
Open:	Every day, noon–1 A.M.

Atmosphere / setting: A social gathering place as much as an eatery. Booths line the walls; woodwork and plants throughout. The long bar is one of the more popular ones in North Beach. Between the entry and the sidewalk is an outdoor dining and lounge area. Excellent for people-watching.

House specialties: Pizza, pasta, grilled seafood, and steak; casseroles and stews; Spanish-style paella; duck breast gumbo; market steak with white truffle oil.

Other recommendations: Pizza with wild mushrooms.

Summary & comments: This place is a San Francisco landmark and tradition. Many local writers have used it as their writing studio or general hangout. The young man or woman studiously scribbling away while quaffing black coffee may be someone you'll be reading soon. Enrico's devotees will argue to the death that Irish coffee was invented here. Every night of the week patrons ensconce themselves in the outdoor lounge and fend off the San Francisco fog with this warm and cheering draught. Who cares where it was invented; this is the place to drink it.

Eulipia

Zone 14   South Bay
374 South First Street, San Jose
(408) 280-6161

Eclectic	
★★½	
Expensive	
Quality 77	Value D

Reservations:	Accepted
When to go:	Any time
Entree range:	$12–25
Payment:	Major credit cards
Service rating:	★★½
Friendliness rating:	★★★
Parking:	Valet
Bar:	Full service
Wine selection:	Good
Dress:	Casual
Disabled access:	Yes
Customers:	Local
Lunch:	Tuesday–Friday, 11:30 A.M.–4:30 P.M.
Dinner:	Tuesday–Thursday, 5:30–9 P.M.;
	Friday and Saturday, 11:30 A.M.–10 P.M.;
	Sunday, 4:30–9 P.M.

Atmosphere / setting: Walls of exposed brick juxtaposed with pastel colors. Trendy yet understated with a long copper bar. Originally a hangout for arty types who came here to drink Italian sodas and cuss and discuss, it's now a leading-edge restaurant and cultural beacon.

House specialties: Deliberately unfocused (or broad view) menu includes Philly cheese steak sandwich with chipotle mayo; rack of lamb with cabernet demi-glace; chicken breast with brie. Don't let it scare you. Most of it is good.

Entertainment & amenities: Upstairs is a popular nightclub of a very civilized variety. People dress up, act politely, and enjoy themselves without embarrassing themselves. A wide variety of bands play here including salsa, reggae, swing, and the band that played in the movie *The Mask.*

Summary & comments: The Eulipia has its ups and downs, its mood swings. But its essential character, that of a place where people seek a new way, or a better way, or just a different way to enjoy life, never changes.

FENG NIAN

Zone 9   Waterfront Crescent
2650 Bridgeway, Sausalito
(415) 331-8102

Chinese
★★½
Inexpensive / Moderate

Quality 79   Value B

Reservations:	Necessary only for large parties
When to go:	Any time
Entree range:	$6.25–18
Payment:	MC, VISA
Service rating:	★★★
Friendliness rating:	★★★
Parking:	Free lot
Bar:	None
Wine selection:	House
Dress:	Casual, informal
Disabled access:	Good
Customers:	Local, business, ethnic
Lunch:	Monday–Saturday, 11:30 A.M.–3 P.M.; closed Tuesday
Dinner:	Wednesday–Monday, 5:30–10 P.M.; closed Tuesday

Atmosphere / setting: Feng Nian's dining area consists of two capacious carpeted rooms with Chinese screens and lanterns, white linens, dark wood, and red brocade chairs: standard Chinese restaurant decor. There's a lounge with reading materials for those waiting for takeout. The sound level is generally low, even on busy evenings.

House specialties: Vegetarian egg rolls and pot stickers; sizzling rice seafood soup; honey-glazed walnut prawns; Peking duck with pancakes, green onions, and plum sauce; Mongolian lamb; moo shu pork or vegetables; spicy string bean seafood; garlic sauce eggplant; spinach sautéed in garlic and oil; ginger beef.

Other recommendations: Feng Nian chow fun with prawns, beef, pork, chicken, and vegetables; steamed vegetables and tofu for those controlling their oil intake; garlic broccoli; twice sizzling beef; General Chow chicken.

Summary & comments: Feng Nian's large, well-executed menu has made it one of the two most popular Chinese restaurants in Marin for many years. The kitchen can be depended upon to turn out flavorful, light dishes in Szechuan, Mandarin, and Hunan styles. The service is generally brisk and efficient. Feng Nian rarely disappoints; yet neither can the food be termed superlative.

Fior d'Italia

Zone 6   North Beach
601 Union Street
(415) 986-1886

Italian
★★★½
Moderate
Quality 85   Value A

Reservations:	Accepted
When to go:	Any time
Entree range:	$10.75–22
Payment:	VISA, MC, AMEX, D, DC
Service rating:	★★★
Friendliness rating:	★★
Parking:	Valet
Bar:	Full service
Wine selection:	Very good
Dress:	Business
Disabled access:	Good
Customers:	Local, tourist
Open:	Every day, 11 A.M.–10:30 P.M.

Atmosphere / setting: Old North Beach. Spacious and well lit, with starched napery, big leather booths, and roomy tables. The bar is old wood and the walls are hung with much memorabilia. It can be quiet or boisterous, depending on the crowd. Situated on the corner of Union and Stockton, it opens out onto Washington Park where, on foggy nights, it becomes a beacon for the hungry.

House specialties: Lengthy list of Italian classics. Hot and cold antipasti; pasta, risotto, and polenta; veal, chicken, beef, and fish. A separate and lengthy dessert menu that features a lot of fresh fruit preparations. The regular special dinner is called the 1886 and is priced at $18.86.

Other recommendations: A long list of single malt Scotch whiskeys, and a list of grappas, an Italian grape distillate.

Summary & comments: Established in 1886, this is the oldest Italian restaurant in the United States. At its current location since 1952, it was originally where Enrico's is today. Having survived all of the city's earthquakes and social upheavals for 110 years, a certain sedate, unflappable quality has sunk into the place. It's as though the restaurant knows it will still be here after you're gone. That breeds both a justifiable confidence and a reluctance to rush.

First and Last Chance Saloon

<table>
<tr><td colspan="2">American
★★
Moderate</td></tr>
<tr><td>Quality 78</td><td>Value A</td></tr>
</table>

Zone 13   Oakland
56 Jack London Square
(510) 839-6761

Reservations:	Not accepted
When to go:	Any time
Entree range:	Varies
Payment:	Cash
Service rating:	★★
Friendliness rating:	★★★
Parking:	Garage
Bar:	Full service
Wine selection:	House
Dress:	Casual
Disabled access:	No
Customers:	Local
Open:	Monday–Thursday, noon–midnight; Friday and Saturday, noon–1 A.M.; Sunday, noon–8 P.M.

Atmosphere / setting: An old, small waterfront saloon that survived the 1906 earthquake almost intact. The foundations sank, producing the sharp tilt in the floor. Watch that first step. Tourists and locals alike love its authentic American West ambiance. Jack London is said to have drunk deeply, and often, in here.

House specialties: You can't buy any food here other than chips, Slim Jims, and beef jerky. But the bartenders will send out to any restaurant in Jack London Square. They have all the menus behind the bar. If you've got a hankering for fried fish, a bucket of clams, a steak or prime rib, or Indonesian curry, but don't want to lose your seat at the bar, this is your place.

Entertainment & amenities: The unisex rest room is equipped with a speaker attached to a microphone behind the bar. If you're a gentleman too gussied up, or a lady too beautiful, you may receive some public comment from the bartender.

Summary & comments: This is a fine place to start or end an evening. Directly opposite is Jack London's log cabin, shipped down from the Yukon. For some reason foreigners think it's a replica; they can't believe it's real. But it's the genuine article, certified by Canada.

The Fish Market

	Seafood
Zone 14 South Bay	★★½
3150 El Camino Real, Palo Alto	Moderate
(415) 493-9188	
	Quality 78 Value B

Reservations:	Not accepted
When to go:	Any time
Entree range:	$8.50–16.75
Payment:	Major credit cards
Service rating:	★★
Friendliness rating:	★★
Parking:	Free lot
Bar:	Beer, wine
Wine selection:	Limited
Dress:	Casual, business
Disabled access:	Good
Customers:	Local, business
Open:	Monday–Thursday, 11 A.M.–9:30 P.M.;
	Friday and Saturday, 11 A.M.–10 P.M.;
	Sunday, noon–9:30 P.M.

Atmosphere / setting: The warehouse look of a dockside sail locker turned cannery row eatery. Big open space with lots of brightwork, nautical hodgepodge, and the smell of the sea. A lot of good photographs of landing piers, fishing boats, and fish hang on the walls. The busy kitchen is separated from the dining room by large window panes.

House specialties: Fish, fish, fish, with a menu a foot-and-a-half long. Rarely is any terrestrial creature served here unless you count Idaho trout as a land animal. Most entrees are cooked over mesquite, though you can request other means. The menu changes daily with the catch.

Other recommendations: They smoke their own fish here, and the sturgeon is superb at $6.50. Also, as the name implies, there is a fish market here where you can buy the same raw material the cooks are using.

Summary & comments: Palo Alto is the mother ship of a small chain that boasts its own fishing fleet and its own oyster farm. With outside purchases and the catch landed by the boats Pilikia and Temptation, the Fish Market hauls in 180,000 oysters, 9,000 pounds of rainbow trout, and 90 tons of fish and shellfish every month. These people know fish! And they know how to cook it and serve it, too. Preparations are simple, relying on the natural taste of fresh, perfect fish served with potatoes, pasta, salad, and sourdough bread. Although reservations are not accepted, you can phone ahead for the wait list.

Fleur de Lys

Zone 4   Financial District
777 Sutter Street
(415) 673-7779

French	
★★★★	
Expensive	
Quality 95	Value B+

Reservations:	Accepted
When to go:	Any time
Entree range:	$28–30
Payment:	Major credit cards
Service rating:	★★★★
Friendliness rating:	★★★★
Parking:	Valet
Bar:	Full service
Wine selection:	Excellent
Dress:	Dressy
Disabled access:	Yes
Customers:	Local, tourist
Dinner:	Monday–Thursday, 6–10 P.M.;
	Friday and Saturday, 6–10:30 P.M.

Atmosphere / setting: With the interior designed to look like the inside of a silken tent, it recalls a movie set about a sheik or a medieval joust. With a lot of mirrors and cubby holes, the decor is very busy, but never too much; it's somehow just right, lending a good feel for a good dinner. It's exotic, colorful, entertaining, yet not distracting.

House specialties: A lot of seafood selections: broiled bass fillet with bits of lobster wrapped in spinach and served with a sauce of beets and chives; salmon with horseradish; lobster salmi; salmon with golden caviar and chives. Also roast lamb chops; veal with onion rings (really good onion rings); duck in spinach leaves with a juniper and pancetta sauce. A very reasonably priced wine list, considering the venue.

Other recommendations: The Menu Gourmand offering a fixed selection of appetizer, fish, entree, and dessert; or the larger Menu Prestige. Both will contain costs in a costly restaurant.

Summary & comments: One of the best, most fun restaurants in town. The service is extremely attentive and formal, yet, like the decor, is never too much. Matching the service and decor is the food presentation: always pleasing to look at, taking advantage of the natural colors and textures of the food, but not too sculpted or contrived.

Honors / awards: *Esquire* Restaurant of the Year 1987.

Fog City Diner

Zone 6   North Beach
1300 Battery Street
(415) 982-2000

American	
★★★	
Moderate	
Quality 89	Value B+

Reservations:	Accepted
When to go:	Off hours
Entrée range:	$7–20
Payment:	Major credit cards
Service rating:	★★★
Friendliness rating:	★★★½
Parking:	Street
Bar:	Full service
Wine selection:	Good, extensive
Dress:	Casual
Disabled access:	Yes
Customers:	Local, tourist
Lunch/Dinner:	Sunday–Thursday, 11:30 A.M.–11 P.M.;
	Friday and Saturday, 11:30 A.M.–midnight

Atmosphere / setting: Very crowded, lively, and popular. As Fats Waller said, "The joint is jumpin." Don't come here for a quiet and romantic dinner. The decor has elements of an old Route 66 diner and a downtown bar and grill, both from pre–WWII San Francisco.

House specialties: For big appetites try the "Large Plates." Chicken on a biscuit with Virginia ham, morels, and cream gravy; rabbit with ancho chile succotash. For lesser stomachs: grilled pasilla pepper stuffed with polenta and five cheeses; garlic custard with mushrooms and walnuts; crab cakes; excellent salads.

Other recommendations: Strawberry rhubarb pie.

Summary & comments: You can come here with a huge appetite for both food and merriment and leave satisfied and not too much the poorer for it. Normal meal times equal long lines snaking out the front door and a crush at the bar. Sometimes this place is too popular for its own good.

Fontina

Zone 12   Berkeley
1730 Shattuck Avenue
(510) 649-8090

Italian	
★★½	
Inexpensive	
Quality 79	Value C+

Reservations:	Not accepted
When to go:	Any time
Entree range:	$5.95–10.95
Payment:	Major credit cards
Service rating:	★★★
Friendliness rating:	★★
Parking:	Street
Bar:	Beer, wine
Wine selection:	Limited but good
Dress:	Casual
Disabled access:	Yes
Customers:	Local
Open:	Sunday–Thursday, 11:30 A.M.–9 P.M.;
	Friday and Saturday, 11:30 A.M.–10 P.M.

Atmosphere / setting: Exposed brick walls in what may have once been a warehouse. Sophisticated lighting system can be adjusted to take advantage of weather and seasons. In cold weather a fireplace burns in the center of the room.

House specialties: Italian standards: fettucini alfredo; ravioli; linguine pomodoro (especially recommended); pollo marsala; linguine vongole; calamari; scampi; veal picatta.

Other recommendations: Good dinner salads.

Entertainment & amenities: Live classical jazz on Wednesday nights.

Summary & comments: On each table sits a large bottle of extra virgin olive oil, a small bowl of freshly grated cheese, and a mound of finely minced fresh garlic. Sweet butter is served on request. With this you could make a satisfying meal of the excellent bread. Service is not showy, but eager and efficient. The tomato sauces are made in-house from fresh, vine-ripened tomatoes, and you can taste the difference.

Frankie Johnnie & Luigi Too

Italian	
★★½	
Inexpensive	
Quality 79	Value A

Zone 14   South Bay
939 West El Camino Real,
   Mountain View
(415) 967-5384

Reservations:	Accepted
When to go:	Any time
Entree range:	$7.95–13.95
Payment:	Major credit cards
Service rating:	★★
Friendliness rating:	★★★
Parking:	Free lot
Bar:	Beer, wine
Wine selection:	Limited but good
Dress:	Casual
Disabled access:	Yes
Customers:	Families, students, couples
Open:	Monday–Thursday, 11 A.M.–midnight; Friday and Saturday, 11 A.M.–1 A.M.; Sunday, noon–midnight

Atmosphere / setting: 1950s diner with a small touch of elegance. Cozy booths in the front dining areas and a heated patio in the rear (the roof leaks in the rain). Always an upbeat, happy crowd and helpful, friendly staff.

House specialties: Italian staples and some of the best pizza in the South Bay. Osso buco verdure (lamb shanks braised with vegetables); scampi.

Other recommendations: New York–style lasagna made with the restaurant's own sausage.

Summary & comments: It's a smallish place, and on weekends you can often count on waiting in the line that snakes around the corner into the parking lot. It's worth it. You'll know when you first walk in and smell the heady aromas of garlic, yeast dough, sausage, and cheese. The owners are the sausage kings of the South Bay, producing some of the tastiest links anywhere. You'll find the same quality, and higher prices, at their upscale restaurant, Nicolino's.

FRINGALE

Zone 7 SOMA/Mission	French
570 Fourth Street	★★★★
(415) 543-0573	Moderate
	Quality 95 Value A

Reservations:	Highly recommended
When to go:	Any time, but quietest at late lunch on weekdays
Entree range:	Lunch, $7–12.75; dinner, $9–18
Payment:	All major credit cards
Service rating:	★★★★
Friendliness rating:	★★★★
Parking:	Street
Bar:	Full service
Wine selection:	Limited but good
Dress:	Informal
Disabled access:	Good
Customers:	Local, business, tourist
Lunch:	Monday–Friday, 11:30 A.M.–3 P.M.
Dinner:	Monday–Saturday, 5:30–10:30 P.M.

Atmosphere / setting: White wine and honey and sunlight; rarely does a restaurant manage to strike a chord balanced so perfectly between the warmth of wheat loaves and the sparkle of chilled champagne. Fringale is captivatingly simple and frequently crowded; to soak up the soul of the southwestern French provinces, go for lunch after 1 P.M. on a weekday.

House specialties: Creative interpretations of French-Basque fare: potato and goat cheese galette; sheep's milk cheese and prosciutto terrine with figs and greens; steamed mussels with garlic and parsley; roast rack of lamb; steamed salmon with braised leeks and fried onions; New York steak with red wine butter.

Other recommendations: Pork tenderloin confit with onion and apple marmalade; fillet of tuna Basquaise; all desserts including Biarritz rocher au chocolat; hazelnut and roasted almond cake with chocolate sauce; iced Armagnac and coffee parfait.

Summary & comments: Gerald Hirigoyan, the consummate young chef at Fringale, achieves near perfection with this disarming little bistro, attracting crowds with his low-priced but highly skilled and artful cooking. Casual and elegant; subtle and robust; earthy and delicate: all the shadings and flavors of the culinary spectrum are eloquently embraced. The cluster of parties waiting near the door can be intimidating, so do make an advance reservation. Fringale is well worth the trouble.

Honors / awards: *Esquire* Best New Restaurants 1992.

The Ganges

Zone 8   Richmond/Avenues
775 Frederick Street
(415) 661-7290

	Vegetarian Indian
	★★★
	Inexpensive
Quality 80	Value A

Reservations:	Recommended on weekends
When to go:	Any time
Entree range:	3-course dinners, $9.50–13.50
Payment:	MC, VISA
Service rating:	★★★½
Friendliness rating:	★★★★
Parking:	Street
Bar:	Beer, wine
Wine selection:	House
Dress:	Casual
Disabled access:	Good
Customers:	Local, business
Dinner:	Tuesday–Saturday, 5–10 P.M.

Atmosphere / setting: Like an island of sanity in a chaotic world, the Ganges' austere setting, further becalmed on weekends by live sitar music on the red-curtained stage at the front of the room, houses a surprise package. Even at peak hours, this is a restful spot.

House specialties: Extremely light, non-greasy vegetarian Indian cooking, including ground lentil dababs; green chili fritters; steamed savory garbanzo dumplings; curries including homemade cheese cooked with peas; garbanzo beans with onions, mushrooms, and spices; baby potatoes stuffed with fresh spices; eggplant with onions and spices; stuffed zucchini and cauliflower with potatoes and onions.

Other recommendations: Mango lassi, a mango and yogurt drink; sheera pudding, shreekhand yogurt and sour cream dessert with rosewater and saffron.

Summary & comments: By the delicacy of its cooking and the economy of its dinners, the Ganges puts most Indian restaurants to shame. Throw in the vegetarian menu, helpful staff, and gentle atmosphere, and you have a real alternative to busy city dining. The Ganges, like the jewel hidden in the lotus blossom, is a rare find.

GARDEN CiTY

Zone 14   South Bay
360 South Saratoga Avenue, San Jose
(408) 244-4443

American	
★★½	
Moderate	
Quality 77	Value C+

Reservations:	Accepted
When to go:	Any time
Entree range:	$13.95–54.95
Payment:	Major credit cards
Service rating:	★★½
Friendliness rating:	★★★
Parking:	Lot
Bar:	Full service
Wine selection:	Fair
Dress:	Dressy
Disabled access:	Yes
Customers:	Local
Lunch:	Monday–Saturday, 11:30 A.M.–5 P.M.
Dinner:	Every day, 5–11 P.M.

Atmosphere / setting: Las Vegas West. Dim lights and a nightclub atmosphere set within the biggest gaming house in town; there is definitely the feel of glitz and excess. Bigger is better, biggest is best, too much is not enough. Big tables, big portions, big everything. It's big!

House specialties: Big steaks. Meat and potatoes perfectly rendered. No pretensions to haute cuisine, nothing trendy. The management knows what the patrons come for and that's what they give 'em: three inch–thick prime rib; monster steaks; big spuds with all the fixin's; grilled fish for those who didn't come for red meat.

Entertainment & amenities: Live jazz during dinner hours. Watching the well- (sometimes overly) dressed people doing the mating dance.

Summary & comments: If you're too wired for the quiet and romantic, or if you need a shot of party vibes with your main course, this might be the place. Most of the customers have been here many times before and will be here many times more seeking that special combination of animal protein and animal magnetism. It's not a meat market, but it is a good place for meat and meeting.

Gate Five

Zone 9   Waterfront Crescent
305 Harbor Drive, Sausalito
(415) 331-5355

American	
★★★½	
Moderate	
Quality 85	Value C

Reservations:	Recommended on weekends
When to go:	Lunch, weeknight dinners
Entree range:	$7–17
Payment:	AMEX, MC, VISA
Service rating:	★★★½
Friendliness rating:	★★★½
Parking:	Free lot
Bar:	Full service
Wine selection:	Moderate
Dress:	Informal, casual
Disabled access:	Good
Customers:	Local, business, tourist
Brunch:	Weekends, 9 A.M.–2:30 P.M.
Lunch:	Monday–Friday, 11:30 A.M.–2:30 P.M.; bar menu until 5 P.M.
Dinner:	Every day, 5–10 P.M.

Atmosphere / setting: Gate Five occupies a spacious square building with wood-paneled walls, high ceilings, a few scattered nautical touches, and two crackling fireplaces on chilly days and evenings.

House specialties: Portuguese kale soup; oysters on the half shell; steamed mussels and clams in white wine; clam chowder with crackers. Mixed seafood grill; paella with scallops, prawns, chicken, and linguica; grilled swordfish with asparagus; sautéed petrale sole with garlic, capers, olives, roasted fennel, and Yukon gold potatoes.

Other recommendations: Grilled and roasted vegetable plate; grilled eggplant and hummus sandwich; warm Indian pudding with vanilla ice cream.

Summary & comments: About as straightforward as a restaurant can be, Gate Five specializes in the Cape Cod–style cooking of chef/owner Peter Morency's childhood, updated to incorporate California ingredients and tastes. The seafood is delicately handled and presented. Service is fast and solicitous. Prices seem a bit high, but still within the moderate range. Gate Five offers a few special deals: kids under ten eat free on Mondays, and drinks are discounted on Thursday evenings; sometimes there's live jazz on the weekends. Call for a calendar.

Gertie's Chesapeake Bay Cafe

Zone 12 Berkeley	Seafood
1919 Addison Street	★★★
(510) 841-2722	Moderate
	Quality 88 Value B+

Reservations:	Accepted
When to go:	Pre-/posttheater
Entree range:	$10.95–17.95
Payment:	Major credit cards
Service rating:	★★★
Friendliness rating:	★★★½
Parking:	Validated lot
Bar:	Beer, wine
Wine selection:	Good
Dress:	Casual
Disabled access:	Good
Customers:	Local, business
Lunch:	Monday–Friday, 11:30 A.M.–2:30 P.M.
Dinner:	Monday–Thursday, 5:30–9 P.M.;
	Friday and Saturday, 5–10 P.M.

Atmosphere / setting: Set back from the street in a shady courtyard, Gertie's makes you feel as though you're about to enter a secret grotto. Upon arrival, though, you find yourself in a very modern, almost hi-tech, cafe awash in a pink light glow. The floor is black-and-white tiled, the long counter is framed with an art deco pink neon light, and there's pink butcher paper on the top of the white linen tablecloths. It's hard to make all this sound cozy, but it is. Somehow, it just is.

House specialties: Maryland and Louisiana seafood: heavenly crab cakes served with french fries, cole slaw, and tartar sauce; beer-steamed shrimp in the shell; seafood chili; seafood pot pie; pecan breaded fried catfish; gumbo; soft-shell crabs in season; grilled chicken or steak; pork chops with hot and sweet pepper jam.

Other recommendations: Bouillabaisse; crab soup; excellent soups of the day; shrimp sandwiches.

Summary & comments: The staff will go out of their way to make children feel welcome, seating them at their own tables or at the counter and bringing them crayons to color on the butcher-paper table covers. They seem to add to the controlled party atmosphere. Being only a block from Berkeley Rep, this is a good place for dinner before or after theater. In good weather, lunch takers can be seated on the patio.

Ginger Island

Zone 12   Berkeley
1820 Fourth Street
(510) 644-0444

Pan-Asian
★★½
Moderate

Quality 77   Value C+

Reservations:	Recommended
When to go:	Any time
Entree range:	$7.50–17.50
Payment:	VISA, MC, AMEX, DC
Service rating:	★★
Friendliness rating:	★★★
Parking:	Free lot
Bar:	Full service
Wine selection:	Limited but good
Dress:	Casual
Disabled access:	Good
Customers:	Local, business
Open:	Sunday–Thursday, 11:30 A.M.–9:30 P.M.; Friday and Saturday, 11:30 A.M.–11 P.M.

Atmosphere / setting: South China Sea with overtones of Polynesian and Southern California beach club. A little schizophrenic and hard to pigeonhole but not unpleasant.

House specialties: Indonesian satay of chicken; Chinese eggplant with ginger-sesame glaze; fried squid with Thai dipping sauce; mixture of fried potato, yam, and taro; clay pot short ribs; Thai red curry noodles; tea-smoked duck.

Other recommendations: Ginger Island hamburger with Southeast Asian salsa.

Summary & comments: Want to take your friends to a restaurant of a kind they've never been to before? In the location of the former 4th Street Grill, this is the place. The "Pan-Asian" style is mostly an interesting mixing, matching, and blending of Thai and southern Chinese, all spoken with a California accent. Ingredients are always fresh and of the best quality. The cook's favorite spice is obviously ginger.

GREENS

Zone 5   Marina
Building A Fort Mason
  (Marina Boulevard and Buchannan)
(415) 771-6222

Vegetarian
★★★★
Moderate
Quality 99   Value A

Reservations:	Necessary
When to go:	Lunch
Entree range:	$10–13
Payment:	Major credit cards
Service rating:	★★★
Friendliness rating:	★★★
Parking:	Lot
Bar:	Beer, wine
Wine selection:	Very good
Dress:	Business
Disabled access:	Yes
Customers:	All walks of life
Brunch:	Sunday, 10 A.M.–2 P.M.
Lunch:	Monday–Friday, 11:30 A.M.–2:15 P.M.
Dinner:	Monday–Saturday, 6–9:30 P.M.

Atmosphere / setting: Full view of the Golden Gate Bridge bordered by the southern promontories of Marin county. Very large and airy, the restaurant was formerly an enclosed pier. Polished wood floors, lovely paintings on the walls, and very comfortable lounging area. Very serene atmosphere.

House specialties: Mesquite-grilled winter vegetables; salad of watercress and escarole, sierra beauty apples, and walnuts tossed with walnut vinaigrette; cubed winter squash baked in parchment with fresh thyme and garlic.

Other recommendations: Dessert: chocolate sabayon cake crème chantilly.

Summary & comments: No health food, no hippie food, no orange and parsley garnish, but the very finest in vegetarian cuisine. This is not a PC restaurant; no one is on a crusade here. Its reason for being is the best of dining without meat.

Griffin's

	American
Zone 10 Suburban Marin	★★★½
23 Ross Common, Ross	Moderate / Expensive
(415) 925-9200	Quality 86 Value C+

Reservations:	Recommended on weekends
When to go:	Any time, but especially in good weather
Entree range:	Brunch, $7.95–12.95; lunch, $6.95–13.95; dinner, $10.95–16.95
Payment:	AMEX, MC, VISA
Service rating:	★★★★
Friendliness rating:	★★★★
Parking:	Street
Bar:	Beer, wine
Wine selection:	Good
Dress:	Informal
Disabled access:	Good
Customers:	Local, business
Brunch:	Sunday, 10:30 A.M.–2:30 P.M.
Lunch:	Tuesday–Saturday, 11 A.M.–2:30 P.M.
Dinner:	Tuesday–Saturday, 5–9 P.M.

Atmosphere / setting: Recessed from the street in a miniature arcade in tiny, tony Ross, Griffin's spun-sugar pink interior borders on the cloying, but a few impressionist prints spark it up satisfactorily. The brick-paved outdoor patio, with tiny lights twinkling in the treetops, adds considerable charm.

House specialties: Seasonal changing menu: grilled breast of duck with fresh raspberries and sliced pears; grilled fillet of salmon with leeks and champagne sauce; filet of beef on grilled polenta with peppers and black olives; fresh steamed vegetable platter glazed with sherry wine vinaigrette.

Other recommendations: Nightly specials; rack of lamb with rosemary and mint; angel hair pasta with scallops, fresh basil, and tomatoes.

Summary & comments: Trust exclusive old-money Ross to have cached a quiet, romantic little restaurant in its barely-there town center. Griffin's isn't stunning, fashionable, or budget conscious, but it's secluded and solicitous, and it serves respectable portions. Salads are bright and large enough to share; entrees are artfully composed and tastefully seasoned. The tray of dessert choices is presented nestled among pink blossoms. The service is genuine and personable. Griffin's won't quite knock your socks off, but you will probably leave replete and refreshed.

Guaymas

Zone 9   Waterfront Crescent
5 Main Street, Tiburon
(415) 435-6300

| Mexican |
| ★★★½ |
| Moderate |
| Quality 85   Value C+ |

Reservations:	Recommended
When to go:	Any time
Entree range:	$8.95–17.50
Payment:	AMEX, MC, VISA
Service rating:	★★★
Friendliness rating:	★★½
Parking:	Street; validated in public lot weekdays
Bar:	Full service
Wine selection:	Good
Dress:	Casual
Disabled access:	Good
Customers:	Local, tourist, business
Brunch:	Sunday, 10:30 A.M.–1 P.M.
Lunch/Dinner:	Sunday–Thursday, 11:30 A.M.–9:30 P.M.; Friday and Saturday, 11:30 A.M.–10:30 P.M.

Atmosphere / setting: Guaymas' smashing location on the Tiburon ferry landing is its most winning feature. The dining area, a spacious, open room with windows overlooking the decks and the bay, sports a fireplace for chilly evenings. Baskets heaped with fresh fruits and vegetables lend a festive air. Small tables line the windows of the bar area where appetizers are available. Hold out for a table closest to the water views or on either of the two heated outdoor decks.

House specialties: Margaritas; designer tequilas and Mexican beers; fresh handmade corn tortillas with a trio of intriguing red and green salsas; mesquite-grilled shrimp in lime juice and cilantro; chicken in a mole sauce of chocolate, chilies, fruits, and spices; dessert plates of colorful Mexican cookies, or suspiro de monga, a puffy cinnamon-dusted floating island.

Other recommendations: Tiny appetizer tamales of chicken or pork with pumpkin seed and guajillo chile sauce; crisp corn tortilla pots filled with crab-meat and avocado; sopa de tortilla; spit-roasted meats and fowl.

Summary & comments: Although the tab can add up alarmingly, a leisurely meal on the deck at Guaymas is as tonic as a vacation. The views of zigzagging sails and distant city skyline mingle agreeably with the scents of Mexican cooking; this is waterfront dining at its breezy best. The cuisine isn't subtle, but the flavors are authentic, fresh, and varied, and the portions are generous. On busy summer weekends, the service and preparation have a harried quality.

The Half Day Cafe

<table>
<tr><td colspan="2">American
★★★
Inexpensive

Quality 83   Value B</td></tr>
</table>

Zone 10   Suburban Marin
848 College Avenue, Kentfield
(415) 459-0291

Reservations:	Accepted for dinner only
When to go:	Breakfast and lunch, especially weekdays
Entree range:	Breakfast, $3.95–7.25; lunch, $6.75–8.50
Payment:	MC, VISA
Service rating:	★★★
Friendliness rating:	★★★
Parking:	Free lot
Bar:	Beer, wine
Wine selection:	Fair
Dress:	Casual
Disabled access:	Good
Customers:	Local, business, student
Breakfast:	Monday–Friday, 7–11:30 A.M.; Saturday and Sunday, 8–11:30 A.M.
Lunch:	Every day, 11:30 A.M.–2:30 P.M.
Dinner:	Every day, 5–9:30 P.M.

Atmosphere / setting:　In a spaciously renovated brick garage, the Half Day's huge windows, high open-beamed ceilings, and hanging greenery provide a cheery, convivial setting for an eclectic breakfast and lunch crowd. In addition to the busy tables, there's a lunch counter overlooking the open kitchen, and, in good weather, off-street garden seating too.

House specialties:　Huge, fruit-studded muffins and scones with frothy bowls of latte; Cajun scrambled eggs; scrambled tofu Mexicana; amaretto French toast. Lunch includes soups and chowders; warm goat cheese salad with oranges; steamed fresh vegetables and brown rice; blackened burger with Cajun mayonnaise.

Other recommendations:　Personalized omelets with a choice of 20 ingredients, including egg substitutes if desired; huevos rancheros; Belgian waffles; whole grain cereals. For lunch: Chinese chicken salad; Cajun Caesar with blackened chicken breast; grilled vegetable quesadilla; tempeh or garden burgers.

Summary & comments:　The Half Day is a local favorite for breakfast and lunch, now open for dinner as well. If you have the time (waits are often 30 minutes), the food is worth the wait, with offerings to suit any palate or dietary need. The portions are enormous, and the ambiance is lively, at once comfortable and energetic. Some celebrity-watching is in order here: George Lucas has been spotted, as well as an assortment of Marin County actors and rock stars.

Hamburger Mary's

Zone 7   SOMA / Mission
1582 Folsom Street
(415) 626-5767 or 626-1985

American
★½
Inexpensive

Quality 69   Value C

Reservations:	Accepted; weekends for parties of 5 or more only
When to go:	Any time
Entree range:	$4–9.50
Payment:	All major credit cards
Service rating:	★★★
Friendliness rating:	★★★½
Parking:	Street
Bar:	Full service
Wine selection:	House
Dress:	Casual
Disabled access:	Good
Customers:	Local, tourist, business
Open:	Tuesday–Thursday, 11:30 A.M.–midnight; Friday, 11:30–1 A.M.; Saturday, 10–1 A.M.; Sunday, 10 A.M.–midnight; Specials available after 5 P.M.

Atmosphere / setting: Like the lair of a demented antique dealer: baby bottles and broken chandeliers; hand-painted mirrors and headless mannequins; chromium starbursts and a life-sized cardboard Elvis; road signs and street signs and soda pop posters and sheet music; stained-glass windows and junk-shop furniture; all jumbled together and set to driving rock and roll. There's a breakfast counter in front; a barroom to the rear, and a separate, you should pardon the expression, dining area in the corner.

House specialties: Breakfast all day, and burgers: with mushrooms, chili, bacon, blue cheese, and / or avocado, and served on whole-wheat toast.

Other recommendations: Vegetarian burgers, soups, and sandwiches; salads; club, B.L.T., or crab-salad sandwich. Chipped beef on toast.

Summary & comments: "Seat yourself at any available table" reads the sign at the door. Doing so in this relic from the 70s is like wandering through the fun house: you have no idea what may appear around the next corner. The food at Hamburger Mary's is, however, unremarkable. There are better burgers, with fresher accompaniments, to be had in most restaurants around town. Perhaps the best reason to go to Mary's, then, is to eat breakfast at any time of day in an atmosphere which promotes the impression that you're still dreaming.

Harpoon Louie's

Zone 7 SOMA/Mission	Bar & Grill
55 Stevenson Street	★★
(415) 543-3540	Inexpensive
	Quality 77 Value B

Reservations:	Not accepted
When to go:	Lunch
Entree range:	$4–6
Payment:	VISA, MC, AMEX
Service rating:	★★
Friendliness rating:	★★★★
Parking:	Street
Bar:	Full service
Wine selection:	House
Dress:	Casual
Disabled access:	Yes
Customers:	Local, business
Lunch:	Monday–Friday, 11 A.M.–3 A.M.

Atmosphere / setting: A neighborhood tavern in an old brick building. The walls are hanging with old photos of old stars and local sports figures and a big shouting-for-attention oil painting of a leggy nude. Pretty much a male hangout, but ladies are just as welcome as gents.

House specialties: Hamburgers and big schooners of draught beer; fried fish of the day; pasta; salads. The menu changes daily, but you can get yourself on the mailing list and learn of advance changes if you want to be a regular. Everything is cooked to order.

Other recommendations: The blue plate special. Free hot dogs at happy hour.

Summary & comments: Harpoon Louie's is a neighborhood-type place that considers itself part of the community. Following the Loma Prieta earthquake of 1989, Louie's fed locals on the street. Service can be slow, so don't go there when you're pressed for time. Go there when you can linger and enjoy.

HARRY DENTON'S

Zone 7   SOMA / Mission
169 Steuart Street
(415) 882-1333

New American
★★★★
Moderate

Quality 90   Value A

Reservations:	Highly recommended
When to go:	Any time
Entree range:	$7.95–16.95
Payment:	Major credit cards
Service rating:	★★★★
Friendliness rating:	★★★★
Parking:	Valet nightly
Bar:	Full service
Wine selection:	Excellent
Dress:	Casual, business
Disabled access:	Good
Customers:	Local, tourist, business
Breakfast / Brunch:	Monday–Friday, 7–10 A.M.; Saturday and Sunday, 8 A.M.–3 P.M.
Lunch:	Monday–Friday, 11:30 A.M.–3 P.M.
Dinner:	Every day, 5:30–10 P.M.

Atmosphere / setting: Harry's has just about everything: fashionable location on Steuart Street, the city's new Restaurant Row, adjacent boutique hotel, smashing view of the Bay Bridge, gorgeous flowered carpets, dark wood wainscoting, Victorian bar, red velvet, and oodles of antiques. The mood can range from serene to wild. On weekends the party can approach the greatest of Gatsby proportions.

House specialties: Chicken and artichokes with white beans; pot roast with buttermilk mashed potatoes and gravy; grilled filet mignon with cracked pepper and cognac; Australian lamb T-bones with polenta.

Other recommendations: Harry's Southside Burger; oak-fired pizzas; Nona's lasagna; creamed spinach; buttermilk onion rings.

Summary & comments: Harry Denton's may be the perfect all-purpose city restaurant: sophisticated and glamorous, yet relaxed and casual; ideal for breakfast by the Bay in jeans and T-shirt or dancing the night away in tux or tiara. The cuisine is big, brassy, Barbary Coast fare; and Harry encourages serious partying once the music begins. "Dancing on the bar is prohibited unless accompanied by Harry." But the place can be subtle and decorous on early weeknights. Even the rest rooms have savoir faire. If it gets too crowded, you can stroll down the avenue where there are five glittering restaurants within two blocks.

The Heights

Zone 8   Richmond/Avenues
3235 Sacramento Street
(415) 474-8890

French
★★★★★
Expensive

Quality 97   Value B+

Reservations:	Highly recommended; required on weekends
When to go:	Any time
Entree range:	$18–24; 6-course tasting menu, $55
Payment:	AMEX, MC, VISA
Service rating:	★★★★½
Friendliness rating:	★★★★½
Parking:	Street
Bar:	Beer, wine
Wine selection:	Limited but good
Dress:	Informal, dressy
Disabled access:	Limited
Customers:	Local, business, tourist
Dinner:	Tuesday–Sunday, 5:30–10 P.M.

Atmosphere / setting: Set back from cultured Sacramento Street in a renovated Victorian home, tiled floors, arched windows and doorways, and white plaster walls bring to mind a modern Moorish air. The interior rooms overlook the chef's herb garden, softly lit for romantic effect.

House specialties: Weekly changing menu, with offerings such as crayfish, hedgehog mushrooms, and potato gnocchi in lobster sauce; seared yellowfin tuna with eggplant puree and sauce aromatique; grilled beef tenderloin with baby artichokes and black truffle sauce; lamb ragout with fennel-tomato concasse.

Other recommendations: Apple crisp with cinnamon ice cream; warm Valrhona chocolate cake with liquid center, ice cream, and chocolate sauce; puff pastry Napoleon with mango parfait and mango sorbet.

Summary & comments: Chef Charlie Solomon carries impressive credentials: he trained with Alain Ducasse at the Louis XV in Monte Carlo, with Jean-Louis Palladin at the Watergate in Washington, D.C., and came to San Francisco via the eminent Bouley in Manhattan. His suave little undertaking in Pacific Heights makes a highly personal, civilized statement about fine dining, from the complimentary amuse geules before the meal to the hand-dipped chocolates which arrive with the check. By wisely undercutting the potential hauteur of the setting with breezy cotton slipcovers and fruit baskets lining the hallways, Solomon and his partner have achieved an smart nonchalance. His splendid cuisine is thus enabled to shine through, with able assistance from an urbane hosting staff and precise, unaffected service.

Helmand

Afghani
★★★
Inexpensive
Quality 85   Value A

Reservations:	Accepted
When to go:	Any time
Entree range:	$8.95–14.95
Payment:	VISA, MC, AMEX
Service rating:	★★★★
Friendliness rating:	★★★
Parking:	468 Broadway
Bar:	Full service
Wine selection:	Fair
Dress:	Casual
Disabled access:	Yes
Customers:	Local, business, tourist
Lunch:	Monday–Friday, 11:30 A.M.–2:30 P.M.
Dinner:	Monday–Thursday, 6–10 P.M.;
	Friday and Saturday, 6–11 P.M.

Atmosphere / setting: Named for a river in Afghanistan; the rooms are decorated in classical Persian-style simplicity and the tables are set with Western, though not stuffy, formality. Beautiful Persian rugs are laid everywhere and the walls are hung with Afgan portraits. Softly played Afghani strings and flutes fill the background.

House specialties: Afghani food is heavily influenced by its neighbors, India and Persia. It's based on flatbreads and rice, fresh vegetables, lamb, and chicken cooked in not-too-assertive spice mixtures. Tomatoes or yogurt are the most common bases for sauces. Dishes include rack of lamb with Persian spices; chicken sautéed with yellow split peas; potatoes and garbanzo beans in vinaigrette with cilantro; meat pies flavored with onion; leek-filled ravioli.

Other recommendations: A good number of meatless dishes and salads.

Summary & comments: This is a good family restaurant, and as such is a bell weather for the changing face of its neighborhood, which used to be the heart of the city's topless district. For the money and the great size of the portions served, this is one of the best restaurant deals in town. And it's the only Afghani restaurant in town. You'll find it crowded on weekends.

Henry's World Famous Hi-Life

Barbecue	
★★	
Inexpensive	
Quality 77	Value A

Zone 14   South Bay
301 West Saint John Street, San Jose
(408) 295-5414

Reservations:	Not accepted
When to go:	Any time
Entree range:	$10–12
Payment:	Major credit cards
Service rating:	★★
Friendliness rating:	★★★
Parking:	Street
Bar:	Full service
Wine selection:	House
Dress:	Casual
Disabled access:	No
Customers:	Local
Lunch:	Tuesday–Friday, 11:30 A.M.–2:30 P.M.
Dinner:	Every day, 5–9 P.M.

Atmosphere / setting: Originally a flop house for Italian laborers in the orchards and canneries of the area. It got to be known more for its kitchen than its accommodation and by degrees evolved into an Italian restaurant serving a little barbecue to a place serving nothing but barbecue and good times. It still looks a little like a flop house. The bar is crammed with memorabilia and patrons, and the jukebox and its selections are from another era. The dining room looks a little like a mess hall with a brick fire pit.

House specialties: Ribs. More than anything the Hi-Life is known for ribs. Barbecued slowly in the oak-fired pit and served with a small bowl of sauce that's good enough to eat with a spoon. Also chicken, steak, and great garlic bread.

Other recommendations: Sautéed mushrooms; barbecued onions.

Summary & comments: Flop house in a lowbrow neighborhood though it is, it's not unusual to see Rolls Royces and Jaguars parked on the street outside, next to the pick-ups, economy cars, and restored 1950s Chevys. Most of the crowd are regulars and they take an affectionate family attitude toward the place. During the floods of 1995 the Hi-Life was threatened by the rising waters. Neighborhood patrons and the San Jose Sharks hockey team came out spontaneously to sandbag the place. Life wouldn't be the same without the Hi-Life.

HiqH TEch BurriTo

<table>
<tr><td></td><td>Mexican</td></tr>
<tr><td>Zone 10   Suburban Marin</td><td>★★</td></tr>
<tr><td>118 Strawberry Village</td><td>Inexpensive</td></tr>
<tr><td>   Shopping Center, Mill Valley</td><td></td></tr>
<tr><td>(415) 388-7002</td><td>Quality 77   Value A</td></tr>
</table>

Reservations:	Not necessary
When to go:	Any time
Entree range:	$2.85–5.95
Payment:	Cash, ATM cards
Service rating:	★★★
Friendliness rating:	★★★
Parking:	Free shopping center lot
Bar:	Beer
Wine selection:	None
Dress:	Casual
Disabled access:	Good
Customers:	Local, tourist
Open:	Monday–Wednesday, 11 A.M.–9 P.M.;
	Thursday–Saturday, 11 A.M.–10 P.M.;
	Sunday, noon–9 P.M.

Atmosphere / setting: Hole-in-the-wall takeout with sidewalk tables in a tree-shaded shopping center.

House specialties: Classic burritos with choice of steak, chicken, vegetables, or beans and cheese. Specialty combinations, including grilled steak and chicken, or grilled steak and prawns. Fajitas, which are burritos without the rice and beans. Cajun and barbecue burritos. Many burritos are designated "heart healthy" by American Heart Association.

Other recommendations: Children's-sized burritos, whole-wheat tortillas upon request; black beans or pintos; guacamole and chips; customized burritos.

Summary & comments: The burrito is the fast food of the '90s: large, power-packed portions, low in fats, high in complex carbohydrates, available in cholesterol-free and vegan versions. High Tech's are state-of-the-art; they do basically one thing, and they do it very well. If you call in your order, you go to the head of the line to pick it up. The cafe tables are pleasant on summer evenings, but, of course, the real way to eat a burrito is to slurp it behind the wheel of your car, dripping juices in your lap as you drive. High Tech is replicating itself; look for new branches in other locations.

HONG KONG FLOWER LOUNGE

	Chinese
	★★½
	Inexpensive
	Quality 79 Value B

Zone 8   Richmond/Avenues
5322 Geary Boulevard
(415) 668-8998

Reservations:	Accepted
When to go:	Dinner
Entree range:	$8–20
Payment:	MC, VISA, AMEX
Service rating:	★★★
Friendliness rating:	★★★
Parking:	Street
Bar:	Full service
Wine selection:	Fair
Dress:	Casual
Disabled access:	Yes
Customers:	Local, business
Lunch:	Monday–Friday, 11 A.M.–2:30 P.M.
Lunch/Dinner:	Saturday and Sunday, 10:30 A.M.–9 P.M.
Dinner:	Monday–Friday, 5–9 P.M.

Atmosphere / setting: A lively, colorful, and festive atmosphere. The whole place is dominated by red, the Chinese color for luck and prosperity. In the entryway the green tile roof gives a feeling of spaciousness along with a bit of the serenity one might find in a Chinese temple.

House specialties: Cantonese cookery, emphasizing the freshness of ingredients and cooking techniques designed to bring out their natural flavors and colors with a minimum of seasoning. Many different dim sums; pan-fried minced pigeon with artfully trimmed lettuce wrappers and plum sauce; duck fried with chile and celery; shredded beef in black pepper sauce; chicken with black-bean sauce; fried prawns with walnuts.

Other recommendations: Live fish swimming in the tank. Choose your own.

Summary & comments: This place is exceedingly popular at lunch, and you may have to wait in line. Consider coming for dinner. Generally the food is really superb, though there might be one or two clunkers on the menu on a given night. Kids seem to love it here. It's a good place to bring the family, especially for lunch on weekends.

HORIZONS

Zone 9   Waterfront Crescent
558 Bridgeway, Sausalito
(415) 331-3232

California
★½
Moderate

Quality 69   Value C

Reservations:	Recommended on weekends
When to go:	Sunny days, clear evenings
Entree range:	$6.75–17.50
Payment:	AMEX, MC, VISA
Service rating:	★★½
Friendliness rating:	★★½
Parking:	Free valet
Bar:	Full service
Wine selection:	House
Dress:	Casual
Disabled access:	Limited
Customers:	Tourist, local
Brunch:	Saturday and Sunday, 10 A.M.–midnight
Lunch/Dinner:	Monday–Thursday, 11 A.M.–9 P.M.;
	Friday, 11 A.M.–midnight;
	Saturday and Sunday, 10 A.M.–midnight

Atmosphere / setting: Only the name and the clientele have changed since the Kingston Trio's 1960s jazz club, The Trident, became Horizons in 1980. The rock stars, groupies, and coke dealers are gone, but the redwood interior, featuring barrel-arched windows and balustrades, rainbow canopies, and the mural-painted ceiling, remains the same as when Janis Joplin held court in her velvet hat and feather boa. The historic building, constructed in 1898 by the San Francisco Yacht Club, has a thousand tales to tell. As does the view: smack on the water, with 180 degrees of classic San Francisco Bay—Belvedere, Angel Island, Alcatraz, and the city itself.

House specialties: Dungeness crab cakes, cocktail, or salad; almond chicken salad; seafood gratinée; bouillabaisse with garlic toasts; linguine with clam sauce; grilled salmon sandwich. Tequila sunrise; piña colada; Irish coffee.

Other recommendations: Burgers, clam chowder, mud pie.

Summary & comments: The main reasons to visit Horizons are the open air view, the nostalgia factor, and the weekend music and dancing. The ample portions of standard California/American fare satisfy but probably won't delight. On weekday afternoons off-season, the deck is a pleasant place to reminisce for those whose personal memories intersect with the Trident's glory days.

House of Bamboo

Zone 2   Civic Center
601 Van Ness
(415) 928-0889

<table>
<tr><td>Chinese</td></tr>
<tr><td>★★½</td></tr>
<tr><td>Moderate</td></tr>
<tr><td>Quality 76   Value B</td></tr>
</table>

Reservations:	Accepted
When to go:	Pretheater
Entree range:	$9.95–19.95
Payment:	Major credit cards
Service rating:	★★★
Friendliness rating:	★★
Parking:	Validated
Bar:	Full service
Wine selection:	Fair
Dress:	Casual
Disabled access:	Yes
Customers:	Local, tourist
Lunch:	Sunday–Friday, 11 A.M.–4:30 P.M.
Dinner:	Sunday–Thursday, 4:30–10 P.M.;
	Friday and Saturday, 4:30–11 P.M.

Atmosphere / setting: Comfortable and cheery blend of Chinese and California designs. At center, black marble tables are flanked by red chairs on jade carpet, while other sections have comfortable booths.

House specialties: This restaurant matches Chinese and Southeast Asian to California cookery. For instance ma-por pork and green onion tortilla is an adaptation of ma-po dofu, a spicy hot mix of bean curd and minced pork; pan-fried black filet prepared with black beans and sun-dried tomatoes.

Other recommendations: Nam yee roasted chicken with oyster mushrooms.

Summary & comments: Casual atmosphere with waiters in blue jeans serving generous portions at affordable prices. Close to ballet, opera, and symphony.

House of Prime Rib

Zone 2   Civic Center
1906 Van Ness
(415) 885-4605

American	
★★★½	
Expensive	
Quality 89	Value B+

Reservations:	Necessary
When to go:	Dinner only
Entree range:	$19.75–23.65
Payment:	Major credit cards
Service rating:	★★★
Friendliness rating:	★★★½
Parking:	Valet
Bar:	Full service
Wine selection:	Good
Dress:	Business, dressy
Disabled access:	Yes
Customers:	Local, business, tourist
Dinner:	Monday–Thursday, 5:30–10 P.M.; Friday, 5–10 P.M.; Saturday, 4:30–10 P.M.; Sunday, 4–10 P.M.

Atmosphere / setting: Plush. Large, comfortable rooms with booths, alcoves, and tables set with heavy napery. A mirrored bar with hardwood floor and fireplace in the lounge. Wall adorned with murals and heavy draperies.

House specialties: Prime rib, of course. You can have it thick cut or "English cut," several thinner slices that some people say brings out more of the flavor. The jury is out on this, but either taste is accommodated here. Baked or mashed potato; creamed spinach; generous tossed salad.

Other recommendations: Fresh catch of the day for the odd patron who prefers not to have red meat.

Summary & comments: This is a temple to red meat. One of the older restaurants in town, it would be hard to find more civilized surroundings for indulging in that most primitive of appetites. The meat is wheeled to your table on a silver steam cart and the great haunch is displayed to you in all its glory. "Thick cut, Madam? English cut, Sir?" It can make one proud to be a carnivore.

Hunan Village

Zone 1   Chinatown
839 Kearny Street
(415) 956-7868

Chinese	
★★★	
Inexpensive	
Quality 83	Value B+

Reservations:	Recommended on weekends
When to go:	Any time
Entree range:	$6.50–20
Payment:	AMEX, MC, VISA
Service rating:	★★★½
Friendliness rating:	★★★½
Parking:	Street, public pay lots
Bar:	Beer, wine
Wine selection:	House
Dress:	Casual
Disabled access:	Good
Customers:	Local, business, tourist
Open:	Monday–Sunday, 11:30 A.M.–9 P.M.

Atmosphere / setting: Not fancy, but cheerful and welcoming; Hunan Village is painted in shades of peach, green, and burnt orange, with murals depicting the misty landscapes of the Hunan province of China. Carpeting helps keep this busy restaurant quiet during peak hours.

House specialties: Spicy dishes from Hunan, many of which have been incorporated into standard Chinese menus: Hunan crab; Kung Pao shrimp, chicken, or squid; cashew prawns; tea-smoked duck or chicken; Hunan smoked pork; Hunan Village beef. Black mushrooms with greens; shrimp and tofu special hot pot; moo shi entrees; honey-glazed walnut prawns; Peking duck.

Summary & comments: Once seated in Hunan Village's hideous orange vinyl chairs, you will be handed a surprisingly classy menu, which recounts the legend of the crane and the pepper, an explanation of the use of fiery spices in Hunan cuisine. The rice paper pages offer extensive calligraphic listings of moderately priced dishes, all of which are prepared with a confident hand, assertively seasoned, and sauced to sparkling perfection. In the bewildering maze of restaurants that inhabit Chinatown, Hunan Village is an excellent choice.

HUNG YEN

Zone 7   SOMA / Mission
3100 18th Street
(415) 621-8531

Reservations:	Not accepted
When to go:	Lunch
Entree range:	$3.75–7.50
Payment:	Cash
Service rating:	★★
Friendliness rating:	★★
Parking:	Lot
Bar:	Beer, wine
Wine selection:	House
Dress:	Casual
Disabled access:	Limited
Customers:	Local
Open:	Monday–Friday, 9 A.M.–9 P.M.; Saturday, 10 A.M.–9 P.M.; Sunday, closed

Atmosphere / setting: It used to be a Mexican restaurant, and you can still tell upon entering—but don't let the decor distract you from the food. At the corner of Harrison and across the street from PG&E, this is an ideal place to meet for a really fine Vietnamese lunch.

House specialties: Hung Yen is most famous for its spicy beef noodle soup: a broth scented with lemongrass and chilies, beef sliced so paper thin that the broth cooks it, noodles, onions, and fresh mint or basil. At $3.75 it's one of the best lunch bargains you'll find anywhere in the city.

Other recommendations: A full range of Vietnamese fare: fried noodle or rice dishes; combination plates; excellent vegetarian dishes; deep fried imperial rolls; lemon beef salad; prawn curry; and fried pineapple. Soups and stir-fries are the most common preparations.

Summary & comments: According to the extensive menu, "Hung Yen does party. Up to sixty people." It also lists "Ten dishes to die for." In good weather diners often avail themselves of the covered patio (which has even more Mexican ambience than the interior). Despite the confused decor, if you concentrate on the dishes in front of you, you could believe you're in Saigon.

Il Fornaio

Italian
★★★
Moderate
Quality 85　　Value B

Zone 10　　Suburban Marin
223 Town Center, Corte Madera
(415) 927-4400

Reservations:	Accepted
When to go:	Any time
Entree range:	$7.50–14.95
Payment:	All major credit cards
Service rating:	★★★½
Friendliness rating:	★★★½
Parking:	Free shopping center lot
Bar:	Full service
Wine selection:	Excellent
Dress:	Informal
Disabled access:	Good
Customers:	Local, business, tourist
Brunch:	Saturday and Sunday, 9 A.M.–3 P.M.
Lunch / Dinner:	Sunday–Friday, 11:30 A.M.–10 P.M.;
	Saturday, 11:30 A.M.–11 P.M.

Atmosphere / setting:　Saunter into Il Fornaio, and presto, you're in a sun-drenched courtyard in Tuscany. Frescoes of forest scenes, farm life, fruit, and flowers festoon the arched ceilings; massive dark wood frames the windows and mirror behind the well-stocked bar; shades of ochre, cream, and pale green reflect the suffused lighting. The garlands of garlic and peppers, jars of olives, hemp-strung cheeses and fragrant sausages; the snowy napery and heavy china; and the musical Italian accents all enhance the trattoria atmosphere.

House specialties:　Pizza with gorgonzola, basil, and pine nuts; dome-shaped bombai pizza with prosciutto, grana cheese, arugula, and truffle oil; carpaccio with capers and olive oil; lasagna with duck ragout, fresh herbs, and bechamel sauce; rotisserie rabbit in Italian bacon; baby pork ribs with Tuscan white beans and spinach.

Other recommendations:　Lobster-filled pasta with lemon cream sauce and leeks; mesquite-grilled veal chop with sage and rosemary; hot coffee drinks with liqueurs and whipped cream; tiramisu.

Summary & comments:　Il Fornaio is the oldest and perhaps the most authentic of the tidal wave of Italian trattorii which swept the Bay Area during the last ten years. The cuisine is earthy and robust, utilizing a palate of darker, richer flavors: lots of rosemary, sage, balsamic vinegar, red wine. The breads, baked on the premises, are outstanding. Bakery opens for coffees and pastry at 8 A.M.

Honors / awards:　*San Francisco Focus* Best Italian 1990.

161

Il Fornaio Panetteria

	Italian bakery
Zone 9 Waterfront Crescent	★★★
1 Main Street, Tiburon	Inexpensive
(415) 435-0777	Quality 85 Value A

Reservations:	Not accepted or necessary
When to go:	Any time, but especially weekdays or early mornings
Entree range:	$4–5
Payment:	MC, VISA
Service rating:	★★★
Friendliness rating:	★★½
Parking:	Street or public lot
Bar:	None
Wine selection:	None
Dress:	Casual
Disabled access:	Good
Customers:	Tourist, local, business
Breakfast:	Coffee and pastry from 6 A.M.
Lunch:	Every day, 11 A.M.–7 P.M.
Dinner:	Panini, salads, and frittati until 7 P.M.

Atmosphere / setting: Fabulously located Italian cafe with black-and-white tiled floors, indoor and outdoor wrought steel tables and chairs, classical Italian music, and the beautiful Tiburon shoreline for picnicking.

House specialties: Italian coffees, pastries and cookies, sandwiches, and salads. Try the panini de pescatore; a sweet buttery breakfast cake stuffed with fennel seeds and candied fruit; the vegetable sandwich on foccacia; or the baby pizza.

Other recommendations: Crusty olive rolls, lemon triangles, gelato.

Summary & comments: A soaring success from the moment its doors opened in 1993, Il Fornaio's location is so logical, one wonders why a great cafe didn't land there sooner. The pace can get a little hectic on sunny weekends, when the staff starts to look deranged and the floor and tables take on a sticky texture. But even at those times you can grab your latte and sandwich and head for the Tiburon green, where the people-watching only gets better on busy days. The only reason not to stop at Il Fornaio is if you're already too full from a meal somewhere else.

INdiA PAlACE

Indian
★ ★ ½
Moderate
Quality 78　　Value D

Zone 10　　Suburban Marin
707 Redwood Highway, Mill Valley
(415) 388-3350

Reservations:	Not usually necessary
When to go:	Any time
Entree range:	Lunch buffet, $6.95; dinner entrees, $7.95–16.95; combination dinners, $16.95–20.95
Payment:	All major credit cards
Service rating:	★ ★ ★
Friendliness rating:	★ ★ ½
Parking:	Free lot
Bar:	Beer, wine
Wine selection:	Fair
Dress:	Informal, casual
Disabled access:	Good
Customers:	Local, business, tourist
Brunch:	Sunday buffet, 11:30 A.M.–2 P.M.
Lunch:	Buffet, 11:30 A.M.–2 P.M.
Dinner:	Every day, 5–9:30 P.M.

Atmosphere / setting: Considering its location in the Travelodge just off Highway 101, the India Palace is rather plush, with pale pink napery and upholstered chairs lending a more formal tone than one might expect in a motel restaurant. It's fairly easy to relax once you're settled, however.

House specialties: Tandoori chicken, lamb, and seafood; prawn curries; vegetarian entrees including bengan bartha, roasted eggplant with tomatoes and onions; sag paneer, fresh spinach with herbs and cheese; malai kokta; cheese balls in gravy; and mixed vegetable curries. Several delicious varieties of housemade Indian breads. Try the Kabuli nan, with nuts, raisins and fennel, or the aloo paratha, stuffed with potatoes and peas.

Summary & comments: The India Palace is not cheap, since except for the combination dinners, all dishes are served a la carte. The cuisine is somewhat lighter and less oily than some Indian fare, and the spicing is fairly mild. Tandoori dishes are tender and attractively presented. If you like Indian food and are willing to spend around $20 per person for it, you will probably enjoy dinner here. The $6.95 lunch buffet is $2 more than those in San Rafael; you pay for the southern Marin location and more elegant trappings.

Italian Colors Ristorante

	Italian
	★★★
	Moderate
	Quality 89 Value B+

Zone 13   Oakland
2220 Mountain Boulevard
(510) 482-8094

Reservations:	Recommended on weekends
When to go:	Any time
Entree range:	$8.25–11.95
Payment:	VISA, MC, AMEX
Service rating:	★★½
Friendliness rating:	★★★
Parking:	Free lot
Bar:	Full service
Wine selection:	Good
Dress:	Casual, business
Disabled access:	Good
Customers:	Local, business
Lunch:	Monday–Friday, 11:30 A.M.–2 P.M.
Dinner:	Every day, 5:30–9:30 P.M.

Atmosphere / setting: A spacious and airy southwest Italian villa. At first glance, its earthtone walls and ample wood might suggest southwestern America.

House specialties: Pan Italian with California flair, featuring pasta and grills. Marinated and broiled pork medallions with onion, apple, and cranberry. Venetian-style fish stew. Herb-roasted chicken. Pizza and pastas include spaghetti salsiccia, linguine vongole, and fettucini with smoked chicken. Vegetarian pizzas and pizzas with smoked meats.

Other recommendations: Salads are large and creative, using a variety of vinaigrettes, smoked meats, and nuts. Oven-roasted red potatoes are a popular side dish.

Summary & comments: Colors is an active part of its community. It contributes to local schools and other programs. Patrons feel very much at ease here, as though they haven't quite left home and yet they've still gone out to dine. The staff are a happy crew and enjoy working here.

Izzy's Steak and Chop House

Zone 5   Marina
3345 Steiner Street
(415) 563-0487

American
★★★
Moderate
Quality 85   Value A

Reservations:	Accepted
When to go:	Any time
Entree range:	$6.95–19.95
Payment:	Major credit cards
Service rating:	★★★
Friendliness rating:	★★★
Parking:	Street
Bar:	Full service
Wine selection:	Good
Dress:	Casual
Disabled access:	Yes
Customers:	Local, business, tourist
Dinner:	Monday–Saturday, 5:30–11 P.M.;
	Sunday, 5–10 P.M.

Atmosphere / setting: A modernized version of an old-time steak house. It can sometimes fill to overflowing with locals who come for beef, booze, and merriment. You'll see a lot of back-slapping, glad-handing, laughing, and carrying on here. In the bar where patrons wait in no particular hurry, the generations mix as the big drinks flow.

House specialties: Aged Black Angus beef in he-man size portions: New York steak; pepper steak; Cajun-style blackened steak; untampered with, unalloyed steak; steak.

Other recommendations: Creamed spinach. Huge and tasty desserts.

Summary & comments: Many of the patrons are regulars, live in the neighborhood, and know each other. When they meet here it's party time. Don't come for quiet, and don't come over-dressed. Come hungry and happy.

Jazzed

Zone 10   Suburban Marin
816 Fourth Street, San Rafael
(415) 455-8077

Reservations:	Not accepted
When to go:	Any time, but especially Tuesday–Saturday nights for live jazz
Entree range:	$4.95–6.50
Payment:	Cash only
Service rating:	★★
Friendliness rating:	★★★
Parking:	Street, public lots
Bar:	None
Wine selection:	None
Dress:	Casual
Disabled access:	Good
Customers:	Local
Open:	Sunday, 9 A.M.–6 P.M.; Tuesday, 9 A.M.–10 P.M.; Wednesday–Thursday, 9 A.M.–11 P.M.; Friday and Saturday, 9–1 A.M.

Atmosphere / setting: Comfortable, open, and friendly coffee house; live jazz performances most nights. No smoking and no alcohol allowed.

House specialties: Limited menu, including coffee drinks and sodas; spinach and feta calzone; quiches; muffaletta sandwiches; and a house garden salad. Nice selection of pastries and desserts.

Summary & comments: Jazzed is a nice concept: part coffee house, part community arts forum, and offering a nonsmoking environment in a venue where that's hard to find. A great, informal stop for nondrinkers, nonsmokers, and underage jazz lovers.

JENNIE LOW'S

Zone 10   Suburban Marin
38 Miller Avenue, Mill Valley
(415) 388-8868

Chinese	
★★½	
Inexpensive	
Quality 79	Value C

Reservations:	Recommended on weekends
When to go:	Any time
Entree range:	Lunch special, $5.68; entrees, $6.28–17.18
Payment:	AMEX, MC, VISA
Service rating:	★★½
Friendliness rating:	★★½
Parking:	Street or public lots, metered in daytime
Bar:	Beer, wine
Wine selection:	House
Dress:	Casual, informal
Disabled access:	Good
Customers:	Local, business, tourist
Lunch:	Monday–Saturday, 11:30 A.M.–3 P.M.
Dinner:	Every day, 4:30–9:30 P.M.

Atmosphere / setting: Generally pleasant, but small and sometimes crowded and noisy; upscale decor with few Chinese touches.

House specialties: Fried wonton skins filled with crab, green onions, and cream cheese; vegetarian egg rolls and pot stickers; sizzling rice soup; pine-nut chicken with vegetables; calamari batter-fried and glazed with honey; moo shi pork; asparagus beef with black-bean sauce.

Other recommendations: Noodle soups; vegetable chow mein.

Summary & comments: Jennie Low's advertises home-style cooking combining Cantonese, Mandarin, Hunan, and Szechuan influences, a sort of Chinese cuisine bonne femme. Many of the dishes are quite sweet, such as the chicken salad dressed primarily with hoisin sauce; inquire to ascertain the sweetness in any given dish. Others, like the vegetable and tofu dishes, are a little bland, but this can be remedied with a pot of chili paste or oil. Jennie's soups are especially delicate and flavorful. Jennie's is a local favorite, but her housewifely cuisine, while fresh and restrained, lacks the zing of some of the less well-heeled Chinese joints in the city. Jennie's has opened a branch in the Vintage Oaks Center in Novato.

Joe LoCoco's

Zone 10   Suburban Marin
300 Drakes Landing Road, Greenbrae
(415) 925-0808

	Italian
	★★★½
	Moderate
Quality 89	Value B

Reservations:	Recommended on weekends
When to go:	Any time
Entree range:	$8.95–18.95
Payment:	AMEX, D, DC, MC, VISA
Service rating:	★★★
Friendliness rating:	★★½
Parking:	Free lot
Bar:	Full service
Wine selection:	Excellent
Dress:	Informal
Disabled access:	Limited
Customers:	Business, tourist, local
Lunch:	Monday–Friday, 11:30 A.M.–3 P.M.
Dinner:	Monday–Saturday, 5:30–10 P.M.;
	Sunday, 5–9 P.M.

Atmosphere / setting: In spite of the requisite peach stucco walls, tile floors, and cast vertigris railings, Joe LoCoco's evokes a more polished urban look and feel than most Marin County Italian eateries. This atmosphere attracts special occasion and business customers, along with the livelier patrons of its adjoining cabaret, the Coconut Room.

House specialties: LoCoco's menu is self-described as hearty peasant fare. If peasants everywhere could enjoy standards like prawns with saffron, rack of lamb with rosemary, risotto with quail and blueberries, or Maine lobster with champagne, this would certainly be a better world. Admittedly, osso buco and bouillabaisse have peasant origins, as do many of the pastas and antipasti.

Other recommendations: Spaghetti alla carbonara; excellent mixed antipasti; a light, airy tiramisu.

Summary & comments: Joe LoCoco's enjoys a wide reputation, in part due to the connections and promotional efforts of its proprietor. The plethora of excellent contemporary Italian restaurants in both Marin and San Francisco makes it difficult to choose one over another, but Joe LoCoco's maintains a dependably high standard. The soft light, spaciously placed tables, and view encourage both affable business dealings and romantic evenings. The addition of the cabaret venue provides an entertainment option as well.

John's Grill

Zone 3   Union Square
63 Ellis Street
(415) 986-DASH

	Steak House
	★★★
	Moderate
	Quality 80 Value A

Reservations:	Accepted
When to go:	Any time
Entree range:	$13.95–39.95
Payment:	AMEX, MC, VISA
Service rating:	★★★
Friendliness rating:	★★★
Parking:	Street
Bar:	Full service
Wine selection:	Good
Dress:	Casual, business
Disabled access:	No
Customers:	Local, business, tourist
Open:	Monday–Saturday, 11 A.M.–10 P.M.; Sunday, 5–10 P.M.

Atmosphere / setting: 1930s at its best. Dark wood everywhere and brass trim. Walk in and you are transported to another—many would say better—San Francisco. Sepia photographs of celebs and local potentates cover the west wall. Deep and narrow with booths and small tables; the general feeling is one of cozy intimacy and . . . conspiracy.

House specialties: Steaks, chops, and seafood. Dungeness crab cakes (a must at any historic place in the city); fried oysters; sanddabs; Sam Spade's lamb chops; pork chops with apple sauce; a giant porterhouse steak; broiled calves' liver; chicken Jerusalem.

Other recommendations: Variety of salads; clam chowder; oysters Wellington.

Summary & comments: "Spade went to John's Grill, asked the waiter to hurry his order of chops, baked potato, sliced tomatoes . . . and was smoking a cigarette with his coffee when. . . ." Open since 1908, this landmark restaurant was the setting for Dashiel Hammet's novel *The Maltese Falcon*. To dine, or drink martinis, here is to imbibe both the history and the literature of the city.

Jose's Caribbean Restaurant

	Caribbean
	★★½
	Inexpensive
	Quality 78 Value C+

Zone 14   South Bay
2275 El Camino Real, Palo Alto
(415) 326-6522

Reservations:	Accepted
When to go:	Any time
Entree range:	$6.50–7.75
Payment:	Major credit cards
Service rating:	★★
Friendliness rating:	★★★
Parking:	Street
Bar:	Full service
Wine selection:	Adequate
Dress:	Casual
Disabled access:	No
Customers:	Local
Lunch:	Monday–Friday, 11 A.M.–2 P.M.
Dinner:	Every day, 5–11:30 P.M.

Atmosphere / setting: A funky, tropical, airy sort of place that reminds you of one of Carmen Miranda's hats. There's nothing here that overtly says "toucan" but you keep looking for one. Very laid back and friendly in a not-too-hurried sort of way.

House specialties: A mix of dishes from around the Caribbean and South America: tangy Cuban-style barbecued ribs; Argentine pizzas; Bolivian empandas, a sort of calzone or meat pie stuffed with meat and potato and savory sauce; black beans and rice.

Entertainment & amenities: Regular performances of jazz, salsa, and reggae. Call for schedules.

Summary & comments: It started small and caught on. Recently expanded to include the full bar and dance floor, Jose's has become a regular stopping place for well-known bands and the people who like to dance to them. With its food, drink, entertainment, and welcoming hosts, it's a good place to spend the whole evening.

Kincaid's Bayhouse

Zone 13   Oakland
1 Franklin Street, Jack London Square
(510) 835-8600

Seafood	
★★★	
Moderate	
Quality 85	Value A

Reservations:	Recommended
When to go:	Any time
Entree range:	$10.95–20.95
Payment:	VISA, MC, AMEX, DC
Service rating:	★★★
Friendliness rating:	★★★
Parking:	Garage
Bar:	Full service
Wine selection:	Good
Dress:	Business
Disabled access:	Good
Customers:	Local, tourist, business
Brunch:	Sunday, 10:30 A.M.–3 P.M.
Lunch:	Every day, 11:15 A.M.–3 P.M.
Dinner:	Monday–Thursday, 5–10 P.M.;
	Friday and Saturday, 5–10:30 P.M.;
	Sunday, 3–9 P.M.

Atmosphere / setting: Polished hardwood trim, Italian marble bar and counters, flagstone floors. At the water's edge of Jack London square, the estuary flows by one side of the ample bar and the marina lies toward another side. The dining area is split-level, large, and airy, yet has intimate seating arrangements. The open kitchen displays a large roastery and gives a feeling of warmth against the chill of the sea and fog.

House specialties: Spit roasts, pasta, and seafood. The spit roaster is a six-foot firebox fueled with hardwood embers that burn at a constant 350°, allowing meats to roast slowly while turning and basting in their own juices. Kincaid's also has a searing grill and a hardwood broiler burning aromatic applewood.

Other recommendations: Superb crab cakes served with beurre blanc, Thai sweet / sour sauce, and pickled ginger.

Summary & comments: Upon entering Kincaid's you are enveloped by the rich aroma of roasting meats and sizzling fish. It's not a veggie place. A good happy hour bar provides a great place to meet friends after work. A good place to bring visitors for its view and central location on the square. From here you can easily catch the cross-bay ferry or watch the boats come and go.

Kirk's

Zone 14   South Bay
1330 Sunnyvale-Saratoga Road,
   Sunnyvale
(408) 446-2988

<table>
<tr><td></td><td>American</td></tr>
<tr><td></td><td>★½</td></tr>
<tr><td></td><td>Inexpensive</td></tr>
<tr><td>Quality 68</td><td>Value B</td></tr>
</table>

Reservations:	Not accepted
When to go:	Any time
Entree range:	$4.20–6.90
Payment:	Cash, personal checks
Service rating:	★
Friendliness rating:	★★
Parking:	Lot
Bar:	None
Wine selection:	None
Dress:	Casual
Disabled access:	Yes
Customers:	Local, working
Open:	Every day, 11:15 A.M.–9 P.M.

Atmosphere / setting: Plain, unadorned, tile-floored, vinyl and cinder block burger joint. Come in and eat, don't look.

House specialties: Arguably some of the best, biggest, juiciest burgers in the county. Good shakes, too.

Other recommendations: Get it to go.

Summary & comments: All they do here is get the best meat they can find, grill it to your specs over mesquite charcoal, and leave the rest to you. You can dress it as you wish with onions, jalapeños, catsup, etc., but no iceberg lettuce.

La Fiammetta

Zone 2   Civic Center
1701 Octavia Street
(415) 474-5077

Italian	
★★★	
Moderate	
Quality 85	Value A

Reservations: Accepted
When to go: Any time
Entree range: $9–10
Payment: VISA, MC
Service rating: ★★★½
Friendliness rating: ★★★
Parking: Valet
Bar: Beer, wine
Wine selection: Good
Dress: Business
Disabled access: Yes
Customers: Local, business
Dinner: Tuesday–Thursday, 6–10 P.M.;
                      Friday and Saturday, 6–10:30 P.M.

Atmosphere / setting: Approaching this restaurant on a corner in a quiet, tree-filled neighborhood, the light beckons and promises gentility without snobbery. Inside, the white tablecloths and wall fixtures all bespeak both form and function, a simple form of elegance not strained.

House specialties: A standard menu of some two dozen items supplemented by daily specials, particularly fish. Radicchio wrapped in pancetta; antipasto plate; seafood risotto; housemade cheese-filled ravioli with a light tomato sauce; gnocchi with a variety of sauces.

Other recommendations: Pressed chicken grilled with herbs; deeply flavorful casserole of duck, sausage, and beans; veal chop in mushroom sauce; rabbit in olive sauce.

Summary & comments: This is a rather small place with rather small prices, bent on being able to attract many customers who will keep coming back. Everything is of the best quality and affordably priced. This place is an act of love.

La Petite Auberge

	French
	★★½
Zone 10 Suburban Marin	Moderate
704 Fourth Street,	
San Rafael	Quality 78 Value C
(415) 456-5808	

Reservations:	Recommended on weekends
When to go:	Any time
Entree range:	Champagne brunch, $12.95; dinner, $13.95–23.95
Payment:	All major credit cards
Service rating:	★★★
Friendliness rating:	★★
Parking:	Street
Bar:	Full service
Wine selection:	Good
Dress:	Informal
Disabled access:	Good
Customers:	Local, business
Brunch:	Sunday, 11 A.M.–2 P.M.
Lunch:	Friday and Sunday, 11 A.M.–2 P.M.
Dinner:	Tuesday–Sunday, 5–9:30 P.M.

Atmosphere / setting: Small and dated, decorated in French provincial style, with pink tablecloths and silk wisteria vines bedecking the skylight, and a slightly dingy, 1950s vintage lounge.

House specialties: Quenelles in champagne sauce; veal sweetbreads with mushrooms and Madeira; rabbit with mustard; frog legs Provençale; duck with orange glaze; Châteaubriand.

Other recommendations: Roasted chicken with tomatoes and garlic; bouillabaisse; rack of lamb; steak with peppercorns.

Summary & comments: La Petite Auberge has been operating continuously for 36 years, and neither the decor, the menu, nor the service appear to have changed much during that time. This is the competently executed French fare traditional to stateside restaurants of the 50s and 60s. The only acknowledgment of the passing of time is the addition of pasta to the menu.

Lalime's

Zone 12   Berkeley
1329 Gilman Street
(510) 527-9838

	Mediterranean
	★★★
	Expensive
	Quality 89 Value B

Reservations:	Recommended
When to go:	Any time
Entree range:	$10.75–17.25
Payment:	VISA, MC
Service rating:	★★★
Friendliness rating:	★★★
Parking:	Street
Bar:	Beer, wine
Wine selection:	Very good
Dress:	Business, casual
Disabled access:	Good
Customers:	Local, regional
Dinner:	Monday–Thursday, 5:30–9:30 P.M.

Atmosphere / setting: Unique! Splashes of modern art and abstractly painted walls in a setting reminiscent of the South of France or the North of Italy; dotted with lovely floral arrangements. It sounds cacophonous but it isn't. It's actually quite soothing without being dull. A split-level building with most of the dining area in the lower front. A small bar area in the rear accommodates overflow crowds.

House specialties: The fixed-price menu changes every day and is planned weeks in advance. The management sends a two-month menu to all on its considerable mailing list. The selections are French / Italian inspired with such as coquille St. Jaques; chicken roasted with whole lemon and rosemary served on ricotta and herb cannelloni; and grilled beef filet with green peppercorn sauce. But they also serve baby-back ribs, cioppino, crab ravioli, and flank steak with mango barbecue sauce.

Other recommendations: A brief à la carte menu is available at each dinner.

Entertainment & amenities: Occasional wine tastings accompany the meals.

Summary & comments: Haig and Cindy Lalime Kirkorian are not simply operating a restaurant. They are, in a way, entertaining at home and endeavoring to be socially and civically active. The menu they send to their mailing list includes a newsletter with comment on upcoming events and dinners; news of their family; and thoughts on food, its preparation and consumption, and its place in social and political life and history. Very Berkeley. Very good food. The influence of Alice Waters of Chez Panisse is apparent.

Lark Creek Inn

Zone 10   Suburban Marin
234 Magnolia Avenue, Larkspur
(415) 924-7766

New American
★★★★½
Expensive

Quality 95   Value B

Reservations:	Required on weekends, recommended other times
When to go:	Any time
Entree range:	Lunch, $8.75–14; dinner, $14–24
Payment:	All major credit cards
Service rating:	★★★★
Friendliness rating:	★★★★
Parking:	Free lot
Bar:	Full service
Wine selection:	Excellent
Dress:	Informal
Disabled access:	Good
Customers:	Local, tourist, business
Brunch:	Sunday, 10 A.M.–2 P.M.
Lunch:	Monday–Friday, 11:30 A.M.–2 P.M.
Dinner:	Monday–Thursday, 5:30–9:30 P.M.;
	Friday and Saturday, 5–10 P.M.;
	Sunday, 5–9 P.M.

Atmosphere / setting: The picturesque Lark Creek Inn, a turn-of-the-century mansion at the mouth of a redwood canyon, emanates a mellow, gentrified warmth. Two dining rooms are simply furnished; windows overlook the gardens and redwood forest. In summer, diners lounge outdoors at garden tables.

House specialties: Brunch: huckleberry soufflé cakes with Meyer lemon curd; Dungeness crab Cobb salad; corned beef hash with poached eggs. Lunch: grilled quail salad with roasted peppers and pecans; onion flatbread with house-cured gravlax and scallion crème fraiche. Dinner: oak-roasted chicken with spinach and mashed potatoes; grilled double-cut pork chop; whole steamed Dungeness crab.

Other recommendations: Butterscotch pudding with shortbread cookies; cream puff sundae with banana ice cream; devil's food cake with espresso ice cream.

Summary & comments: Executive chef Bradley Ogden has decamped to Market One, his new restaurant in San Francisco, but the Lark Creek Inn carries on in the territory he staked out: outstanding versions of classic American fare utilizing fresh produce, meats, poultry, fish, and game from local farmers, ranchers, and fishermen. For overall excellence, Lark Creek reigns as Marin's prime special occasion restaurant.

Las Camelias

Zone 10   Suburban Marin
912 Lincoln Avenue, San Rafael
(415) 453-5850

Mexican	
★★½	
Inexpensive	
Quality 77	Value B

Reservations:	Recommended on weekends
When to go:	Any time
Entree range:	$8.95–11.95
Payment:	AMEX, MC, VISA
Service rating:	★★★
Friendliness rating:	★★★
Parking:	Street
Bar:	Beer, wine
Wine selection:	House
Dress:	Casual
Disabled access:	Good
Customers:	Local, business
Lunch/Dinner:	Monday–Saturday, 11:30 A.M.–9:30 P.M.
Dinner:	Sunday, 3–9:30 P.M.

Atmosphere / setting: Casual Mexican with an old hacienda ambiance: tiles, worn wood, flowers, and pottery.

House specialties: Chile relleno with sautéed onions, zucchini, corn, and cinnamon-walnut cream sauce; pozole with chicken and pork; seafood brochette; sautéed shrimp marinated in tequila, ginger, and garlic; carne asada, charbroiled beef with salsa.

Other recommendations: Grilled chicken salad with avocado, jicama, and cilantro cream dressing; Mexican chocolate cake.

Summary & comments: Las Camelias offers a thoughtful take on traditional Mexican dishes. As evidenced by the white bean frijoles and blue corn pozole, the cuisine gives a nod to current trends without giving way to trendiness. The results are Mexican comfort food; unaffected, inexpensive, and toothsome. There's an ease and an unhurried, yet efficient feel to the service.

LE TROU

Zone 7   SOMA / Mission
1007 Guerrero Street
(415) 550-8169

	French
	★★½
	Moderate
	Quality 79 Value B

Reservations:	Accepted
When to go:	Any time
Entree range:	$11.95–18.95
Payment:	Cash
Service rating:	★★★
Friendliness rating:	★★★
Parking:	Street
Bar:	Beer, wine
Wine selection:	Limited but good
Dress:	Casual, business
Disabled access:	Yes
Customers:	Local, business
Dinner:	Tuesday–Saturday, 6–9 P.M.

Atmosphere / setting: A little neighborhood restaurant in France. Almost homey in its unpretentious yet comfy decor. Earthenware knickknacks on shelves and doodads on the walls; nice china though not all matching, but it cannot be said that this mixture detracts from the warm domestic charm. The name "Le Trou" means "The Cave." In this case a very cozy cave.

House specialties: The menu changes seasonally. Menus are focused on a particular style of various regions of France, so whatever your table orders will be a better match than the china. Selections may include choucroute garni; simply fried fish with lime and capers deglazing; zucchini flan with herbs; rich, thick soups; chicken with walnuts and cream.

Other recommendations: Strawberries with red wine and honey; sweet dessert wines.

Summary & comments: Le Trou is operated by a local cooking teacher, and this is where his lessons are put to practical use. The emphasis is on the food and in maintaining its consistently high quality. The small staff dedicate their efforts to that, and anything else is gravy.

Left Bank Cafe

Zone 10   Suburban Marin
507 Magnolia, Larkspur
(415) 927-3331

French Bistro	
★★★★	
Moderate	
Quality 91	Value B

Reservations:	Recommended
When to go:	Any time
Entree range:	$5.50–19.50
Payment:	MC, VISA
Service rating:	★★★½
Friendliness rating:	★★★★
Parking:	Street, public lot
Bar:	Full service
Wine selection:	Limited but good
Dress:	Informal, casual
Disabled access:	Good
Customers:	Local, tourist, business
Brunch:	Sunday, 10 A.M.–3 P.M.
Lunch/Dinner:	Monday–Thursday, 11:30 A.M.–11 P.M.;
	Friday and Saturday, 11:30 A.M.–midnight

Atmosphere / setting: The Left Bank is a brasserie in the grand tradition: mirrored Victorian bar; splashy turn-of-the-century French prints; high cream and white walls; lots of brass and wood; plus a sidewalk cafe. The setting is at once luxe and relaxed, and the staff is friendly and knowledgeable.

House specialties: Left Bank specializes in updated renditions of French brasserie fare, described as Cuisine Grandmere. There are numerous appetizer dips and spreads for bread, called tartines: salmon rillettes; olive tapenade; onion marmalade; and brandade de Morue. Steamed mussels; leek and onion tart; and charcuterie are other appetizers. Salads are of new potatoes, mussels, and roasted artichokes; oxtail terrine, or seared tuna. Entrees include prawns Provençale with tomatoes and garlic; roast rabbit and couscous with winter vegetables. Profiteroles with chocolate sauce, tarte Tatin, and lemon tart for dessert.

Other recommendations: Sandwiches of marinated lamb with aïoli, or rare tuna with lemongrass and ginger on lemon focaccia; plats du jour.

Summary & comments: This Belle Epoque cafe, open since mid-1994, filled a gap in the local restaurant scene. It's the Left Bank's combination of casually glamorous service all day and modestly priced, creative Gallic fare that provides so much leeway; one can drop in for a sandwich in jeans, dressed to kill for a momentous occasion, or linger over dessert in the sidewalk cafe after a movie. Watching the clientele, as well as what they're eating, is part of the concept, and facilitates some friendly banter between customers. Eat, drink, expound, enjoy.

Lefty O'Doul's

Zone 3   Union Square
333 Geary Street
(415) 982-8900

Hof Brau	
★★	
Inexpensive	
Quality 75	Value B

Reservations:	Not accepted
When to go:	Any time
Entree range:	$.50–7.75
Payment:	Cash
Service rating:	★★
Friendliness rating:	★★★
Parking:	Street
Bar:	Full service
Wine selection:	House
Dress:	Casual
Disabled access:	Yes
Customers:	Local, business
Open:	Every day, 7 A.M.–midnight

Atmosphere / setting: A rather gritty sports bar with a steam table and a baby grand piano. Directly across the street from the very elegant Compass Rose in the Saint Francis Hotel, Lefty's seems to have been deliberately put there to add counterpoint to the high-toned hostelry and its expensive watering hole.

House specialties: All the usual roasts: beef, turkey, ham. Dinner plates, hot open-face sandwiches. Polish sausage, lasagna, soup, salad, and daily specials.

Summary & comments: Named for the baseball player, this is an institution in the neighborhood. A place full of regulars and hungry shoppers. It's big and cavernous, yet it still maintains an air of cozy familiarity. It's also considered neutral ground by warring factions. When the San Francisco Fortyniners won their first Superbowl there was pandemonium in the streets requiring a huge police presence. The celebrations went on long into the night, exhausting cops, revelers, and paddy-wagon drivers alike. Between skirmishes, members of both sides could be seen recuperating at adjacent tables in Lefty's.

Let's Eat

Zone 9   Waterfront Crescent
Cove Shopping Center, Tiburon
(415) 383-3663

Delicatessen
★★½
Inexpensive

Quality 77   Value C

Reservations:	Not necessary
When to go:	Any time
Entree range:	$4.25–6
Payment:	DC, MC, VISA
Service rating:	★★★
Friendliness rating:	★★★
Parking:	Free lot
Bar:	None
Wine selection:	None
Dress:	Casual
Disabled access:	Good
Customers:	Local, tourist
Open:	Monday–Friday, 10 A.M.–7 P.M.; Saturday and Sunday, 10 A.M.–6 P.M.

Atmosphere / setting: Clean white suburban gourmet takeout and catering deli; two large eat-in tables with cushioned chairs and benches; rows and cases of condiments, confections, and cheeses.

House specialties: Curried turkey salad, Chinese chicken salad; barbecued chicken; chicken breast and roasted pepper sandwich on focaccia; muffaletta; smoked turkey sandwich with brie and Dijon mustard. Moussaka; Nantucket corn pudding; crab cakes rémoulade; tomato, fennel, and white-bean soup. Swedish almond tarts; chocolate-dipped madeleines.

Summary & comments: Located on the road to Tiburon and therefore ideal for packing a picnic lunch for the Tiburon green, Angel Island, or Paradise County Park, Let's Eat offers some very snappy salads, sandwiches, soups, and entrees to eat on the premises or take away for a picnic or dinner. The same owners operate Sweet Things, the bakery next door, so there are numerous dessert options in addition to the daily special entrees, soups, and salads, and the sandwich menu. There's a wine shop on the corner, too, for the complete picnicker.

LuLu

Zone 7   SOMA / Mission
816 Folsom Street
(415) 495-5775

American
★★★½
Moderate

Quality 89   Value B+

Reservations:	Required except in the cafe
When to go:	Any time
Entree range:	$8.50–17.50
Payment:	AMEX, DC, MC, VISA
Service rating:	★½
Friendliness rating:	★
Parking:	Valet, metered street, public lots
Bar:	Full service
Wine selection:	Excellent
Dress:	Casual, informal
Disabled access:	Good
Customers:	Local, business, tourist
Lunch:	Every day, 11:30 A.M.–2:30 P.M.
Dinner:	Every day, 5:30–10:30 P.M.

Atmosphere / setting: Capacious warehouse redux with painted concrete floors, splashy pottery and prints, a behemoth open rotisserie, and a perpetual party pace. This is definitely where it's happening: if you don't believe it, just ask the staff, whose condescending attitude can be a shock. Lulu hosts a pulsating bar scene and a small cafe next door for drop-in business.

House specialties: Highly eclectic menu, incorporating Mediterranean and Southwest influences: whole wood oven–roasted portobello mushroom with polenta; grilled chevre wrapped in grape leaves; duck cannelloni; pork loin with fennel and garlic mashed potatoes; calamari pizza with basil and aïoli; mixed seafood grill with salsa; lamb daube with artichokes.

Other recommendations: Rabbit fricassee Provençale; pork, sage, and hazelnut sausage with crispy polenta.

Summary & comments: Once the food arrives, you'll probably forgive the attitude, since the dishes are vibrant and distinctive, and the party is one of the best in town. Everything's brought to the table on bright, painted platters in ample proportion, and the family-style service provides easy sharing. You can have a grand meal here without spending a fortune. Great oyster selection; desserts are good too.

Mama's Royal Cafe

Zone 13   Oakland
1012 Broadway
(510) 547-7600

American	
★★	
Inexpensive	
Quality 75	Value B

Reservations:	Not accepted
When to go:	Any time
Entree range:	$3.50–9.25
Payment:	Cash
Service rating:	★★
Friendliness rating:	★★
Parking:	Street
Bar:	Beer, wine
Wine selection:	House
Dress:	Casual
Disabled access:	Good
Customers:	Local, business
Breakfast/Lunch:	Monday–Friday, 7 A.M.–3 P.M.; Saturday and Sunday, 8 A.M.–3 P.M.

Atmosphere/setting: Lineal descendent of the 1950s diner, upgraded to reflect a clientele that wants the best.

House specialties: Breakfast and burgers. Eggs Benedict; eggs Florentine; huevos rancheros; French toast; waffles; granola; applewood-smoked bacon and sausage; lox and onions; Dagwood sandwich; crab sandwich; mushroom burger.

Other recommendations: Seemingly infinite permutations on the omelet.

Summary & comments: Most of the customers are regulars. People on their way to work stopping for breakfast, breaking from work or shopping for lunch, or catching an early dinner. The food is very good and very abundant. There is usually a lengthy wait for breakfast on weekends and holidays.

MANKA'S INVERNESS LODGE

Zone 11   Yonder Marin
Calendar Way at Argyle, Inverness
(415) 669-1034

Continental
★★★½
Expensive
Quality 89   Value D+

Reservations:	Recommended
When to go:	Any time
Entree range:	$18–23
Payment:	MC, VISA
Service rating:	★★
Friendliness rating:	★★
Parking:	Free lot, street
Bar:	Beer, wine
Wine selection:	Excellent and impressive
Dress:	Informal
Disabled access:	No
Customers:	Local, tourist
Breakfast:	Every day, 8:30–10:30 A.M.
Dinner:	Tuesday–Sunday, 5:30–9:30 P.M.

Atmosphere / setting: Rustic / elegant hillside bed-and-breakfast lodge; intimate tables in the candlelit reception hall surround a fireside; a few additional tables are scattered near a grand piano; and a brighter, more formal dining area to the rear, with a huge spray of local flora as its focal point. Inverness is an enchanting waterfront hamlet; and the last outpost on the highway to dramatic Point Reyes National Seashore, about a 90-minute drive from San Francisco.

House specialties: Changing nightly menu which usually includes locally harvested oysters and clams, wild mushrooms, fish and game, and varying accompaniments. Noteworthy starters might be a wild mushroom ragout spooned over roast garlic custard, a housemade wild boar sausage with black pepper polenta, and a Gruyère cheese soup deepened with smoked tomato and chipotle cream. Lamb tenderloins served with a demi-glace and garlic cream are succulent, with the two sauces perfectly balanced.

Other recommendations: Chops of red deer with zinfandel jus; house-cured grilled pork chop with apple-cranberry chutney.

Summary & comments: Given the current trend toward economically priced and prix-fixe options in Old World fare, a destination dinner house needs near flawless service and bountiful, beautiful cuisine to justify starters priced at $9–10 and entrees in the $18–25 range. While much of the menu is exquisitely prepared, inconsistencies in service, amplitude, and seasoning, as well as pedestrian dessert choices, can prove disappointing. Manka's secluded rendezvous charm is unparalleled; but the totality falls a slim, significant margin shy of superb.

MARIN COUNTY
FARMER'S MARKET

Zone 10   Suburban Marin
Marin County Civic Center, San Rafael
(415) 456-3276

Eclectic		
★★★		
Inexpensive		
Quality 85		Value A

Reservations:	No
When to go:	Thursday and Sunday mornings
Entree range:	$2–6
Payment:	Cash
Service rating:	★★★½
Friendliness rating:	★★★½
Parking:	Free lot
Bar:	None
Wine selection:	None
Dress:	Casual
Disabled access:	Good
Customers:	Local
Breakfast/Lunch:	Every day, 8 A.M.–1 P.M.

Atmosphere / setting: The Marin County Farmer's Market, which pops up in several additional locations during the summer months, operates yearly in the Civic Center parking lot every Sunday and Thursday morning. A festive, block party atmosphere prevails, especially during summer, autumn, and the December holidays. Call for information about summer schedules and other locations.

House specialties: Free tastes of locally grown fresh and organic produce, juices, dried fruits and nuts, pastas, goat and sheep's milk cheeses, condiments, vinegars, honey, and olive oils. Pancakes, Indian Chai tea, coffee, and fresh breads and pastries. Tamales, sausage sandwiches, and barbecued skewered meats.

Other recommendations: Locally cured smoked salmon, sheep's-milk pecorino cheese, and olives.

Summary & comments: The farmer's market, like the weekly village markets of simpler cultures, draws a cross-section of the Marin community together in an outdoor setting to share food, music, creative inspiration, and local news. It's a block party, a village fair, a festival, and a wonderful opportunity to savor a sense of community life. The food's great, and the vendors are cheerful; there's a balloon sculptor and storyteller who mesmerizes the children, an egg man who sometimes hawks his wares on roller skates, an herbalist, a chiropractor, and a grandmother who sells long-stemmed roses for $5 a dozen. Some of the summer markets take place in the evenings, when the party atmosphere is even more potent.

Marin Joe's

	Italian
	★★½
	Inexpensive / Moderate
	Quality 70 Value C

Zone 10   Suburban Marin
1585 Casa Buena Drive, Corte Madera
(415) 924-2081

Reservations:	Accepted for parties of 10 or more
When to go:	Late nights, late lunch
Entree range:	$6.50–13.75
Payment:	AMEX, MC, VISA
Service rating:	★½
Friendliness rating:	★½
Parking:	Valet, street
Bar:	Full service
Wine selection:	House
Dress:	Casual
Disabled access:	Good
Customers:	Local, business, tourist
Breakfast:	Weekdays, 11–12:45 A.M.
Lunch:	Weekdays, 11 A.M.–4 P.M.
Dinner:	Monday–Saturday, 5 P.M.–12:45 A.M.;
	Sunday, 4 P.M.–12:45 A.M.

Atmosphere / setting: Crowded, dark, noisy throwback to the 50s, with a lousy location, open grill, no decor to speak of, no view, and a generally go-to-hell attitude.

House specialties: Hamburgers; cheese ravioli with porcini mushroom sauce; roasted meats; grilled steaks; liver and onions; spaghetti with meatballs; and the ubiquitous Joe's Special: scrambled eggs with ground beef, spinach, and mushrooms.

Summary & comments: What really happened to Amelia Erhardt? Who can explain the pull of the Bermuda Triangle? And why is Marin Joe's packed every day from noon to midnight? The most amazing assortment of customers flocks through the doors: beer-bellied bikers and spandexed cyclists; polyester tourists and blue-jeaned college kids; bored suburban yuppies and steel-haired businessmen out to lunch with their mink-stoled mistresses. Some say it's the dingily authentic Ike-and-Mamie ambiance, complete with piano lounge. Aficionados swear by the tossed-at-the-table Caesar salads and grilled steaks, chops, and seafood, and also cite the moderate prices. But none of the above seems to justify such heavy traffic, day after day, year after year. Is this the restaurant at the end of the universe? Why do fools fall in love?

186

MASA'S

Zone 3   Union Square
648 Bush Street
(415) 989-7154

	French
	★★★★★
	Expensive
	Quality 99 Value C

Reservations:	Recommended
When to go:	Any time
Entree range:	$15 and up
Payment:	Major credit cards
Service rating:	★★★★★
Friendliness rating:	★★★★
Parking:	Valet
Bar:	Full service
Wine selection:	Excellent
Dress:	Dressy
Disabled access:	Yes
Customers:	Local, tourist
Dinner:	Tuesday–Saturday, 6–9:30 P.M.

Atmosphere / setting: It ain't cheap and it don't look it. But it's never intimidating. How a place can be so grand and yet not stuffy, pretentious, or snobby is hard to fathom, but there it is. The staff are not concerned with impressing or looking down at their patrons, but with seeing that they get the superb gastronomic experience they pay so dearly for.

House specialties: A unique blend of French and California cooking turned out in an elegant fashion that no other restaurant could imitate even if it tried. The result of the Japanese founder's 30 years in French kitchens honing his style and making his mark. The rather short menu may begin with seafood sausage in beurre blanc or housemade foie gras with spinach. Entrees include roasted partridge with cabbage and thyme; veal or beef with marrow and truffles; grilled fish with caviar or herb confit; grilled lobster with quenelles.

Other recommendations: Desserts are worth the trip if you have any sweet tooth. Pineapple in dark caramel sauce; frozen mousses with crushed filberts.

Summary & comments: This is often said to be a New York restaurant that happens to be located in San Francisco. That might be saying a little too much for New York. It is without a doubt one of the best restaurants in the city, indeed, in the state. It could also be the single most expensive. Especially if you have wine with your meal. And the corkage fee is $20! But if you're swimming in money, or content to eat humble fare for a week or two after, it's worth a blow-out splurge.

Max's Opera Cafe

	Deli/Barbecue
Zone 2 Civic Center	★½
601 Van Ness	Moderate
(415) 771-7300	
	Quality 79 Value B

Reservations:	Not accepted
When to go:	Before or after the show
Entree range:	$11.95–14.95
Payment:	Major credit cards
Service rating:	★★½
Friendliness rating:	★★★
Parking:	Street
Bar:	Full service
Wine selection:	Limited but good
Dress:	Casual to dressy
Disabled access:	Yes
Customers:	Theatergoers, tourists, locals
Open:	Monday, 11:30 A.M.–10 P.M.;
	Tuesday–Thursday, 11:30 A.M.–midnight;
	Friday and Saturday, 11:30 A.M.–1 A.M.;
	Sunday, 11:30 A.M.–11 P.M.

Atmosphere/setting: New York deli cum piano bar and cocktail lounge with barbecue on the side. Spacious with high ceilings and a well-lit and large window looking out onto the streets and City Hall. Though it's a broad space, it has a lot of little nooks, booths, and intimate corners.

House specialties: Big deli sandwiches; barbecue with unique sauces, some using subtle hints of Asian spices; pasta with wild mushrooms; pastrami and corned beef, but ask for it "easy on the lean." Takeout orders are available.

Other recommendations: Desserts and salads.

Entertainment & amenities: Many of the staff are aspiring opera singers; they perform, accompanied by the house pianist, during lulls.

Summary & comments: Being situated close to the War Memorial Opera House, Herbst Theater, and Davies Symphony Hall, this is an ideal spot for a pretheater dinner. Service is generally quick and efficient, no fluff or folderol—they know you've got tickets to the show. Unlike much of the city, parking can actually be had on the street now and then.

Mayflower Inne

Zone 10   Suburban Marin
1533 Fourth Street, San Rafael
(415) 456-1011

British Pub
★½
Inexpensive

Quality 69   Value C

Reservations:	For dinner theater only
When to go:	Any time
Entree range:	$6.25–13.50
Payment:	MC, VISA
Service rating:	★★★
Friendliness rating:	★★★½
Parking:	Street
Bar:	Beer, wine
Wine selection:	Fair
Dress:	Casual
Disabled access:	Good
Customers:	Local
Lunch:	Monday–Friday, 11:30 A.M.–3 P.M.
Dinner:	Monday–Friday, 5–9 P.M.;
	Saturday and Sunday, 5–10 P.M.

Atmosphere / setting: Crossbeamed Tudor-style pub with a separate dining room for family dining, singalongs, and mystery dinner theater.

House specialties: Imported and local draught brews; fish and chips; steak and kidney or steak and mushroom pie; Cornish pasty; shepherd's pie; banger and mash; ham and cheese platter.

Other recommendations: Rhubarb pie with whipped cream; sherry trifle; chocolate cake.

Summary & comments: San Rafael's unique neighborhood pub, boisterous, frankly unsophisticated, politically incorrect, and full of good cheer, along with some excellent beer. The grub is hearty and certainly better than its English counterpart: good french fries, peas cooked al dente, and a downright sinful pastry on the steak and kidney pie. The witty ambiance is infectious, if a trifle corny. Children's portions are available, making this Marin's only family bar.

MENARA MOROCCAN

Zone 14   South Bay
41 East Gish Road, San Jose
(408) 453-1983

	Moroccan
	★★½
	Moderate
Quality 77	Value B

Reservations:	Accepted
When to go:	Any time
Entree range:	$9–15
Payment:	Major credit cards
Service rating:	★★★
Friendliness rating:	★★★
Parking:	Lot
Bar:	Full service
Wine selection:	Limited but good
Dress:	Casual
Disabled access:	Yes
Customers:	Local, business
Dinner:	Every day, 6–10 P.M.

Atmosphere / setting: Your standard Moroccan casbah, complete with carpets, hangings, tassels, brassworks, and draperies; cushions on the floor for seating. The large main room has a couple of small alcove-sized rooms for a bit more privacy. All in all it's well done for the style, exuberant but not gaudy.

House specialties: Honeyed lamb with almonds is tops on the menu here; various eggplant dishes and Moroccan salads of marinated vegetables; roast chicken; chicken pastry with raisin and powdered sugar. A fair selection of Spanish wines goes well with the bill of fare.

Other recommendations: The obligatory mint tea poured from a great height with nary a drop spilled.

Entertainment & amenities: Belly dancing! What else? Patrons may join in.

Summary & comments: Moroccan restaurants seem to be all made from the same kit. But this one has a unique something to it that's hard to put a finger on. Maybe it's just the attitude of the staff. They seem to be genuinely happy to be working there.

Mexicali Rose

Zone 13   Oakland
7th & Clay Streets
(510) 451-2450

	Mexican
	★★
	Inexpensive
	Quality 75 Value B

Reservations: Accepted
When to go: Any time
Entree range: $5.75–11.45
Payment: Major credit cards
Service rating: ★★
Friendliness rating: ★★
Parking: Lot
Bar: Full service
Wine selection: House
Dress: Casual
Disabled access: Yes
Customers: Local
Open: Every day, 10–3:30 A.M.

Atmosphere / setting: Very large and well lit, with more red leather booths than tables. Simple Mexican decorations, the kind you see everywhere.

House specialties: All the usual suspects: tacos; burritos; enchiladas etc., etc., etc. Nopales (cactus pads) with eggs is especially good.

Other recommendations: Pork chops.

Summary & comments: This is the oldest restaurant in the city of Oakland. They're doing something right: the bar makes a splendid margarita, the atmosphere is down home, and you can linger and just hang out. Hang out till nearly dawn. You can drink till 2 A.M. and eat till 3:30 A.M. You can just sit with a cup of coffee and a book. No one will chase you away or tell you to hurry.

Mikayla at the Casa Madrona

	American
	★★★★
	Moderate/Expensive
	Quality 92 Value B

Zone 9   Waterfront Crescent
801 Bridgeway, Sausalito
(415) 332-0502

Reservations:	Recommended on weekends
When to go:	Any time
Entree range:	Brunch, $19.95 buffet; dinner, $14.50–21.50
Payment:	AMEX, DC, MC, VISA
Service rating:	★★★★
Friendliness rating:	★★★½
Parking:	Street
Bar:	Beer, wine
Wine selection:	Excellent
Dress:	Informal, business, dressy
Disabled access:	No
Customers:	Local, business, tourist
Brunch:	Sunday, 10 A.M.–2:15 P.M.
Dinner:	Every day, 6–10 P.M.

Atmosphere/setting: Newly renovated, Casa Madrona commands a 180-degree view of San Francisco Bay from its glass-walled aerie. Located at the top of a romantic inn built on a tree-studded hillside in Sausalito, with sliding glass walls and a transparent roof that rolls back in summer for stargazing; this is definitely one of the Bay Area's most stunning settings.

House specialties: Sunday brunch buffet with 40-plus offerings; otherwise nightly changing menu which may include rack of lamb with couscous and red pepper jus; potato-wrapped striped bass with leek fondue; pan-roasted poussin with braised cabbage.

Other recommendations: Grilled quail with roasted beets and horseradish dressing; crème brûlée sampler of espresso, amaretto, and vanilla.

Summary & comments: The Casa Madrona, although past its glory days, has a longstanding reputation as Marin's most romantic dinner venue. The menu design is conservative, with contemporary classic dishes admirably well executed and moderately priced. New chef John State seems to be guiding Casa Madrona ahead with confidence and polish.

Honors/awards: *Wine Spectator* Award of Excellence; AAA Three Diamond Award; *Mobil* Three Star Award, Epicurean Rendezvous.

MILANO

	Italian
	★★★
	Moderate
	Quality 89 Value B

Zone 13   Oakland
3425 Grand Avenue
(510) 763-0300

Reservations: Accepted
When to go: Any time
Entree range: $8.95–12.95
Payment: Major credit cards
Service rating: ★★½
Friendliness rating: ★★½
Parking: Street
Bar: Full service
Wine selection: Fair
Dress: Casual
Disabled access: Yes
Customers: Local, business
Lunch/Dinner: Monday–Friday, 11:30 A.M.–10:30 P.M.;
                       Saturday and Sunday, 5–11 P.M.

Atmosphere / setting: It's been here for a couple of years but it still looks as new as a freshly minted penny. Textured umber walls, a marble bar, flagstone floors, and high ceilings from which hang lamps of copper tubing and molten glass. It's hard to pigeonhole this place, but it has overtones of rustic Italian if you look at it with one eye, American Southwest if you look at it with the other. It's nice.

House specialties: All the usual suspects in an Italian restaurant, but done expertly, with a light hand and an easy touch. Risotto alla Milanese; many seafood pasta dishes; grilled eggplant; fettuccini with four cheeses; salmon with roasted pepper and balsamic vinegar sauce; veal Carciofe; various grills of meat, shellfish, and sausage.

Other recommendations: Superior pizzas from the wood-fired oven.

Summary & comments: This place is jammed every night, so you may want to come early or late. The crowds coupled with all the stone, plaster, copper, and marble surfaces can make for a high noise level, but this is a happy place and no one seems to mind. The strain on the sense of hearing is somehow compensated for by the soft yet illuminating lighting. And the aroma from the wood-burning oven gives it a homey feel.

Miss Pearl's Jam House

Zone 2   Civic Center
601 Eddy Street
(415) 775-5267

	Caribbean
	★★★
	Moderate
Quality 85	Value B

Reservations: Accepted
When to go: Any time
Entree range: $8–12
Payment: Major credit cards
Service rating: ★★½
Friendliness rating: ★★★
Parking: Small lot
Bar: Full service
Wine selection: Good
Dress: Casual
Disabled access: Yes
Customers: Eclectic
Brunch: Sunday, 10:30 A.M.–2:30 P.M.
Lunch: Monday–Friday, 11:30 A.M.–2:30 P.M.
Dinner: Monday–Wednesday, 6–10 P.M.;
                       Thursday–Saturday, 6–11 P.M.;
                       Sunday, 5:30–9:30 P.M.

Atmosphere / setting: Rather wild and eclectic. Located in a hotel that used to be frequented by rock stars. The pool is painted in gaudy colors, the dining room is a jumble of Jamaican stuff, and the staff are efficient but always manage to be laid back.

House specialties: Angry pork (pork chops grilled with jerk sauce); jerk chicken; yucca patties filled with beef and spices; sugar-smoked salmon; Jamaican curried chicken salad.

Other recommendations: Monster sandwiches.

Summary & comments: A bright and exuberant bit of Caribbean color amid the great gray granite bulk of surrounding federal buildings. Don't be afraid of the street people walking by. They are generally harmless.

Momi Toby's Revolution Cafe

Eclectic	
★★	
Inexpensive	
Quality 78	Value C+

Zone 2   Civic Center
528 Laguna Street
(415) 626-1508

Reservations:	Not accepted
When to go:	Any time
Entree range:	$4.25–8
Payment:	Cash
Service rating:	★★
Friendliness rating:	★★★
Parking:	Street
Bar:	Beer, wine
Wine selection:	House
Dress:	Casual
Disabled access:	No
Customers:	Neighborhood
Open:	Monday–Friday, 7:30 A.M.–9:30 P.M.;
	Saturday and Sunday, 8:30 A.M.–10:30 P.M.

Atmosphere / setting: This renovation of a 100-year-old bakery is reminiscent of a Berlin cafe right down to the lamps and the bar. Darkly paneled walls and hardwood floors abound and help provide a comfortable atmosphere for long conversations over coffee, lunch, or dinner.

House specialties: Along with the usual coffee shop fare try enchilada pie; meatless pesto lasagna; taqueria-style burritos; Caesar salad. It would seem at first glance that this is a case of a menu that can't make up its mind, but it all hangs together nicely.

Summary & comments: This is not just a restaurant, it's a local hangout. The regulars are very regular, and people come here often just to relax, linger over their coffee, meet friends, and feel at home.

Moose's

Zone 6   North Beach
1652 Stockton Street
(415) 989-7800

California	
★★★★	
Moderate	
Quality 95	Value A-

Reservations:	Accepted
When to go:	After theater
Entree range:	$13.75–24
Payment:	Major credit cards
Service rating:	★★★★
Friendliness rating:	★★★★
Parking:	Street
Bar:	Full service
Wine selection:	Excellent
Dress:	Business
Disabled access:	Good
Customers:	Local, tourist
Brunch:	Sunday, 10:30 A.M.–2:30 P.M.
Lunch:	Monday–Saturday, 11:30 A.M.–2:30 P.M.
Dinner:	Sunday–Thursday, 5:30–10 P.M.;
	Friday and Saturday, 5:30–11 P.M.

Atmosphere / setting: Streamlined, stripped down, classic San Francisco. Polished brightwork, hardwood, and marble elegance in a minimalist form. Posh without being stuffy or cloistered.

House specialties: A hard-to-pigeonhole mix of Italian, French, and California. Pizza, pasta, and Caesar salad; lamb chops and roasted chicken; smoked meats and crab cakes; mashed potatoes and gravy.

Other recommendations: An occasional special roast of pork. Diners can actually be heard moaning when they eat it.

Summary & comments: Every dish is prepared with the utmost love and care and professionalism. In the open kitchen, where skillful hands are the most valuable tools in the shop, you can watch superior workers practicing their art. Service is so genuinely warm and friendly that it doesn't feel as though you have come to a commercial enterprise, but to somebody's hearth.

Moss Beach Distillery

Zone 14   South Bay
Beach Way and Ocean Boulevard,
    Moss Beach
(415) 728-5595

Seafood	
★ ★ ★	
Moderate	
Quality 80	Value B+

Reservations:	Accepted
When to go:	Sunset
Entree range:	$9.95–20.95
Payment:	Major credit cards
Service rating:	★ ★ ½
Friendliness rating:	★ ★ ½
Parking:	Lot
Bar:	Full service
Wine selection:	Adequate
Dress:	Casual
Disabled access:	Yes
Customers:	Local, tourist
Open:	Monday–Saturday, noon–9 P.M.;
	Sunday, 11 A.M.–8 P.M.

Atmosphere / setting: Originally a prohibition roadhouse and speakeasy. Since it's perched on a promontory overlooking the ocean, the rum runners used to land directly below and discharge their cargo to be taken up into the house and stored for distribution. The bar is always full, happy, and noisy, and the crowd spills out onto the deck overhanging the bluff that slopes into the sea.

House specialties: Mesquite-broiled fish; prime rib and steak; salad bar; pasta with a good variety of sauces including smoked salmon and cream, black or red caviar, smoked chicken and andouille sausage, and garlic prawn with sun-dried tomatoes and feta cheese.

Other recommendations: An extensive bar menu, the most popular item of which is the oyster shooter.

Entertainment & amenities: Occasional live bands.

Summary & comments: The sign on Highway One directing you to this place off the path reads "View, Food, Ghost." It's said that some of the prohibition rummies and a mysterious "blue lady" still stalk the place. The new owners like to play that up. The location and patina of age make that unnecessary. Ask any of the many regulars who come here to gab, watch the sun set, drink, carouse, and feed.

The Mountain Home Inn

American
★½
Moderate

Quality 69   Value D

Zone 10   Suburban Marin
810 Panoramic Highway, Mill Valley
(415) 381-9000

Reservations:	Recommended on weekends
When to go:	Weekend breakfasts and brunches; weeknight dinners
Entree range:	Breakfast, brunch, and lunch, $5.95–10.95; dinner, $10.95–16.75
Payment:	MC, VISA
Service rating:	★½
Friendliness rating:	★★
Parking:	Public lot across highway
Bar:	Beer, wine
Wine selection:	Fair
Dress:	Casual, informal
Disabled access:	Limited, with elevator
Customers:	Tourist, local
Breakfast:	Saturday and Sunday, 8–11:30 A.M.
Brunch:	Saturday and Sunday, 11:30 A.M.–3:30 P.M.
Lunch:	Monday–Friday, 11:30 A.M.–3:30 P.M.
Dinner:	Every day, 5:30–9:30 P.M.; closed Mondays November–April

Atmosphere / setting: The Mountain Home Inn's name is an apt description of the location and decor of this woodsy bed-and-breakfast establishment, perched on the eastern slope of Mount Tamalpais at a major crossroads of hiking trails. There are several dining areas: a patio with panoramic views of the valley and the bay, a well-appointed lounge and bar, and a cozy fireplace parlor.

House specialties: Contemporary California standard breakfast, lunch, and dinner menu, with omelets and egg dishes, salads, grilled sandwiches, and pasta dishes. Dinner entrees: braised lamb shanks with tomatoes, sherry, and herbs; garlic polenta; poached salmon with julienned vegetables; grilled medallion of beef with black beans, mushrooms, roasted shallots, and Madeira sauce.

Other recommendations: Warm spinach salad with bacon, shallots, and feta cheese; grilled Japanese eggplant with sun-dried tomato vinaigrette.

Summary & comments: At the base of a grand hiking area, one might hope for a great country inn to either start or finish the day, but the lackluster, juvenile service and uninspired cooking at the Mountain Home do not fulfill this expectation. The deck is a pleasant spot for brunch or an après hike sherry or beer.

Nadine's

Zone 13   Oakland
4228 Park Boulevard
(510) 428-5303

	Czech
	★★½
	Moderate
Quality 79	Value C+

Reservations:	Accepted
When to go:	Any time
Entree range:	$9.50–15.75
Payment:	MC, VISA
Service rating:	★★
Friendliness rating:	★★★
Parking:	Street
Bar:	Beer, wine
Wine selection:	Limited but good
Dress:	Casual
Disabled access:	Yes
Customers:	Local, business
Brunch:	Sunday, 9 A.M.–2 P.M.
Lunch:	Tuesday–Friday, 11:30 A.M.–2 P.M.
Dinner:	Tuesday–Saturday, 5:30–9 P.M.;
	Sunday, 5:30–8:30 P.M.

Atmosphere / setting: Nadine's is located in a space that was originally a hardware store or an antique shop or both, depending on whom you talk to. The ceilings are high and cantilevered, the walls are painted in simple off-white and hung with a few posters, and the floor boards have got the look of age. It has that converted warehouse feel, but small and intimate.

House specialties: Czech food is basically meat and potatoes, but it's good. Here you get thick soups made of the freshest ingredients; salads of fruits, nuts, and greens; grilled or pan-roasted meats with demi-glace or reduction sauces; excellent mashed potatoes; vegetables undercooked to perfection.

Other recommendations: The kitchen makes a regular nod to France or Italy with specials such as seafood risotto; grilled salmon with beurre blanc; spinach and pine nut ravioli with mushroom cream sauce; roast loin of lamb in garlic and red wine sauce.

Summary & comments: Tuesday, Wednesday, and Thursday feature a fixed-price dinner for about $20, including appetizer, main course, dessert, and a glass of each of two wines or Czech beer. It's the best bargain in the house. Nadine's was formerly situated for many years in West Berkeley. It seems to have brought a lot of its old clientele to its new location. The lunch crowd is mostly local government workers, but the dinner patrons come from all over.

NAKAPAN

Zone 12   Berkeley
1921 Martin Luther King Way
(510) 548-3050

	Thai
	★★½
	Inexpensive
	Quality 75 Value B+

Reservations:	Accepted
When to go:	Any time
Entree range:	$6.95–9.95
Payment:	VISA, MC, AMEX
Service rating:	★★
Friendliness rating:	★★
Parking:	Street
Bar:	Beer, wine
Wine selection:	House
Dress:	Casual
Disabled access:	Fair
Customers:	Local, business
Lunch:	Monday–Friday, 11:30 A.M.–3 P.M.
Dinner:	Every day, 5–10 P.M.

Atmosphere / setting: With all its exposed beams and wood paneling, especially with a Bay Area fog outside, this place has an unusually "ski-lodgey" feel to it. It's cozy and warm and inviting, and decidedly non-tropical. It's a welcome change from the almost obligatory theme decor of an "ethnic" restaurant.

House specialties: Much seafood, including salmon, cooked Thai style and using a lot of both holy (or sweet), and hot (or Thai) basil leaves. Most of it sautéed or curried, but also stewed in broth or coconut milk. Fried noodles and rice. Delicious appetizers such as satay and tod mun pla, deep-fried spicy fish cakes with cucumber and peanut dipping sauce. By special order, roasted duck in red curry is available. It is arguably the best dish in the house.

Other recommendations: Chef Orowan has hired an assistant who specializes in Cajun fare and offers half a dozen dishes in that style. The jury is still out.

Summary & comments: There are a number of well-known Thai restaurants in the Bay Area and this isn't one of them. It's tucked away on a corner a block north of University Avenue and is easy to miss. One of the well-known places is just around the corner, exuding its glamour and trailing its line of patrons respectfully waiting. At Nakapan there's no fame and no waiting, just the genuine Thai article expertly prepared and served in pleasant surroundings.

200

Nan Yang

Zone 13   Oakland
6048 College Avenue
(510) 655-3298

Burmese
★★★
Moderate

Quality 85   Value A

Reservations:	Accepted for 3 or more
When to go:	Midweek
Entree range:	$7.50–14.95
Payment:	VISA, MC
Service rating:	★★★
Friendliness rating:	★★½
Parking:	Street
Bar:	Beer, wine
Wine selection:	Adequate
Dress:	Casual
Disabled access:	None
Customers:	Local
Lunch:	Tuesday–Saturday, 11:30 A.M.–2:30 P.M.
Dinner:	Tuesday–Saturday, 5–10 P.M.; Sunday, noon–9 P.M.

Atmosphere / setting: Very bright and open with booths lining all the walls. Numerous Burmese artworks and artifacts are on display, but nothing too overt. The style is restrained. It's pleasing to the eye, but doesn't scream for your attention.

House specialties: Garlic and pepper squash soup; curried Indian knish; slow-cooked curries of meat, fish, or fowl; spinach and bamboo shoots with prawns in tamarind sauce; garlic noodles with pork; green mango salad.

Other recommendations: By special order, "see-byan"–style curry, a Burmese approach to curry that incorporates large amounts of oil and produces exceptional flavor and rich texture. Not for small appetites or weak hearts.

Summary & comments: Burmese is a style of cooking that is literally "Indochinese." Being sandwiched between China and India, Burma has equal influences from both countries. In cuisine they are reflected in Chinese cooking methods and equipment, and Indian spices. Dishes tend to be heavily flavored but always well balanced. The use of chilies is discreet, but you can order dishes to your taste.

Nicolino's Garden Cafe

	Italian
Zone 14 South Bay	★★★
1228 Reamwood Avenue, Sunnyvale	Moderate
(408) 734-5323	
	Quality 89 Value B+

Reservations:	Accepted
When to go:	Any time
Entree range:	$9.50–18.95
Payment:	Major credit cards
Service rating:	★★★
Friendliness rating:	★★★½
Parking:	Lot
Bar:	Full service
Wine selection:	Good
Dress:	Business
Disabled access:	Yes
Customers:	Local, business
Lunch:	Monday–Saturday, 11 A.M.–3 P.M.
Dinner:	Monday–Saturday, 5–10 P.M.

Atmosphere / setting: A lot of plant life, brightwork, and deep carpet. Big, comfy, well-upholstered booths and big round tables well set without too much extraneous stuff. A fountain and a baby grand both play in their turns. Not exactly luxurious—a little like someone's over-decorated living room—but nice.

House specialties: Big portions of formal fare from the Puglia region of Italy. Heavy use of cheeses, cream, and tomatoes. Veal Parmesan; Italian sausage with peppers; a variety of pasta dishes with the usual sauces: tomato, pesto, etc. Vegetables are always perfectly fresh, never overcooked, and presented simply.

Other recommendations: Sausage bread. The owners are also some of the best sausage makers around. They wrap a yeast dough around a portion of broken sausage and a good measure of cheese and bake the loaf to golden brown. It sounds a bit like calzone but it isn't. It's addictive. They sometimes offer it as an appetizer, but be careful—it is very filling as well as delicious.

Entertainment & amenities: Opera on Saturday night. The baby grand gets its workout when members of the San Jose Opera come to sing arias and Italian art and love songs.

Summary & comments: There is nothing that quite compares with feasting on really good Italian food and drinking fine Italian wine, all in the company of good friends, while a first-rate tenor and two sopranos sing the drinking song from Verdi's *La Traviata*. Usually two or three singers will appear throughout the evening, sometimes singly, sometimes together. Requests are gladly taken.

No Name Bar

Zone 9 Waterfront Crescent	Bar
757 Bridgeway, Sausalito	★½
(415) 332-1392	Inexpensive
	Quality 69 Value C

Reservations:	Not accepted
When to go:	For food, Sunday afternoons; for music, Wednesday–Sunday nights
Entree range:	$5.50–7.50
Payment:	Cash
Service rating:	★★
Friendliness rating:	★★★
Parking:	Street or public lot
Bar:	Full service
Wine selection:	House
Dress:	Casual
Disabled access:	Limited
Customers:	Local, tourist
Lunch:	Every day, 11 A.M.–4 P.M.

Atmosphere / setting: Dark, narrow bar with a rear garden courtyard.

House specialties: Jazz club sandwich with salami, mortadella, and cheese; California club with turkey, avocado, and Black Forest ham; San Francisco club with roast beef and melted cheese.

Other recommendations: Irish coffee, martini.

Summary & comments: The No Name Bar is your basic bar: small, smoky, funky, TV winking blearily in the corner. Sandwiches are served in the afternoon, but it's too depressing to go during the day except on Sundays, when there's Dixieland jazz. The enclosed garden area behind the main room offers a breath of slightly fresher air, but there's smoking allowed everywhere. The No Name is not for the faint of heart. Why go there at all? Because it's a Sausalito institution; because there's live jazz with no cover until 1 A.M.; because you're not ready to go home yet; because they serve a great Irish coffee, a Ramos fizz, and a decent martini.

NOAH'S NEW YORK BAGELS

Zone 10   Suburban Marin
Bon Air Center, Greenbrae
(415) 925-9971

	Delicatessen
	★★½
	Inexpensive
	Quality 79 Value B

Reservations:	Not necessary
When to go:	Any time
Entree range:	$1.50–5.75
Payment:	Cash or check
Service rating:	★★★½
Friendliness rating:	★★★
Parking:	Free shopping center lot
Bar:	None
Wine selection:	None
Dress:	Casual
Disabled access:	Good
Customers:	Local, business, student
Open:	Monday–Friday, 7 A.M.–7 P.M.;
	Saturday, 7:30 A.M.–7 P.M.;
	Sunday, 7:30 A.M.–5 P.M.

Atmosphere / setting: Noah's looks like a jazzed-up New York subway station, with old-fashioned hexagonal tile floors and tiled trim around the high-ceilinged walls. There are hanging lamps, table and counter seating, and old black-and-white photos on the walls. The shop is bright and inviting, and there's generally upbeat music playing, a reflection of the median age of the staff, many of whom look as though they're on the lam from high school.

House specialties: Fourteen varieties of fresh, pillowy bagels; handmade onion bialys; mini-bagels; knishes; plain and flavored cream cheese schmears, whose slight effervescence is due to a spritz of club soda in the recipe. Four kinds of lox; salmon and whitefish salad; herring in cream or wine sauce.

Other recommendations: Bagel sandwiches; cinnamon or chocolate babka, the buttery, sweet, layered bread; halvah; coffee and espresso drinks, and the Sunday *New York Times.*

Summary & comments: Noah's is a great stop for a quick nosh or sandwich, or bagels and fixings to go. The bagels are huge and very fresh, the bialys are chewy and oniony, and the shop is pleasant and well tended. Early mornings attract a crowd, but the lines move quickly.

North Sea Village

Zone 9   Waterfront Crescent
300 Turney Street, Sausalito
(415) 331-3300

<table>
<tr><td>Chinese</td></tr>
<tr><td>★★½</td></tr>
<tr><td>Moderate</td></tr>
<tr><td>Quality 75   Value C+</td></tr>
</table>

Reservations:	Accepted; recommended for weekend brunch
When to go:	Best for dim sum lunch or brunch
Entree range:	Dim sum, $2.50–5.50 per plate; entrees, $7–26
Payment:	AMEX, MC, VISA
Service rating:	★★½
Friendliness rating:	★★★
Parking:	Free lot
Bar:	Beer, wine
Wine selection:	House
Dress:	Informal
Disabled access:	Good
Customers:	Local, business, ethnic
Brunch:	Monday–Friday, 11 A.M.–3 P.M.; Saturday and Sunday, 10 A.M.–3 P.M.
Lunch:	Monday–Friday, 11 A.M.–3 P.M.
Dinner:	Every day, 5:30–9 P.M.

Atmosphere / setting: North Sea Village is among the most appealing dim sum houses in the Bay Area. Double-decker dining rooms occupy a large old wood-frame boathouse overlooking the Sausalito docks. On sunny Sundays, the marble-tiled foyer fills with Chinese families waiting to sample the excellent selection of dim sum and the views of the harbor. The North Sea's crisp linens and shirred green curtains provide a refreshing departure from tradition.

House specialties: Hong Kong–style seafood fresh from the tanks: lobster with ginger and scallions, crab with black-bean sauce, steamed fresh rock cod, salt-baked prawns. Dim sum specialties include steamed chive, shrimp, or pork dumplings; barbecue pork puffs; stuffed crab claws; shrimp toasts; and broccoli rabe with oyster sauce.

Other recommendations: Sizzling prawns with chili; chicken Macao in a clay pot; Hunan eggplant; minced squab in lettuce cups.

Summary & comments: The high proportion of Chinese wielding their chopsticks at the North Sea Village gives testament to the authenticity of the fare. Frequently the English level of the staff is minimal; this can be a problem if you wish to ascertain the exact ingredients in a dish. The dim sum are attractively presented, fresh, and flavorful, and along with the view and the fresh seafood, they are the North Sea Village's main attraction.

Oakland Grill

Zone 13   Oakland
3rd and Franklin Streets
(510) 835-1176

American	
★★	
Inexpensive	
Quality 77	Value A

Reservations:	Not accepted
When to go:	Any time
Entree range:	$4.50–12.95
Payment:	VISA, MC, AMEX
Service rating:	★★
Friendliness rating:	★★
Parking:	Street
Bar:	Beer, wine
Wine selection:	House
Dress:	Casual
Disabled access:	Fair
Customers:	Local
Open:	Monday–Friday, 6 A.M.–9:30 P.M.;
	Saturday and Sunday, 8 A.M.–9:30 P.M.

Atmosphere / setting: Down by the railroad tracks, just across from the early morning produce market. This is a working people's diner of a kind only to be found in the Bay Area. It has elegance. Large picture windows, polished wood tables, plants that recall a fern bar, and a long counter overlooking a first-class grill.

House specialties: Anything imaginable for breakfast, including the Ono Yoko, scrambles, and omelets made of the egg whites only. Lunch of hamburgers, sandwiches, soups, and salads including Crab Louie. For dinner the Fork Lift Special Steak, Chicken Kiev, and seafood of the day.

Other recommendations: Pork chops with fried apples, dinner crêpes. Many daily specials.

Entertainment & amenities: In the early morning, watching the produce shippers unload their goods from the rail cars and trucks while the eager buyers buy. Few restaurants have a view like this, one that Rembrandt might have studied.

Summary & comments: It's a grill! A pancake, burger, and steak joint that reflects its regular clientele: working people, both blue and white collar, who have a sense of style and demand good food at good prices. The breakfast crowd have been coming here for years and know the staff by name.

Olema Farm House

Zone 11 Yonder Marin	American
Highway 1, Olema	★★½
(415) 663-1264	Moderate
	Quality 75 Value C+

Reservations:	Recommended on weekends
When to go:	Any time
Entree range:	Breakfast, $4.50–7.50; lunch, $4.25–11.95; dinner, $10.25–18.95
Payment:	AMEX, MC, VISA
Service rating:	★★★
Friendliness rating:	★★★
Parking:	Free lot
Bar:	Full service
Wine selection:	Fair
Dress:	Casual
Disabled access:	Good
Customers:	Tourist, local
Breakfast/Brunch:	Every day, 8 A.M.–1 P.M.
Lunch:	Every day, 11:30 A.M.–9 P.M.
Dinner:	Sunday–Thursday, 8 A.M.–9 P.M.; Friday and Saturday, 8 A.M.–10 P.M.

Atmosphere/setting: Historic farmhouse, built in 1856, with cowhide-upholstered barroom, stained-glass chandeliers, and quieter adjoining dining rooms. Locals gather in the bar, which houses a collection of antique bottles.

House specialties: Barbecue oysters; clam chowder and oyster stew; Portuguese fish stew; tournedos of beef; prime rib with horseradish sauce on weekends.

Other recommendations: Fried calamari; spinach salad with feta, walnuts, and sun-dried tomatoes; catch of the day; oyster sandwich.

Summary & comments: Any restaurant which has held onto its pink neon cocktail glass roadhouse signs aims to maintain a few traditions, and the Olema Farm House does just that. The bar is a genuine old-time saloon, while the dining rooms have a country boardinghouse feel. Although it is located a few miles from the coast, the Olema Farm House includes on its menu a selection of offerings from the local oyster farms and fisheries, as well as chicken, beef, and pork. The cooking reflects the atmosphere: hefty portions of home-style vittles with some refreshing, original turns to the sauces and side dishes. There's usually a crowd for weekend dinners; reservations are a must.

Oliveto

Zone 13   Oakland
5655 College Avenue
(510) 547-5356

	Italian
	★★★½
	Moderate
	Quality 89 Value A-

Reservations:	Recommended
When to go:	Any time
Entree range:	$14–16.50
Payment:	VISA, MC, AMEX, DC, checks
Service rating:	★★★
Friendliness rating:	★★★★
Parking:	Street, BART lot after 4 P.M.
Bar:	Beer, wine
Wine selection:	Very good
Dress:	Casual
Disabled access:	Good
Customers:	Local
Lunch:	Monday–Friday, 11:30 A.M.–2 P.M.
Dinner:	Monday–Saturday, 5:30–10 P.M.;
	Sunday, 5:30–8:30 P.M.

Atmosphere / setting: Italian villa style with hand-rubbed walls and lime-stone bar, yet still a simple country decor to contrast the richness and variety of the cuisine. Elaborate seasonal flower arrangements add a touch of elegance. Built in two levels with a casual cafe below. The restaurant proper looks out over the street and provides good people-watching.

House specialties: Rustic cooking of northern Italy. Liberal use of olives and olive oil. In keeping with its theme, an olive mix, with excellent Acme bread, is served when diners are seated. Consulting chef Paul Bertoli cooks Tuesdays and Thursdays. Specialties include warm pigeon salad with vinaigrette, Tuscan bread soup, chicken cooked under a brick (ask about it), halibut with artichokes and wild onion. Portions are large.

Other recommendations: The bread is served with butter, but you can ask for the really remarkable San Giusto extra virgin olive oil at a small price.

Entertainment & amenities: Occasional classical guitar.

Summary & comments: The staff is kept well informed in daily meetings where all aspects of the menu are discussed in detail. You can try to play stump-the-waiter here, but you will lose the game. The whole kitchen is open to view from the bar, and the thoroughly professional staff are a pleasure to watch. It's also a good place to enjoy a before- or after-dinner drink from the well-balanced list of cordials and aperitifs.

Orchid

Thai
★★★½
Inexpensive
Quality 89   Value B

Zone 10   Suburban Marin
726 San Anselmo Avenue, San Anselmo
(415) 457-9470

Reservations:	Recommended for dinner
When to go:	Any time
Entree range:	Lunch, $4.95–5.95; dinner, $6.95–8.95
Payment:	MC, VISA
Service rating:	★★★
Friendliness rating:	★★★
Parking:	Street, public lot
Bar:	Beer, wine
Wine selection:	House
Dress:	Casual, informal
Disabled access:	Good
Customers:	Local, business
Lunch:	Monday–Friday, 11:30 A.M.–2:30 P.M.
Dinner:	Every day, 5–10 P.M.

Atmosphere / setting: Simple and tasteful with brass and copper Thai touches. Orchid is small and locally popular. It's cramped for large parties but fine for more intimate dining. There's an enclosed porch in front whose windows open onto the sidewalk in summer.

House specialties: Satays with peanut sauce; fried calamari with dipping sauce; seafood and vegetable hot pot; prawns sautéed with chili, onions, and sweet basil; eggplant sautéed with garlic and black-bean sauce.

Other recommendations: Delicious takes on curries, noodles, soups, and other standard Thai offerings.

Summary & comments: Orchid's owner-chef Tom Thongnopneva was chef for 13 years at San Francisco's popular French bistro Le Central before opening his own place some 10 years ago. The menu at Orchid, while classically Thai, reflects the chef's training: every dish is a little more delicate, a little more subtle than the usual, yet still bursting with explosive Thai flavors and colors. Orchid is an excellent choice for Thai cuisine.

Original Joe's

Zone 14   South Bay
301 South First Street, San Jose
(408) 292-7030

Italian	
★½	
Inexpensive	
Quality 67	Value C-

Reservations:	Not accepted
When to go:	Any time
Entree range:	$8.95–23
Payment:	Major credit cards
Service rating:	★★
Friendliness rating:	★★
Parking:	Street
Bar:	Full service
Wine selection:	Debatable
Dress:	Casual
Disabled access:	Yes
Customers:	Local
Open:	Every day, 11–1:30 A.M.

Atmosphere / setting: Tacky, somewhat neglected, aging diner. Looks something like a Denny's that no one has taken care of. Bottom-lit plants, pink fluorescent overhead lights, brown naugahyde booths. A long counter faces the stoves and diners get a very close view of the cooks at work. The staff are well dressed and you get the feeling that this place once had a certain cache.

House specialties: Diner fare: steaks; fried chicken; sweetbreads; corned beef and cabbage; eggplant Parmesan; unremarkable pastas.

Summary & comments: Despite the depressing decor, the unremarkable food, a wine list that carries some downright bad selections, and a seedy bar that seems to serve its drinks in thimbles, this place won't die. It's an institution, a revered relic! It's packed almost every night, and if you want a booth you usually have to wait in the bar drinking from egg cups. You want to grieve for this place when you look at it, but it needs no sympathy; it's doing fine.

Original Joe's

Zone 3   Union Square
144 Taylor Street
(415) 775-4877

	American
	★★
	Inexpensive
	Quality 78 Value B

Reservations:	Accepted
When to go:	Any time
Entree range:	$6.25–18
Payment:	Major credit cards
Service rating:	★★
Friendliness rating:	★★★
Parking:	Lot
Bar:	Full service
Wine selection:	Fair
Dress:	Casual
Disabled access:	Yes
Customers:	Local, tourist, regular
Open:	Every day, 10:30–12:30 A.M.

Atmosphere / setting: This is the original Original Joe's. It's one of the oldest places in the neighborhood, and many will say it looks like it. Most of the staff seem to date from the same year. The menu, the decor, and the patrons never seem to change either. Red plastic booths, a long bar, and a counter overlooking the kitchen; low lights and some plants. A certain hominess prevails, perhaps borne of old familiarity.

House specialties: Italian meat and potatoes. Joe's buys whole sides of beef and then ages and cuts them in-house. From these come the monster steaks and hamburgers that the regulars eat in quantity. Also: overcooked pasta with superior sauce; thick-cut french fries; corned beef and cabbage; prime rib.

Summary & comments: The neighborhood has gone down in recent years, so you should park in the lot or nearby on the street. Unlike the OJ's in San Jose, the bar here serves up a man-size drink in a convivial atmosphere.

Pasticceria Rulli

	Italian bakery
	★★★½
Zone 10 Suburban Marin	Inexpensive
464 Magnolia, Larkspur	
(415) 924-7478	Quality 89 Value A

Reservations:	No
When to go:	Any time
Entree range:	$2.95–3.50
Payment:	Cash, local check
Service rating:	★★★★
Friendliness rating:	★★★★
Parking:	Street, public lot
Bar:	Beer, wine
Wine selection:	House
Dress:	Casual
Disabled access:	Good
Customers:	Local, tourist
Breakfast/Brunch:	Monday–Saturday from 7:30 A.M.; Sunday from 8 A.M.
Lunch:	Every day from 11 A.M.
Dinner:	Sunday–Thursday until 10 P.M.; Friday and Saturday until 11 P.M.

Atmosphere / setting: Simply the most elegant coffee and pastry shop around: murals, crystal chandeliers, polished wood, brass and glass pastry cases filled with exquisite, jewel-like confections. There's usually classical Italian music playing as well.

House specialties: Tiny Italian cookies sold by the pound; breakfast breads and rolls; fruit tarts, chocolate tortes, and cream cakes; housemade fruit jelly confections and candied chestnuts; assorted sandwiches on fresh focaccia or panini with grilled eggplant, fresh mozzarella, gorgonzola, and baked prosciutto and walnuts; grilled tuna with olives and capers; egg and spinach frittati with fontina cheese and bell peppers. Espresso, cappuccino, latte; Italian sodas; still or sparkling wines by the glass.

Summary & comments: This is a luxurious, yet very affordable stop for a hot or cold Italian sandwich; pastry or cookie; and coffee drink or glass of wine. The romantic atmosphere is an invitation to linger over a hot beverage and newspaper or book, or just to daydream yourself to Italy for an hour or so. Everything in the pastry cases literally begs to be tried; and, unlike some Bay Area Italian baked goods, these taste as good as they look.

Honors / awards: Gary Rulli, the proprietor, was a finalist for the Coppa Italia, Italy's prestigious pastry award.

212

Pat O'Shea's Mad Hatter

Bar and Grill	
★★	
Inexpensive	
Quality 75	Value A

Zone 8 Richmond/Avenues
3848 Geary Boulevard
(415) 752-3148

Reservations:	No way
When to go:	Any time
Entree range:	$7–12
Payment:	VISA, MC
Service rating:	★★
Friendliness rating:	★★★
Parking:	Small lot, street
Bar:	Full service
Wine selection:	House
Dress:	Casual
Disabled access:	Yes
Customers:	Local, tourist
Brunch:	Sunday, 11 A.M.–3 P.M.
Lunch:	Monday–Saturday, 11:30 A.M.–3 P.M.
Dinner:	Every day, 4–10 P.M.

Atmosphere / setting: A sports bar since 1937 whose motto has always been, "We cheat tourists and drunks!" This is a proper bar with proper television sets showing proper games to proper sports drinking proper drinks. You won't find ferns or silk wall hangings, but wooden floors and pictures of sports greats. It just happens to serve great food.

House specialties: The cook is a proper chef from proper restaurants who decided he would have more fun in a bar. He produces a limited but faultless selection that leans heavily on meat and potatoes. Two-third pound burgers; carrot soup; grilled swordfish or other catch of the day; pasta with whatever is on hand; simple but excellent salads. Altogether superb pub grub. Also a very good selection of beers and cocktails that bring mixology up to the status of art.

Summary & comments: Since before WWII serious sports people have been coming here and making it their office away from the office. Sports writers are especially in evidence and are hailed by name by the staff. In addition, you will see every kind of person come through here to watch a game, have a drink, hold forth in Western fashion at the bar and tell tall tales. It's a "Cheers" with food.

The Pelican Inn

Zone 11 Yonder Marin	British Pub
Muir Beach	★★½
(415) 383-6000	Moderate
	Quality 78 Value C+

Reservations: Recommended on weekends
When to go: Weekday lunches and dinners;
                        off-season weekends
Entree range: Sunday brunch, $13.75; lunch, $5.95–7.95;
                        dinner, $11.95–19.50
Payment: MC, VISA
Service rating: ★★★
Friendliness rating: ★★★
Parking: Free lot
Bar: Beer, wine
Wine selection: Fair
Dress: Casual, informal
Disabled access: Good
Customers: Local, tourist
Brunch: Sunday, 11:30 A.M.–3:30 P.M.
Lunch: Tuesday–Friday, 11:30 A.M.–3 P.M.;
                        Saturday, 11:30 A.M.–3:30 P.M.
Dinner: Tuesday–Friday, 6–9 P.M.;
                        Saturday and Sunday, 5:30–9 P.M.

Atmosphere / setting: English Tudor country house set amidst beautifully tended lawns and gardens, one quarter mile from picturesque Muir Beach. Interior is dark, with low beamed ceilings and a sometimes too toasty fireplace. The beer and wine bar is a local hangout; on busy weekend evenings the mug-toting crowds spill out the door into the gardens.

House specialties: Prime rib with Yorkshire pudding; mixed grill of chicken breast, banger, lamb chop with kidney; scampi with sherry, mushrooms, roasted red peppers, and garlic. Entrees come with a small salad or soup. Sunday lunch is a gargantuan buffet with sliced-to-order roasts and hams.

Other recommendations: Escargots with anisette and garlic butter; pâté with wild mushrooms. Children's portions of some entrees.

Summary & comments: The grounds are so entrancing, one is immediately drawn inside. Unfortunately, the interior is stuffy and a bit airless even when empty, so it's a good thing that the weather in Muir Beach is often cool and foggy. The Pelican is a casual, unpretentious place; the menu is savory and satisfying.

PERRY'S

Zone 5   Marina
1944 Union Street
(415) 922-9022

American
★★
Inexpensive

Quality 75   Value B+

Reservations:	Not accepted
When to go:	Any time
Entree range:	$7.50–17.50
Payment:	Major credit cards
Service rating:	★★★
Friendliness rating:	★★★
Parking:	Street
Bar:	Full service
Wine selection:	Fair
Dress:	Casual
Disabled access:	Yes
Customers:	Local, business, singles
Brunch:	Saturday and Sunday, 9 A.M.–3 P.M.
Open:	Every day, 9–2 A.M.

Atmosphere / setting: Sports bar, singles meeting place, business rendez-vous, bar and grill: a pleasant American "bistro." Congenial long bar surrounded by checker-clothed tables on a bare wood floor. Wide windows overlooking fashionable Union Street. The back has a pleasant patio for quieter dining.

House specialties: Burgers; shoestring fries; one of the few places in town serving sautéed calves' liver with bacon and onions; grilled double chicken breast; New York steak; linguine with clams.

Other recommendations: Apple Brown Betty.

Summary & comments: This bar has always been a great place to meet people, friends or strangers. Go for a cocktail before or a cordial after dinner, or a late snack after dancing.

Phnom Penh House

	Cambodian
	★★
	Inexpensive
	Quality 79 Value B+

Zone 13   Oakland
251 8th Street
(510) 893-3825

Reservations:	Recommended for 4 or more
When to go:	Any time
Entree range:	$5.85–7.85
Payment:	VISA MC
Service rating:	★★
Friendliness rating:	★★
Parking:	Street
Bar:	Beer, wine
Wine selection:	House
Dress:	Casual
Disabled access:	No
Customers:	Local
Lunch/Dinner:	Sunday–Thursday, 11 A.M.–9:30 P.M.;
	Friday and Saturday, 11 A.M.–10 P.M.

Atmosphere/setting: A small family-run operation at the edge of Oakland's Chinatown district. The decor is more functional than inspired, but pleasant enough with Cambodian wall hangings and calendars. In simple terms, Phnom Penh is a square room with tables and chairs wherein some very good food is served.

House specialties: The unique lemongrass- and coconut-based curries of Cambodia; piquant salads; aromatically sauced fish and fowl; and spicy soups. Don't come here looking for dull.

Other recommendations: Pork-filled crêpes; vegetarian duck or abalone; grilled eggplant; crunchy green beans.

Summary & comments: A clean, well lighted place for food. The service is no great shakes, though friendly. The beer is always cold, and the curries are as hot as you like. You'll know you're in a good place for Cambodian food when you walk in and find that half the patrons are Cambodian ex-pats. At night the neighborhood looks a bit dingy, but it's as safe as any other, and you can usually park near the door.

Pho An Dao

Zone 13 Oakland	Vietnamese
280 East 18th Street	★★
(510) 836-1566	Inexpensive
	Quality 77 Value B+

Reservations:	Not accepted
When to go:	Any time
Entree range:	$2.99–3.95
Payment:	Cash only
Service rating:	★½
Friendliness rating:	★½
Parking:	Street
Bar:	Beer, wine
Wine selection:	House
Dress:	Casual
Disabled access:	Fair
Customers:	Local, ethnic
Open:	Every day, 9 A.M.–9 P.M.

Atmosphere / setting: A clean, well-lighted place, open and airy. Formica tables and aluminum chairs. A simple eatery, the only decorations being a few plants and a large fish tank.

House specialties: Eighteen variations on the Vietnamese national dish, Pho—noodle soup generally made from a clear stock of beef brisket and subtly spiced with anise. The noodles are placed into a deep bowl and dressed with paper-thin slices of raw beef. Boiling hot stock poured over the meat quickly cooks it. Diners then dress the soup as they wish with sliced chilis, bean sprouts, fresh basil leaves, and various condiments. In Vietnam this soup is eaten any time of day or night.

Other recommendations: Variations include chicken and seafood stocks with corresponding meats. Also available are spring rolls and spicy Vietnamese meatballs.

Summary & comments: An excellent bargain, a full belly, a satisfied palate, as quick as any fast food place and all for under $5.

Piazza D'Angelo

Zone 10　Suburban Marin	Italian
22 Miller Avenue, Mill Valley	★★★½
(415) 388-2216	Moderate
	Quality 87　　Value B

Reservations:	Recommended; required on weekends
When to go:	Any time
Entree range:	$6.95–12.95
Payment:	AMEX, MC, VISA
Service rating:	★★
Friendliness rating:	★
Parking:	Street, public lots metered during the day
Bar:	Full service
Wine selection:	Extensive
Dress:	Casual, informal
Disabled access:	Good
Customers:	Local, tourist, business
Brunch:	Saturday and Sunday, 10:30 A.M.–3 P.M.
Open:	Every day, 11:30 A.M.–11 P.M.

Atmosphere / setting:　Oozing casual/chic, Piazza D'Angelo instantly emerged as the fashionable place to dine in downtown Mill Valley. The inviting outdoor patio tables, the companionable bar, and the simple Mediterranean dining rooms set a cultured yet comfortable stage. There are tantalizing aromas, cubist paintings, and lots of pretty people here.

House specialties:　Brunch: Fluffy omelet with gorgonzola and grilled polenta; baked eggs or risotto with asparagus, basil, and tarragon; grilled flank steak with green peppercorns. Lunches feature homemade pastas: ravioli with Swiss chard, watercress, and Parmesan in bechamel; pizza with smoked salmon and mascarpone; grilled chicken breast sandwich with radicchio; salad with fennel, cannellini beans, and balsamic vinegar. Dinner plates include sautéed pork scallopini with prosciutto, sage, and fontina; baked whole salmon trout filled with eggplant, tomato, and mushrooms; grilled Sicilian sweet sausages and Calabrian spicy sausage with polenta and braised cabbage.

Other recommendations:　Gigantic crème brûlée and sugar-dusted tarts.

Summary & comments:　Piazza D'Angelo is definitely in with the in crowd. Few Marin restaurants combine such fashionable atmosphere, tempting food preparation, and reasonably priced options and stay open until 11 every night. During October the Mill Valley Film Festival sweeps the town, and D'Angelo's glitters with international film personalities. Occasionally the service can be spotty, and even downright rude, if you've been classified as unimportant or unhip.

PJ's Oyster Bed

Zone 8   Richmond/Avenues
737 Irving Street
(415) 566-7775

	Seafood
	★★★
	Moderate
	Quality 87 Value B

Reservations:	Accepted
When to go:	Any time
Entree range:	$7.98–22.95
Payment:	Major credit cards
Service rating:	★★★
Friendliness rating:	★★★½
Parking:	Street
Bar:	Beer, wine
Wine selection:	Adequate
Dress:	Casual
Disabled access:	Yes
Customers:	Local, tourist
Brunch:	Saturday and Sunday, 11 A.M.–3:30 P.M.
Lunch/Dinner:	Monday–Friday, 11:30 A.M.–10 P.M.;
	Saturday and Sunday, 11 A.M.–10 P.M.

Atmosphere/setting: Casual, comfortable, upbeat atmosphere. The always intriguing counter seating as well as table service.

House specialties: Wide selection of oyster dishes and many Cajun specialties. New Orleans–style gumbo.

Other recommendations: Try the alligator. It's good.

Summary & comments: San Francisco has always been a hot-bowl-of-soup kind of town, given its "distinctive" weather, and PJ's clam chowder fits the bill for a respite from those chilling winds and damp fogs.

Honors/awards: Voted Best Seafood Restaurant 1994 by the *Bay Guardian*.

PlumpJack Cafe

Zone 5   Marina
3127 Fillmore
(415) 563-4755

	Mediterranean
	★★★
	Moderate
	Quality 83 · Value B

Reservations:	Accepted
When to go:	Any time
Entree range:	$16–18
Payment:	Major credit cards
Service rating:	★★★
Friendliness rating:	★★★
Parking:	Street
Bar:	Beer, wine
Wine selection:	Very good
Dress:	Casual, business
Disabled access:	Yes
Customers:	Everybody from home and abroad
Lunch:	Monday–Friday, 11:30 A.M.–2 P.M.
Dinner:	Monday–Saturday, 5:30–10 P.M.

Atmosphere / setting: The decor recalls the theater in which the world first saw Sir John Falstaff, otherwise known as "Plump Jack." But this setting is a lot cleaner and warmer than Shakespeare's Globe Theater.

House specialties: An imaginative menu based on old favorites. Bruschetta; duck confit; lemongrass brûlée.

Other recommendations: Numerous Mediterranean specialties.

Summary & comments: PlumpJack has received plaudits from all the major food pundits in the Bay Area and some from beyond. One patron from England carried a clipping of the place for weeks before finding his way here. Its excellent wine list alone makes it worth a visit.

Red's Java House

Zone 4   Financial District
Pier 30
No phone

Dive	
★	
Inexpensive / Cheap	
Quality 65	Value A

Reservations:	No way
When to go:	Daytime
Entree range:	$2.70–4.65
Payment:	Cash
Service rating:	★
Friendliness rating:	★
Parking:	Street
Bar:	Beer
Wine selection:	None
Dress:	Work clothes
Disabled access:	No
Customers:	Local, workmen
Open:	Every day, 6 A.M.–5 P.M. or at staff's discretion

Atmosphere / setting: The chief attraction here is the view. In front you can see the East Bay and the Bay Bridge over your morning coffee. Behind you lies the bulk of the city. Red's 40-year history can be seen hanging on the walls in its scores of black-and-white photos of people and patrons from the waterfront. All else is tacky and dirty.

House specialties: Double burgers; double hot dogs; devilled egg sandwiches.

Other recommendations: What many will argue is a great cup of coffee.

Summary & comments: A place of historical value as a gathering place for working people during the glory days of the San Francisco waterfront. Down to your last dollar? Eat here.

The Rice Table

Zone 10 Suburban Marin	Indonesian
1617 Fourth Street, San Rafael	★★★
(415) 456-1808	Moderate
	Quality 83 Value B

Reservations:	Recommended
When to go:	Any time
Entree range:	$13.75–19.95
Payment:	MC, VISA
Service rating:	★★★★
Friendliness rating:	★★★½
Parking:	Street
Bar:	Beer, wine
Wine selection:	House
Dress:	Casual
Disabled access:	Good
Customers:	Local, business, tourist
Dinner:	Tuesday–Sunday, 5:30–9:30 P.M.

Atmosphere / setting: Welcome to Indonesia: batiks, bamboo, ceiling fans, and fringed parasols. One expects a warm breeze or tropical shower to waft through at any moment. The Rice Table is one square, peaceable room with a mural, a few hovering deities, and some soft, gentle flute music.

House specialties: The Rice Table special is a complete dinner, including ten authentic dishes served with rice, lumpia rolls, pickled vegetables, sambal sauces, and roasted coconut. The dishes, which can be ordered separately, include marinated and grilled pork or chicken skewers; fried shrimp with tamarind; chicken curry; a spicy beef stew; fried rice noodles; mushrooms with tamarind and tofu; sweet and sour pork; lamb curry; and barbecued chicken with chili sauce.

Summary & comments: The Rice Table aims to duplicate the feasts of the Dutch colonists, who selected their favorites from among hundreds of island dishes. Over 25 years old, the Rice Table continues, with second generation family ownership, to offer a skilled, cordial entry into the world of Indonesian cooking. Once the only Indonesian restaurant in the Bay Area, it now has peers, but none in Marin County, and none providing this unusual combination of ceremony and quietude, seasoned with deft hands from the Spice Islands.

Ristorante Dalecio

Zone 10 Suburban Marin	Italian
340 Ignacio Boulevard, Novato	★★½
(415) 883-0960	Moderate
	Quality 78 Value C

Reservations: Recommended on weekends
When to go: Any time
Entree range: $10.95–18.95
Payment: All major credit cards
Service rating: ★★★
Friendliness rating: ★★★
Parking: Free lot
Bar: Full service
Wine selection: Excellent
Dress: Informal
Disabled access: Good
Customers: Local, business, tourist
Lunch: Monday–Saturday, 11:30 A.M.–3 P.M.
Dinner: Monday–Saturday, 3–10 P.M.; Sunday, 5–10 P.M.

Atmosphere / setting: Dalecio's spacious dining rooms and outdoor patio handily cover all the bases of Italian kitsch: plastic grapes and straw-wrapped wine bottles; Cinzano umbrellas; black-jacketed waiters; a brick-walled wine cellar; accordion music piped into the bathrooms. The results are a bit dated, but not unpleasantly so. The patio is very inviting on warm evenings.

House specialties: Homemade pastas with choices of sauce, many of which are rich in oil, cream, egg, and butter; carpaccio with capers and Parmesan; veal scallopini with mushrooms and marsala; grilled prawns with lemon and olive oil; filet mignon with fresh rosemary.

Other recommendations: Zabaglione with strawberries and cream.

Summary & comments: Suburban Italian with excellent homemade pastas, mostly very rich sauces and entrees. Nicely presented fresh salads. Professional but not genuinely friendly service. They play the tarantella softly here, but they do play it. Dalecio's offers an old-fashioned Italian evening, harkening back to the Italian restaurants of 20 years ago.

Honors / awards: Wine list has received *Wine Spectator*'s Award of Excellence.

RISTORANTE ECCO

Italian	
★★★½	
Moderate	
Quality 85	Value C

Zone 7   SOMA / Mission
101 South Park
(415) 495-3291

Reservations:	Recommended
When to go:	Any time
Entree range:	Lunch, $5.75–12.25; dinner, $10–16.50
Payment:	AMEX, D, MC, VISA
Service rating:	★★★½
Friendliness rating:	★★★★
Parking:	Street
Bar:	Full service
Wine selection:	Limited but good
Dress:	Informal
Disabled access:	Good
Customers:	Local, business, tourist
Lunch:	Monday–Friday, 11:30 A.M.–2:30 P.M.
Dinner:	Monday–Saturday, 5:30–10 P.M.

Atmosphere / setting: Toasted brown walls and sepia prints, pungent aromas, and a peaceful hubbub; Ecco carries the old world serenity of its South Park location indoors. There's a tile-floored bar with tables and a softer-edged dining room with windows overlooking the quiet boulevard.

House specialties: Exquisite antipasto selections; vitello tonnato; chickpea fritters with eggplant vinaigrette; roasted salmon with herb crust; pork chop with sage butter and polenta; shrimp and mussels over linguine cake in tomato curry broth.

Other recommendations: Daily risotto and seafood specials; desserts including hazelnut chocolate ice cream sandwich and pecan, pine nut, and hazelnut tart with orange cream.

Summary & comments: Dinner on South Park Boulevard provides a stroll into a bygone era, and Ecco's streamlined service and soothing decor quietly preserve the magic of the neighborhood. The Italian menu is competently carried out, and the specials, such as tuna risotto, are unusual. This is generally forceful, highly aromatic Italian fare.

Ristorante Fabrizio

Zone 10   Suburban Marin
455 Magnolia Avenue, Larkspur
(415) 924-3332

Italian	
★★★½	
Moderate	
Quality 87	Value B

Reservations:	Recommended on weekends
When to go:	Any time
Entree range:	Lunch, $5.50–10.95; dinner, $9.95–15.75
Payment:	MC, VISA
Service rating:	★★★½
Friendliness rating:	★★★½
Parking:	Free lot
Bar:	Beer, wine
Wine selection:	Moderate
Dress:	Informal
Disabled access:	Good
Customers:	Local, business
Lunch:	Monday–Saturday, 11:30 A.M.–4 P.M.
Dinner:	Monday–Saturday, 4–10 P.M.;
	Sunday, 5:30–10 P.M.

Atmosphere / setting: Simplicity itself: a white room, white napery, and large color photographs on the walls. A small wine bar, a basket of vegetables, and a dessert tray. Fabrizio's minimalist design has a bit of a formal feel, but once inside, it's easy to relax.

House specialties: Northern Italian seasonally changing menu, with specials: tortelli with crab; roast pork loin with spinach and mustard sauce; fresh sea bass with rosemary. For dessert, try the silky baked cream.

Other recommendations: Spaghettini pescatora; sautéed prawns in garlic and lemon butter; veal with wild mushrooms.

Summary & comments: Smaller and less elaborate than some of its local counterparts, Fabrizio offers another choice in Marin's bouquet of contemporary Italian comestibles. The chef's hand is light and self-assured, and the plates arranged simply but attractively. Fabrizio tends to be quiet, but soothing and cheering, and they pour a generous glass of wine.

Robata Grill

	Japanese
	★★★½
	Moderate
	Quality 85 Value C

Zone 10   Suburban Marin
591 Redwood Highway, Mill Valley
(415) 381-8400

Reservations:	Accepted
When to go:	Any time
Entree range:	$10.50–16.95
Payment:	AMEX, MC, VISA
Service rating:	★★★½
Friendliness rating:	★★★½
Parking:	Free lot
Bar:	Beer, wine
Wine selection:	House
Dress:	Casual
Disabled access:	Limited
Customers:	Local, business, family
Lunch:	Monday–Friday, 11:30 A.M.–2 P.M.
Dinner:	Sunday–Thursday, 5:30–9:30 P.M.;
	Friday and Saturday, 5:30–10 P.M.

Atmosphere / setting: Robata's location is nothing special, but the interior is reassuringly handsome, furnished in royal blue, white, and wood tones, with flying Japanese masks and fabric panels, saké barrels, and the giant wooden oars traditional to the robata, which originated in Northern coastal villages where fishermen, grilling over an open fire, passed their catch from boat to boat on their oars. Seating is at the lively sushi bar, or at quieter tables and banquettes around the room.

House specialties: Many small dishes from the sushi bar and grill: lightly seared salmon sashimi with ponzu sauce; steamed shrimp dumplings; broiled skewered shrimp; butter sautéed scallops; slices of beef filet wrapped around asparagus; lamb chops sautéed in garlic butter; barbecued rice balls; grilled vegetables.

Other recommendations: Udon or soba, Japanese noodles with tempura or chicken; steamed soybeans; any of the special sushi rolls.

Summary & comments: Robata's great variety of small appetizers allows diners to sample and share the colors and flavors of Japanese cuisine. The dishes are light, simply presented, and visually pleasing, and they complement each other in infinite combinations. It's hard to limit yourself, and although the individual dishes are not high priced, the bill adds up quickly. On weekdays, Robata does have a lower-priced lunch menu, usually featuring a combination of small dishes for around $7.95, a couple of sushi combos, rice and noodle dishes, tempura, and teriyaki plates.

Rockridge Cafe

	American
Zone 13 Oakland	★★
5492 College Avenue	Inexpensive
(510) 653-1567	Quality 75 Value B

Reservations:	Not accepted
When to go:	Any time
Entree range:	$3–9.95
Payment:	VISA, MC
Service rating:	★★
Friendliness rating:	★★½
Parking:	Street
Bar:	Beer, wine
Wine selection:	House
Dress:	Casual
Disabled access:	Good
Customers:	Locals, students, shoppers
Open:	Monday–Saturday, 7:30 A.M.–10 P.M.;
	Sunday, 8 A.M.–10 P.M.

Atmosphere / setting: Originally a small burger and hot dog stand seating about six. Decor is plain and simple but homey with wooden floors and comfortable tables.

House specialties: The style is cafe fare but the execution is something more refined. Blue corn meal chile relleno; Acadian cassoulet; pizza, pasta, and calzone; tomato, basil, and cheese tart; Apache lamb stew; Baja chicken salad.

Other recommendations: Really good burgers.

Summary & comments: In continuous operation since 1973. Operating 358 days a year. You can get an outstanding breakfast or lunch and a good dinner as well as breads and pastries baked on the premises. On weekends breakfast is served till 2 P.M. Whole pies can be ordered with one day's advance notice. Although reservations are not the norm, they will be taken for parties of six or more. A good place for lunch while shopping or for dinner before the theater.

Rooney's

Zone 9   Waterfront Crescent
38 Main Street, Tiburon
(415) 435-1911

New American	★½
Moderate	
Quality 69	Value C+

Reservations:	Recommended on weekends
When to go:	Any time
Entree range:	$8.50–14.95
Payment:	DC, MC, VISA
Service rating:	★★½
Friendliness rating:	★★½
Parking:	Validated in public lot
Bar:	Beer, wine
Wine selection:	Fair
Dress:	Casual, informal
Disabled access:	Good
Customers:	Tourist, local
Brunch:	Sunday, 7 A.M.–1 P.M.
Lunch:	Monday–Friday, 11:30 A.M.–3:30 P.M.; weekends, 11:30 A.M.–4 P.M.
Dinner:	Wednesday–Sunday, 5:30–9 P.M.

Atmosphere / setting: Small, pleasant cafe with an outdoor garden deck; no waterfront views.

House specialties: Dungeness crab cakes; crab sandwich with melted cheese; salad of pears, endive, Stilton, and toasted pecans; sautéed rock shrimp on greens with sweet red peppers; hot Greek salad, grilled lamb sausage with tomatoes, Greek olives, sizzling vinaigrette, and feta cheese; sautéed crab legs with pasta, tomatoes, and garlic; grilled calamari sandwich with basil and tomatoes.

Summary & comments: Rooney's features some interesting salads, and their lunch sandwiches are especially good. When all the waterfront cafes are full, Rooney's is usually a good bet. The food is better, and better priced, at lunch than at dinner.

Rosmarino

Zone 8   Richmond/Avenues
3665 Sacramento Street
(415) 931-7710

Italian	
★★★	
Moderate	
Quality 84	Value B-

Reservations:	Recommended on weekends
When to go:	Any time
Entree range:	Brunch, $4.50–9.50; lunch, $6.50–11.50; dinner, $11–16
Payment:	AMEX, MC, VISA
Service rating:	★★★
Friendliness rating:	★★★½
Parking:	Street, metered during day
Bar:	Beer, wine
Wine selection:	Good
Dress:	Casual, informal
Disabled access:	Good
Customers:	Local, business
Brunch:	Sunday, 10 A.M.–2:30 P.M.
Lunch:	Tuesday–Saturday, 11:30 A.M.–2 P.M.
Dinner:	Tuesday–Saturday, 5:30–10 P.M.

Atmosphere / setting: A small and understated but usually bustling trattoria with outdoor heated patio, Rosmarino boasts an especially delightful location, hidden away behind a flower shop on a quiet block of exclusive antique shops and boutiques. The proprietors are open and welcoming.

House specialties: Pastas and risotto of the day; braised beef short ribs with roasted squash, leeks, and polenta; grilled swordfish with sauce Grabiche and artichoke confit; braised salmon with bacon and savoy cabbage. For brunch: frittata with housemade fennel sausage and sweet bell peppers; buttermilk soufflé pancakes with fresh fruit; fried polenta with poached eggs, sautéed chard, and Parmesan.

Other recommendations: Luncheon sandwiches; desserts.

Summary & comments: Rosmarino is casual and friendly, located in a lovely neighborhood, and offers a very good wine list. The menu is somewhat limited, but not unsophisticated, and there are nightly specials. It's not a great big night in the city, but for a little night on the town, Rosmarino is a fine choice.

Rossetti

Italian
★★★½
Moderate
Quality 88   Value B

Zone 10   Suburban Marin
510 San Anselmo Avenue, San Anselmo
(415) 459-7937

Reservations:	Recommended for weekend dinners
When to go:	Any time
Entree range:	Lunch, $6.95–8.25; dinner, $7–13.25
Payment:	MC, VISA
Service rating:	★★★
Friendliness rating:	★★★
Parking:	Street, public lots
Bar:	Beer, wine
Wine selection:	Limited but good
Dress:	Casual, informal
Disabled access:	Good
Customers:	Local, business, tourist
Lunch:	Tuesday–Saturday, 11:30 A.M.–2:30 P.M.
Dinner:	Thursday–Saturday, 5:30–9 P.M.

Atmosphere / setting: Toasty wheatstraw painted walls; terra cotta tile floors and blond wood tables and chairs; dried flower garlands and groupings of wine bottles and preserved pomegranates. The blaze of the open wood-fired pizza oven at the back of this small room beckons as cheerily as the pungent scents of rosemary and garlic.

House specialties: Daily risotto, homemade pasta, and lasagna specials; wood-fired pizzas with chevre, walnuts, and prosciutto; soft polenta with portobello mushrooms; saltimbocca alla Romana; pork loin roast braised in milk with wild mushrooms; potato gnocchi with fresh tomato and garlic sauce. Addictive cheese breadsticks. Tartuffo: a cocoa-powdered ball of chocolate mousse surrounding a walnut sized nubbin of frozen zabaglione.

Other recommendations: Tuscan cannellini beans with tomatoes and olive oil; salad of field greens and gorgonzola prawns, feta, and mint; focaccia sandwiches of grilled fish and tomatoes, or roasted vegetables and arugula.

Summary & comments: The Rossetti family moved their fabulous Italian take-out around the corner to a smaller shop in order to remodel this location as a snazzy osteria; their always luxuriantly creative takes on salads, pizzas, and lasagnas have, if anything, improved with the new setting. There are delicious offerings for vegetarians, even those trying to avoid dairy products, and also specials for the diet conscious and heart healthy. The menu is an unusual mix of thoughtful care and spontaneous inspiration seasoned with gleeful abandon.

Royal Thai

<table>
<tr><td></td><td>Thai</td></tr>
<tr><td>Zone 10　Suburban Marin</td><td>★★½</td></tr>
<tr><td>610 Third Street, San Rafael</td><td>Inexpensive</td></tr>
<tr><td>(415) 485-1074</td><td>Quality 76　Value B</td></tr>
</table>

Reservations:	Recommended on weekends
When to go:	Any time, or for lunch specials
Entree range:	Lunch, $4.95–6.95; dinner, $5.95–11.95
Payment:	AMEX, MC, VISA
Service rating:	★★★
Friendliness rating:	★★★½
Parking:	Free lot under freeway
Bar:	Beer, wine
Wine selection:	House
Dress:	Casual, informal
Disabled access:	Good
Customers:	Local, business, tourist
Lunch:	Monday–Friday, 11 A.M.–2:30 P.M.
Dinner:	Every day, 5–10 P.M.

Atmosphere / setting:　Huddled under the highway in the cluster of renovated Victorians called the French Quarter, Royal Thai is entered through a wrought iron gate into a brick courtyard. Inside the resemblance to the Crescent City stops, other than, perhaps, in the slightly canted floors. The decor is simple, with a few Thai prints and the omnipresent royal portraits.

House specialties:　Salmon barbecue with chili and basil; marinated pork and prawns with spicy sauce; spinach leaf salad with seven ingredients and tamarind sauce; skewered squid with spicy green sauce; spicy beef, chicken, and pork with eggplant, sweet basil, and green pepper.

Other recommendations:　Grilled pork chop with garlic and pepper; boneless duck in honey sauce; sautéed squid with fresh chili, garlic, and basil; trout or pompano fried in batter with spicy sauce.

Summary & comments:　The oldest of Marin's Thai restaurants, and a branch of a popular San Francisco eatery, Royal Thai is perhaps handicapped by its unimpressive location. The food, however, is generally quite good, light in oil and moderately seasoned, and the service is efficient and friendly.

Ruby's

Zone 7 SOMA/Mission	Italian
489 Third Street	★★½
(415) 541-0795	Inexpensive
	Quality 79 Value C+

Reservations:	Accepted
When to go:	Dinner
Entree range:	$8.50–14
Payment:	AMEX, VISA, MC
Service rating:	★★★
Friendliness rating:	★★★★
Parking:	Street
Bar:	Beer, wine
Wine selection:	Limited but good
Dress:	Casual
Disabled access:	Yes
Customers:	Local
Open:	Monday–Thursday, 11:30 A.M.–10:30 P.M.; Friday and Saturday, 11:30 A.M.–11:30 P.M.; Sunday, 3–10 P.M.

Atmosphere / setting: Bare and worn wooden floors, walls of indeterminate color and what seems to be a slight lean to them do not deter the patrons of Ruby's. Nor should it. This is one of the friendliest, most convivial places in town. The regulars are mostly a youngish crowd who come here in big numbers for lunch. People outside the neighborhood are beginning to discover it for dinner.

House specialties: If you eat pizza here, it will never be the same for you. Be prepared to be dissatisfied with most others. This is no mere conglomeration of cheese and tomato on dough with some sausage and veg thrown on top. The crust is made from cornmeal and olive oil, and toppings include roasted garlic with five cheeses, Black Forest ham, pancetta, and smoked ham. Also served are eggplant sandwiches; tangy pork stew; duck confit and Italian sausage; mussels with fennel and leeks; risotto with wild mushrooms.

Other recommendations: A variety of creative salads incorporating such things as fresh fruits, nuts, and cheeses.

Summary & comments: Despite the unassuming interior, this is a hidden gem of a restaurant. If you are looking for an excellent meal in the company of happy people, with nothing in the visual realm to distract you, this is it.

Rue de Main

	French
Zone 13 Oakland	★★
22622 Main Street, Hayward	Moderate
(510) 537-0812	Quality 75 Value C

Reservations:	Recommended
When to go:	Any time
Entree range:	$14–22
Payment:	AMEX, MC, DC, VISA
Service rating:	★★
Friendliness rating:	★★★
Parking:	Free lot
Bar:	Beer and wine
Wine selection:	Good
Dress:	Casual
Disabled access:	Good
Customers:	Local, business
Lunch:	Tuesday–Friday, 11:30 A.M.–2:15 P.M.
Dinner:	Tuesday–Saturday, 5:30–10 P.M.

Atmosphere / setting: Located in a historic building, the interior is painted with murals that depict a Parisian street scene. The effect is to give one the feeling of dining in a sidewalk restaurant, or at least at a window table. The split-level dining area is very roomy, and the lower portion is covered by a skylight and graced with potted palms.

House specialties: A standard French menu featuring such staples as escargots, onion soup, and numerous sautéed dishes in cream- or wine-based sauces. Roast rack of lamb in a garlic herb crust is an exception and one you should try.

Other recommendations: Prawns chablisienne; oysters dumas; at lunch try cassoulet.

Summary & comments: Like most French restaurants, the food is tasty and over-priced. The most remarkable thing about Rue de Main is that it's the only place of its kind for miles around. Jenny Lee and Bill Teng are new owners and very eager to please. While Bill works as chef, Jenny manages the front and is always pleasantly available to chat with her clientele. If you want anything out of the ordinary, simply ask her.

Honors / awards: Chamber of Commerce Gold Medal.

Ruth's Chris Steak House

	American
Zone 2 Civic Center	★★½
1700 California Street	Moderate
(415) 673-0557	
	Quality 78 Value B

Reservations:	Accepted
When to go:	Any time
Entree range:	$17–29
Payment:	Major credit cards
Service rating:	★★★
Friendliness rating:	★★★
Parking:	Street
Bar:	Full service
Wine selection:	Good
Dress:	Casual
Disabled access:	Yes
Customers:	Local, tourist
Dinner:	Sunday–Thursday, 5–10 P.M.;
	Friday and Saturday, 5–10:30 P.M.

Atmosphere / setting: A very proper looking steak house in the best tradition. The dark wood puts you in mind of the cattle ranch, and the well-set, clean tables tell you you're in a place of serious eating. Any doubts are dispelled by the black-and-white-clad waiters who look like real pros.

House specialties: Serious steak. It's all from the Midwest where beef is something more than mere food. Corn-fed, aged USDA prime is what you'll get here. It makes up the top 2% of market beef. You'll taste the difference.

Other recommendations: Barbecued shrimp; pork chops; salmon; chicken; shellfish. Creamed spinach; potatoes au gratin; shoestring potatoes.

Summary & comments: The menu defines what rare means, as well as the other grades of doneness, and the cooks are good about it. You'll get what you order. Portions are big and may look daunting. But they can be so good they seem to disappear.

St. James Infirmary

	Bar and Grill
	★★
	Inexpensive
	Quality 77 Value A

Zone 14   South Bay
390 Moffet Boulevard, Mountain View
(415) 969-0806

Reservations:	Not accepted
When to go:	Any time, though lunch is busy
Entree range:	$1.69–5.09
Payment:	VISA, MC, AMEX
Service rating:	★★
Friendliness rating:	★★
Parking:	Free lot
Bar:	Full service
Wine selection:	House
Dress:	Brooks Brothers to Levis
Disabled access:	None
Customers:	You name it
Open:	Every day, 11:30 A.M.–9:30 P.M.

Atmosphere / setting: Wild, eclectic, exuberant, shocking. Sawdust on the floor, graffiti carved into the furniture, and an 18-foot statue of Wonder Woman. A horse-drawn hearse hangs from the ceiling between a biplane and a reindeer sled. It looks like a carnival fun house done with imagination, verve, and a literary dark side.

House specialties: "Home of Burger Madness." Burgers, fries, sandwiches, and salads.

Other recommendations: Bowl 'o chili, nachos, stuffed jalapeños, and buffalo wings. Everything you'd want from a bar and grill.

Entertainment & amenities: A sound system playing equal parts rock 'n' roll and country western, and a little bit of Mozart and Beethoven.

Summary & comments: Once you get over the shock of entry, you smile. Only good feelings here. Check your weapons and your rank and station at the door. Here all are equal. Suits dine next to blue collars in easy camaraderie; bikers and accountants play darts together; good girls and bad girls quaff beers; and the rest of the world is somewhere far away. Though the kitchen closes at 9:30 P.M., the party goes on at least till the witching hour, and often beyond. Check it out.

Salmagundi

Zone 3   Union Square
442 Geary Boulevard
(415) 441-0894

Cafeteria
★★
Inexpensive
Quality 75   Value B

Reservations:	Not accepted
When to go:	Pre-/posttheater
Entree range:	$5.95–6.95
Payment:	Major credit cards
Service rating:	★★
Friendliness rating:	★★½
Parking:	Street
Bar:	Beer, wine
Wine selection:	House
Dress:	Casual
Disabled access:	Yes
Customers:	Local, tourist
Open:	Sunday–Monday, 11 A.M.–9 P.M.;
	Tuesday–Saturday, 11 A.M.–11 P.M.

Atmosphere / setting: Clean, bright, white, airy, and sparkling. If it weren't for the rich aroma of soup you might think you had walked into an ice cream parlor.

House specialties: Soup. Five kinds of soup and they change every day. Thirty-five different soups every week. Split pea; clam chowder; vegetable; beef noodle; hot and sour; borscht. You name it. All made in-house and fresh every day.

Other recommendations: Sandwiches; salads; lasagna; quiche; daily specials.

Summary & comments: This might be the most famous soup kitchen in town. Across the street from the Geary Theater, it's ideal for a quick dinner before or a snack after the play. Service is fast and efficient, prices are low, and it's a good place to people-watch since the windows look out onto the street.

Salute

Italian
★★½
Moderate
Quality 77   Value B

Zone 10   Suburban Marin
706 Third Street, San Rafael
(415) 453-7596

Reservations:	Recommended on weekends
When to go:	Any time
Entree range:	Lunch, $8.25–13.50; dinner, $9.50–16.25
Payment:	MC, VISA
Service rating:	★
Friendliness rating:	★★
Parking:	Street
Bar:	Full service
Wine selection:	Good
Dress:	Informal
Disabled access:	Good
Customers:	Local, business
Open:	Sunday–Thursday, 11:30 A.M.–11 P.M.;
	Friday and Saturday, 11:30 A.M.–midnight

Atmosphere / setting: Classic urban Italian trattoria with black-and-white tile floors, red leather, and dark wood. Several small dining areas and a massive, traditional bar.

House specialties: Brick-oven pizzas with sautéed greens, sun-dried tomatoes, and fontina; wild mushrooms and roasted garlic; rock shrimp, feta, and red onion; or pear, prosciutto, and goat cheese. Warm prawns wrapped in pancetta with lemon and olive oil; tuna carpaccio with cucumbers and dill; dry-cured beef with shaved Parmesan; squash, ricotta, and goat cheese ravioli in walnut sauce; broiled lamb sirloin with black olive sauce.

Other recommendations: Cannelloni with veal, mushrooms, and herbs; potato gnocchi with beef ragout; braised rabbit with mushrooms, prosciutto, and brandy.

Summary & comments: Perched on the corner of a busy artery in downtown San Rafael, Salute is yet another moderately priced restaurant offering modish and tasty Italian dishes. The service here can be negligent, especially, but not only, during peak hours. The late-night dining is a definite plus.

Sam Woh

Zone 1   Chinatown
815 Washington Street
(415) 982-0596

Chinese	
★½	
Inexpensive	
Quality 69	Value B+

Reservations:	Not accepted
When to go:	Lunch or late night
Entree range:	$3.50–7.50
Payment:	Cash
Service rating:	★
Friendliness rating:	★
Parking:	Street
Bar:	None
Wine selection:	None
Dress:	Casual
Disabled access:	Adequate
Customers:	Local, business
Open:	Every day, 11 A.M.–3 A.M.

Atmosphere / setting: Hole-in-the-wall cum rabbit warren. Three floors of deep narrow rooms with a definite cramped feeling, especially during the lunchtime squeeze. Even when you're alone in the place you feel the need for elbow room. And the decor? There is no decor.

House specialties: All the usual suspects in a Chinese restaurant. Chow mein with a variety of additions; crisp fried noodles; sautéed shellfish; won ton soup; fried rice; etc.

Other recommendations: More of the same.

Summary & comments: The motto hangs from the wall: "No credit card, no fortune cookie, just damn good food!" It's not quite a dive, but almost. And it's one of the most popular places in the neighborhood. Of its kind it might be the most popular place in town. The staff are singularly intolerant, demanding, disputatious, and nearly downright rude. "You! Move over. Somebody else gotta sit down too." That's how you get seated when it's very crowded, as it is every day at noon. Lingering too long after lunch? "You! Watsamatta you? People waiting. You go!" Somehow it's not insulting. Somehow that's just the way they say howdy. There is no wine or beer, but the package store just across the street will sell you a cold one or a bottle of jug wine and wrap it in a brown paper bag to take into the restaurant. They know the drill, and they're quick about it. You hungry now? You go!

Sam's Anchor Cafe

Zone 9   Waterfront Crescent
27 Main Street, Tiburon
(415) 435-4527

American	
★★	
Moderate	
Quality 75	Value C+

Reservations:	Recommended for dinner only
When to go:	Off-season weekdays
Entree range:	$6.95–15.95
Payment:	MC, DC, VISA
Service rating:	★★★
Friendliness rating:	★★★
Parking:	Validated in lot, street
Bar:	Full service
Wine selection:	Moderate
Dress:	Casual
Disabled access:	Good
Customers:	Tourist, local
Breakfast:	Monday–Friday, 11 A.M.–2 P.M.
Brunch:	Saturday and Sunday, 10 A.M.–2 P.M.
Lunch:	Every day, 11 A.M.–4 P.M.
Dinner:	Every day, 4–10 P.M.

Atmosphere / setting: Sam's is one of those ample, busy dockside restaurants you might find in any waterfront town: outdoor decks, full bar, nondescript dining room filling and emptying as the ferries come and go. Usually extremely busy on summer weekends, or during the prime lunch and dinner hours even on weekdays, Sam's is a favorite with young, tanned, and fit tourists who can sniff out a party a mile away. During off-season and off-peak hours, the crying seagulls and lapping waves create a pleasing lull on the outdoor deck.

House specialties: Clam chowder; crab cakes; onion rings; fish and chips; burgers, including tuna burgers and garden vegetable burgers; crab and cheese omelets; baked, broiled, or fried seafood; steak sandwich; crab salad.

Other recommendations: Daily specials are recommended.

Summary & comments: If you like table hopping in a crowd, getting a tan while downing brews and large portions of predictable, moderately priced fare with a sports bar inside so you can check on the game, Sam's is your place. Sam's could be interchanged with its counterpart on either American coast and just keep on cranking out the seafood platters. Late lunch hours on off-season weekdays, a quieter atmosphere prevails; go then if you don't like crowds.

Samurai

Zone 9   Waterfront Crescent
2633 Bridgeway, Sausalito
(415) 332-8245

Japanese	
★★½	
Moderate	
Quality 79	Value B

Reservations:	Recommended on weekends
When to go:	Any time
Entree range:	Lunch, $4.50–6.95; dinner, $9–12
Payment:	AMEX, DC, MC, VISA
Service rating:	★★★½
Friendliness rating:	★★★½
Parking:	Free lot
Bar:	Beer, wine
Wine selection:	House
Dress:	Casual
Disabled access:	Good
Customers:	Local, business, tourist
Lunch:	Tuesday–Friday, noon–2 P.M.
Dinner:	Tuesday–Friday, 5:30–9:30 P.M.;
	Saturday, 5:30–10 P.M.

Atmosphere / setting: Traditional Japanese with black tiled floors, honey-colored wood, glass cases displaying Japanese artwork, blue-and-white fabric-covered cushions. Woodworked partitions separate rooms for larger parties. Samurai stays fairly calm and peaceful even when busy. Convivial sushi bar seating provides contact with the chef.

House specialties: Traditional, well-executed Japanese menu with extensive sushi selections. Try the spicy tuna roll, the futomaki, the Alaskan crab and salmon roll, or the vegetarian sushi combination.

Other recommendations: Vegetarian sukiyaki; marinated spinach salad; sautéed enoki mushrooms with tuna.

Summary & comments: Samurai offers dependably fresh, well-prepared versions of familiar Japanese dishes, with a few original twists, especially in the sushi department. The sushi chefs are usually attentive and friendly to customers at the sushi bar. It's possible to put together a very reasonably priced meal at Samurai, especially if you like a lot of vegetables. The vegetarian sukiyaki is a particular bargain.

Santa Fe Bar & Grill

Zone 12   Berkeley
1310 University Avenue
(510) 841-4740

Southwest
★★★
Moderate
Quality 88   Value A-

Reservations:	Accepted
When to go:	Any time
Entree range:	$13.95–16.95
Payment:	VISA, MC, AMEX
Service rating:	★★½
Friendliness rating:	★★½
Parking:	Free lot
Bar:	Full service
Wine selection:	Good
Dress:	Business
Disabled access:	Good
Customers:	Local, business
Lunch:	Monday–Friday, 11:30 A.M.–3 P.M.
Dinner:	Sunday–Thursday, 5–10 P.M.;
	Friday and Saturday, 5–11 P.M.

Atmosphere / setting: The reconstructed historic Santa Fe railway station. Spanish mission-style interior and exterior, but stripped down to its architectural essence. Clean lines, no fluff or red tiles, whitewashed walls in and out. Simple elegance in the unique southwestern style.

House specialties: Smoked meats, fish, and poultry; corn, beans, and rice; flatbread. Southwestern specialties done to perfection, as well as a good selection of pastas and pizzas. The wood-smoked pork chop is two inches thick and, though sometimes dry, when it's moist it's worth a trip across the bay. If that doesn't float your boat, try the Petaluma duck with basmati rice.

Other recommendations: Ceviche of shellfish, black-bean soup, clam chowder with saffron.

Entertainment & amenities: Live pianists, usually on weekends, but sometimes mid-week. One man, one woman. They often play the music of a chosen decade and dress accordingly.

Summary & comments: This place became famous originally under Jeremia Tower. Though he is gone to other pastures, chef Lars Seebohm is keeping it a regular stopping place for East Bay locals. Easy access from the freeway on one side and the hills from the other doesn't hurt. Being near the Berkeley Rep makes it a good spot for after theater dining.

SHERATON PALACE
GARDEN COURT

Zone 4   Financial District
Market at New Montgomery
(415) 392-8600

New American
★★★★
Expensive

Quality 92   Value C-

Reservations:	Recommended
When to go:	Any time
Entree range:	Breakfast buffet, $17.50; Sunday brunch, $39; lunch, $11.50–18.25; dinner, $18.50–29
Payment:	All major credit cards
Service rating:	★★★½
Friendliness rating:	★★½
Parking:	Hotel garage
Bar:	Full service
Wine selection:	Excellent
Dress:	Informal, dressy
Disabled access:	Good
Customers:	Tourist, business, local
Breakfast:	Monday–Saturday, 6:30–10:30 A.M.; Sunday, 6:30–9:30 A.M.
Brunch:	Sunday, 10 A.M.–1:30 P.M.
Lunch:	Monday–Saturday, 11 A.M.–2 P.M.
Dinner:	Tuesday–Saturday, 6–10 P.M.

Atmosphere / setting: The Sheraton Garden Court may be the most gorgeous Rococo room in San Francisco, with its 40-foot high atrium ceiling and copious lead crystal chandeliers dwarfing the baby grand.

House specialties: Breakfast or Sunday brunch buffet; Japanese breakfast; warm lobster salad or potato-wrapped lobster; venison scallopini with red lentils; pan-roasted boneless quail; organic chicken with buckwheat polenta and chanterelles; rare Muscovy duck breast with sun-dried plum sauce.

Other recommendations: Filet mignon; John Dory with wild mushroom ragout; herb-encrusted monkfish with fingerling potatoes.

Summary & comments: Opulent, plush, hushed, and halcyon; if you've recently won the lottery, the Garden Court's grandeur will no doubt satisfy your need to pamper yourself. But you're definitely paying for the atmosphere and deferential service; the food, while meticulously prepared and admirably presented, is among the highest priced in the city, and can be equaled in quality elsewhere for considerably less. Best bet: stop in for a drink on the way somewhere else. The afternoon teas, topping off with a champagne tea for $19.95, are a luxurious treat.

Smokey Joe's Cafe

<table>
<tr><td>Zone 12   Berkeley</td><td>Diner</td></tr>
</table>

Zone 12   Berkeley
1620 Shattuck Avenue
(510) 548-4616

Diner
★½
Inexpensive

Quality 65   Value B

Reservations:	Not accepted
When to go:	Daytime
Entree range:	$4.35–6.95
Payment:	Cash
Service rating:	★
Friendliness rating:	★★
Parking:	Street
Bar:	Beer, wine
Wine selection:	House
Dress:	Come as you are
Disabled access:	Fair
Customers:	1960s holdovers and real people, too
Breakfast/Lunch:	Every day, 8 A.M.–3 P.M.
Dinner:	Friday and Saturday till 9 P.M.

Atmosphere / setting: Vegetarian hash house, "green" beanery, greasy spoon with no animal fat. A long counter and a few rickety tables. Lots of 60s memorabilia on the walls. A cook who looks like a roady for the Grateful Dead and a waitress with a faraway look in her eye.

House specialties: Breakfast. It's really good, really big, really cheap, and you don't walk away with that too-full feeling. Big omelets, multigrain pancakes, and, the ultimate, the Mex Brex Grande: a Spanish omelet, tortillas, refried beans, and home fries. Also fresh juices, French toast, and stick-to-your-ribs oatmeal.

Other recommendations: Prune juice that doesn't taste like a laxative. For lunch the mushroom sandwich or the Holy Mole Frijole Bowl. Special coffee blend.

Entertainment & amenities: Live music from time to time at night.

Summary & comments: Step inside and leave the present decade at the door. Welcome back to the 60s. No in-your-face politics or drugs, just the groovy side. "Where the elite meet to eat no meat." Just don't meet here for a quick bite, because you also leave the word "quick" at the door. You can book the place for a party (sliding scale) if you have enough friends left over from the Summer of Love. The food really isn't bad, the portions are large, and the prices are low.

Sorabol

Zone 13   Oakland
372 Grand Avenue
(510) 839-2288

	Korean
	★★½
	Inexpensive
	Quality 78 Value B

Reservations: Accepted
When to go: Any time
Entree range: $4.95–12
Payment: Major credit cards
Service rating: ★★
Friendliness rating: ★★
Parking: Street
Bar: Full service
Wine selection: Fair
Dress: Casual
Disabled access: Yes
Customers: Local
Open: Every day, 11 A.M.–9:30 P.M.

Atmosphere / setting: Modern Asian. Touches of Japanese / Korean lightness and airiness in the dining area. A bit more of the red opulence of Chinese in the bar. A lot of nooks and twists and turns and paper screens give a feeling of privacy.

House specialties: Korean grills, pickles, and soups and stews. Most common seasonings are ginger, garlic, sesame, chili, and soy sauce. Dinners come with rice, soup, and a variety of Korean "salads"—cooked, raw, and marinated vegetables tossed in sesame and other spices. Grilled beef and pork; hot and spicy soup; buckwheat noodles; stuffed peppers; lamb with pickled garlic; clay pot dishes.

Summary & comments: Korean restaurants have a tendency toward sameness. Sorabol stands out from the crowd with its varied seating arrangements and comfortable bar. The staff make the effort to provide a total dining experience, not just good food.

244

South Park Cafe

Zone 7 SOMA / Mission	French
108 South Park	★★★½
(415) 495-7275	Moderate
	Quality 87 Value A

Reservations:	Recommended
When to go:	Any time
Entree range:	Lunch, $5.25–10; dinner, $10–14.50
Payment:	MC, VISA
Service rating:	★★★½
Friendliness rating:	★★★½
Parking:	Street
Bar:	Full service
Wine selection:	Limited but good
Dress:	Casual, informal
Disabled access:	Good
Customers:	Local, business, tourist
Breakfast:	Monday–Friday, 7:30 A.M. for pastries and coffee
Brunch:	Saturday and Sunday, 8 A.M.–2:30 P.M.
Lunch:	Tuesday–Friday, 11:30 A.M.–2:30 P.M.
Dinner:	Tuesday–Thursday, 5–9 P.M.;
	Friday and Saturday, 5–10 P.M.

Atmosphere / setting: South Park Cafe's enchanting location on historic South Park Boulevard sets off a pared-down neighborhood bistro ambiance: affable clamor and bustle with relatively bright lighting. It's a very romantic street, but not a romantic restaurant.

House specialties: Small tapas menu from 5–7 P.M.: grilled shrimp; sautéed mushrooms; anchoiade potatoes; steamed mussels. Dinners include grilled duck breast with wild honey and spices; boudin noir with sautéed apples; steamed mussels with saffron cream; roast rabbit with lemon confit.

Other recommendations: Nightly specials, including desserts: apple cake with geranium ice cream and calvados crème anglaise.

Summary & comments: South Park's minimalist approach arrived as fore-runner antidote to the ever more flamboyant and expensive dinner houses of the 80s. Heralding as well the gentrification of quaint South Park Boulevard, the original affluent section of old San Francisco then down at the heels in an industrial neighborhood, South Park offered a small, well-executed bistro menu served in a simple setting for shockingly low prices. Others have followed, spiffing up the neighborhood and spawning a whole restaurant movement.

Speckman's

Zone 7 SOMA / Mission	German
1550 Church Street	★★
(415) 282-6850	Inexpensive
	Quality 75 Value B

Reservations:	Accepted
When to go:	Any time
Entree range:	$6.50–11.95
Payment:	AMEX, VISA, MC
Service rating:	★★½
Friendliness rating:	★★★
Parking:	Street
Bar:	Beer, wine
Wine selection:	House
Dress:	Casual
Disabled access:	Yes
Customers:	Local
Lunch:	Monday–Friday, 11 A.M.–2 P.M.
Dinner:	Monday–Thursday, 5–9 P.M.; Friday, 5–10 P.M.
Lunch / Dinner:	Saturday, 11 A.M.–10 P.M.; Sunday, noon–9 P.M.

Atmosphere / setting: Something of a hole-in-the-wall, but nice. Tucked around a corner in an alley so you wouldn't expect to find it here. But once you're inside, it's a little piece of Germany.

House specialties: Traditional German fare. Assorted sausages and cold plates; leek and potato soup; veal Holstein with anchovies and egg; a very zesty goulash with spaetzle; stuffed beef roll; potatoes in many guises.

Other recommendations: Good selection of beers.

Summary & comments: A simple, comfortable place to really pack it in. It seems incongruous to find a German establishment deep in the Mission district, but the area is richer for it.

Splendido's

	Italian
Zone 4 Financial District	★★★
Embarcadero Center Four	Moderate
(415) 986-3222	Quality 88 Value B+

Reservations:	Recommended
When to go:	Any time
Entree range:	$9.50–22
Payment:	Major credit cards
Service rating:	★★★
Friendliness rating:	★★★
Parking:	Street
Bar:	Full service
Wine selection:	Very good
Dress:	Casual, business
Disabled access:	Yes
Customers:	Local, business
Lunch:	Monday–Friday, 11:30 A.M.–2:30 P.M.
Dinner:	Monday–Wednesday, 5:30–10 P.M.;
	Thursday–Saturday, 5:30–10:30 P.M.

Atmosphere / setting: Definitely an incongruous setting: a Mediterranean-style taverna in a shopping center. And a welcome break it is, too. So many other people think so that it's hard to get in here. You should make reservations even for lunch, and make them a few days in advance.

House specialties: Very creative pizza with onion confit and not too salty anchovy; pan-roasted chicken that's as good as any you'll get in a restaurant, served with fennel potatoes; thin-sliced dried beef with rémoulade and cheese; lamb shanks with beans and lemon.

Other recommendations: A bar menu for those who didn't come with reservations. Super desserts.

Summary & comments: The decor is an island of serenity and charm in the malestrom of retail shopping that is Embarcadero Center. It makes for a perfect psychic transition from the frenzy of personal commerce to the contemplation and enjoyment of a good dinner.

Spoons

Zone 14   South Bay
1555 South Bascom Avenue, Campbell
(408) 559-7400

American
★★½
Inexpensive
Quality 78   Value B

Reservations:	Accepted
When to go:	Early
Entree range:	$4–11
Payment:	Major credit cards
Service rating:	★★
Friendliness rating:	★★★
Parking:	Lot
Bar:	Full service
Wine selection:	Fair
Dress:	Casual
Disabled access:	Yes
Customers:	Local, business
Open:	Sunday–Thursday, 11 A.M.–11 P.M.;
	Friday and Saturday, 11 A.M.–midnight

Atmosphere / setting: Sports bar-taqueria-tap room-bar & grill. Awfully hard to pigeonhole this place, but it's wildly popular. Green stuff, sports paraphernalia, and Mexican gewgaws jostle together in a way that just seems to work. The atmosphere is always of a beach party or one that's just about to happen.

House specialties: All the Tex-Mex mess, the stuff you'd find on a Mexican combination plate, plus buffalo wings; fajitas; Philly cheesesteaks; burgers and fries; pretty good beer-marinated baby-back ribs; brownies with ice cream.

Other recommendations: The "Mugarita," a frozen margarita dispensed from a slurpy machine into a beer mug.

Summary & comments: This place can draw standing-room-only crowds, so if you want to get a seat at the bar or eat before 8 P.M., come early. It's always a fun crowd, and a lot of patrons know each other and/or the staff. A lot of regulars. Mostly a youngish crowd but nobody feels out of place. The food is good though it's nothing to write home about. But taken with the happy atmosphere, it does seem to taste better.

SQUARE ONE

Zone 4   Financial District
190 Pacific Avenue
(415) 788-1110

California
★★★
Moderate

Quality 85   Value A

Reservations:	Accepted
When to go:	Any time
Entree range:	$9.50–23
Payment:	Major credit cards
Service rating:	★★★½
Friendliness rating:	★★½
Parking:	Street
Bar:	Full service
Wine selection:	Excellent
Dress:	Business
Disabled access:	Yes
Customers:	Local, business, tourist
Lunch:	Monday–Friday, 11:30 A.M.–2:30 P.M.
Dinner:	Monday–Thursday, 5:30–10 P.M.;
	Friday and Saturday, 5:30–10:30 P.M.;
	Sunday, 5–9:30 P.M.

Atmosphere / setting: Restrained, understated elegance. Tall glass door opens into a spare room with wood floors, some wall hangings, and some trim. An open kitchen on one side, a waiting area on the other. Function more than form is the purpose here. And the function is to serve superior cooking in surroundings that will not detract.

House specialties: California-style cookery and the most demanding standards of quality. Excellent soups such as potato and leek with croutons and Parmesan; beet with buttermilk, cucumber, and chives. Roasted peppers and arugula; sea bass grilled with Moroccan spice and served with couscous; chicken sautéed with mushrooms, cream, cognac, and prosciutto; roast lamb with mustard mint sauce.

Other recommendations: Peach and raspberry pie.

Summary & comments: The menu announces, "We purchase limited quantities so that we may serve only the freshest food. Occasionally we run out of items on our menu. Please accept out apology should this occur." There is no compromise on freshness or quality here.

STARS

Zone 2 Civic Center	Eclectic
150 Redwood Alley	★★★★½
(415) 861-7827	Expensive
	Quality 95 Value B

Reservations:	Highly recommended
When to go:	Any time
Entree range:	$8–30
Payment:	Major credit cards
Service rating:	★★★★½
Friendliness rating:	★★★★
Parking:	Valet
Bar:	Full service
Wine selection:	Excellent
Dress:	Dressy
Disabled access:	Good
Customers:	Local, tourist, business
Lunch:	Monday–Friday, 11:30 A.M.–2 P.M.
Dinner:	Every day, 5:30–10:30 P.M.;
	late dinner till 11:30 P.M.

Atmosphere / setting: Everything about Stars is seductive: the mysterious location down an almost invisible alley, the nonchalant glamour of the decor, the air of casual and elegant ease. No longer unique, Stars set the tone for a whole generation of swank eateries: a stage set for beautiful, stylish people to watch themselves enjoying life. The magic is that it works for everyone.

House specialties: Oysters Rockefeller; gravlax with peppercorn brioche and ginger cream; oven-roasted mussels with bacon and ancho chiles; lobster risotto with scallops; red pepper soup with crab and basil; sautéed halibut with tangerine vinaigrette; grilled veal loin chop with buttered greens; roast garlic rouille.

Other recommendations: Mesquite-grilled hamburgers and wood-fired pizzas; iced tuna tartare with wasabi cream and peppered mangoes. All desserts.

Summary & comments: Open since 1984, Jeremia Tower's Stars was the flagship voyager into a new constellation of fancy restaurant dining and still shines bright in the firmament. A giant mirrored bar and a star-strewn green carpet, a baby grand piano, and spiffy service all make an evening at Stars one to remember.

Honors / awards: *Travel and Leisure* magazine: Best Restaurants of SF.

THE STATION HOUSE

	American
	★★★
	Moderate
	Quality 85 Value B

Zone 11   Yonder Marin
Main Street, Point Reyes Station
(415) 663-1515

Reservations:	Recommended on weekends
When to go:	Any time
Entree range:	Breakfast, $4.45–6.25; lunch, $5.25–8.95; dinner, $7.25–15
Payment:	MC, VISA
Service rating:	★★★
Friendliness rating:	★★★
Parking:	Street, free lot
Bar:	Full service
Wine selection:	Good
Dress:	Casual, informal
Disabled access:	Good
Customers:	Local, tourist
Breakfast/Brunch:	Every day, 8–11:30 A.M.
Lunch:	Every day, 11:30 A.M.–5 P.M.
Dinner:	Sunday–Thursday, 5–10 P.M.; Friday and Saturday, 5–11 P.M.

Atmosphere / setting: Friendly, easygoing yet sophisticated cafe in a little old West Marin cattle ranching town, complete with feed store and saddlery, which seems to have sprung from a country and western song. The bar is locally popular for televised sports events and live music Fridays, Saturdays, and Sundays.

House specialties: Seasonally changing menu, featuring meat loaf and garlic mashed potatoes; black bean and turkey chili; oysters on the half shell; chicken and sausage pot pie with buttermilk biscuit; tiger prawns with horseradish and chive sauce.

Other recommendations: Fettucini with Tomales Bay mussels; double cheese polenta frilled with garlic, tomatoes, and spinach sauté.

Summary & comments: The Station House, which outgrew its smaller quarters in the historic rail station house down the street to move to its present location, is a favorite with locals and West Marin day trippers alike. Even before a write-up in *Gourmet* a few years back, the cafe was filled to capacity for weekend breakfasts and dinners, which renders advance reservations during those times a must. They do, however, handle the crush with ease and style, managing to maintain a busy yet relaxed pace, and the food remains reliably creative and freshly prepared.

The Stinking Rose

Zone 6   North Beach
325 Columbus Avenue
(415) 781-7673

Italian
★★★
Moderate
Quality 80   Value B

Reservations:	Accepted
When to go:	Any time
Entree range:	$8–18
Payment:	VISA, MC, AMEX, JCB
Service rating:	★★★
Friendliness rating:	★★
Parking:	Street
Bar:	Full service
Wine selection:	Short but good
Dress:	Casual
Disabled access:	Yes
Customers:	Local, tourist
Open:	Sunday–Thursday, 11 A.M.–11 P.M.;
	Friday and Saturday, 11 A.M.–midnight

Atmosphere / setting: The main room is a mix of murals, a Rube Goldberg garlic factory, and toy trains. Garlic braids hang from the ceiling, photos of celebrities smile from the walls, and understatement is nowhere in sight. All is exuberant without being overpowering, rather like the aroma of cooked garlic.

House specialties: "Garlic seasoned with food." The mostly Italian menu is comprised of well-made pastas and seafood that are laden with garlic. The garlic is usually cooked long and slow to mellow it, so you won't step out of here a bane to vampires, but people will know where you've been. Weekly specials include meat loaf with garlic mashed potatoes, paella, and salt cod.

Other recommendations: Forty-clove chicken, pork chops with sweet garlic relish and apples, braised rabbit, vegetarian dishes. Specially marked items can be made without the pungent lily, on request.

Summary & comments: Stats: one and a half tons of garlic and 12,000 mints per month! This is a fun place, one that takes itself not too seriously but not too lightly either. It's dedicated to gustatory enjoyment and other good feelings. The bar is a popular place to meet. Regulars will often come in just for a drink and a deep breath or two. At Candlestick Park you can buy "The Stinking Rose's 40-Clove Chicken Sandwich." Upon learning that Queen Elizabeth II does not eat garlic, the proprietors issued a terse and testy press release to effect that henceforth her Brittanic majesty is banned from the premises!

STOYANOF'S

Zone 8   Richmond/Avenues
1240 Ninth Avenue
(415) 664-3664

Greek
★★★
Inexpensive / Moderate

Quality 85   Value B

Reservations:	Recommended on weekends
When to go:	Dinner
Entree range:	$9.59–13.95
Payment:	AMEX, MC, VISA
Service rating:	★★★
Friendliness rating:	★★★
Parking:	Street
Bar:	Beer, wine
Wine selection:	House
Dress:	Casual
Disabled access:	Good
Customers:	Local, business, tourist
Breakfast/Brunch:	Tuesday–Sunday, 10 A.M.–5 P.M.
Lunch:	Tuesday–Sunday, 11 A.M.–5 P.M.
Dinner:	Tuesday–Sunday, 5–10 P.M.

Atmosphere / setting: Fresh and uncluttered, with a blue ceiling and warm wood floors, slatted chairs, and hewn tables, Stoyanof's evokes the flavor of Greece with a few bright paintings. It's a self-serve cafeteria by day, with a rear garden terrace, but converts to efficient, personable table service in the evenings.

House specialties: Greek appetizers: dolmades stuffed with herbed rice; hummus and tabbouleh; tzatziki, yogurt with cucumbers; and tarama salata, the red mullet roe spread. Smoked eggplant with tomato, sweet peppers, and olive oil; flaky phyllo pastries with spinach, lamb, or cheese; grilled fresh salmon, cod, or sea bass; chicken breast in pastry with nutmeg, cumin, and leeks; shish kebab of beef, lamb, swordfish, or ground lamb with choice of sauces.

Other recommendations: Moussaka in both lamb and vegetarian versions; roast leg of lamb with herb marinade; eggplant stuffed with couscous, pine nuts, currants, and red peppers. Wonderful array of pastries.

Summary & comments: Stoyanof's open, airy ambiance pours through its storefront windows and beckons to passersby on the street. Inside, the scents and colors of Greece are as mesmerizing as ever, and the execution of traditional dishes as well as more innovative specials is carried off skillfully, with a lightness that does not sacrifice the assertive Greek flavors. Stoyanof's has a carefree insouciance that goes well with the comestibles, and would suit admirably after a day in the nearby park or at the beach.

Swan Oyster Depot

Zone 2   Civic Center
1517 Polk Street
(415) 673-1101

Oyster Bar	
★★	
Inexpensive	
Quality 78	Value A

Reservations:	Not accepted
When to go:	Lunch
Entree range:	$3.50–7
Payment:	Cash
Service rating:	★★★
Friendliness rating:	★★★
Parking:	Street
Bar:	Beer, wine
Wine selection:	House
Dress:	Casual
Disabled access:	No
Customers:	Local
Open:	Every day, 11 A.M.–5:30 P.M.

Atmosphere / setting: Really a fishmonger's, this little gem boasts a long marble bar where you sit on ancient stools feasting on the freshest seafood in town. It's an old-time San Francisco neighborhood joint.

House specialties: Raw oysters; shellfish cocktails; seafood salads.

Other recommendations: New England clam chowder with sourdough bread.

Summary & comments: Friendly family members of this Polk street business entertain you with continuous conversation while they shuck, peel, and crack your order of shellfish. It must be one of the few places in town that still serves old-fashioned oyster crackers.

Sweden House Conditori

	Bakery Cafe
Zone 9 Waterfront Crescent	★★★
35 Main Street, Tiburon	Inexpensive
(415) 435-9767	Quality 85 Value B

Reservations:	Not accepted
When to go:	Weekdays
Entree range:	$5–8.25
Payment:	MC, VISA
Service rating:	★★½
Friendliness rating:	★★½
Parking:	Validated in public lot
Bar:	None
Wine selection:	House
Dress:	Casual
Disabled access:	Assisted
Customers:	Local, tourist
Breakfast / Brunch:	Every day, 8 A.M.–3 P.M.
Lunch / Dinner:	Monday–Friday, 11 A.M.–5 P.M.; weekends, 11 A.M.–6 P.M.

Atmosphere / setting: A cozy corner Swedish pastry shop and cafe with flowered wallpaper, collections of antique rolling pins and copper cookware, and fresh flowers on the wooden tables. The tiny deck overlooks Sam's and the harbor.

House specialties: Delectable Scandinavian pastries: princess cake, raspberry almond tarts, linzertorten. Breakfasts are served with Swedish limpa bread. Swedish pancakes with lingonberries; Scandinavian sandwiches with Swedish meat loaf, smoked chicken, avocado, and shrimp. Beer, wine, and coffee drinks.

Summary & comments: Like the other Tiburon eateries with outdoor decks, Sweden House is charming during off hours, and crowded on weekends and during the peaks. But the pastries are authentic Scandinavian treats, and you can take them away to the park if there are no tables available. Don't look for especially friendly service here; it's a businesslike little place.

Tadich Grill

Zone 4   Financial District
240 California Street
(415) 391-2373

American
★★★
Moderate
Quality 89   Value A

Reservations:	Not accepted
When to go:	Any time
Entree range:	$7.50–15
Payment:	Major credit cards
Service rating:	★★★
Friendliness rating:	★★½
Parking:	Street
Bar:	Full service
Wine selection:	Good
Dress:	Casual, business
Disabled access:	Yes
Customers:	Local, business, tourist, day trippers
Open:	Monday–Friday, 11 A.M.–9 P.M.;
	Saturday, 11:30 A.M.–9 P.M.

Atmosphere / setting: 150 proud years in the same location. The oldest restaurant in the city. Brightly lit, but the heavily draped tables and curtained booths give a warm ambiance (if you're lucky enough to get one). Otherwise a seat at the long marble counter affords delightful glimpses into the open kitchen.

House specialties: Seafood. Or anything else you want grilled. Tadich is a place for plain cooking, no fancy sauces or tarted-up presentations. Straightforward and honest Yankee fare.

Other recommendations: Good bar to help you through the long wait for seating.

Summary & comments: A culinary cultural treasure of the city by the bay. Quite possibly built over sunken ships of the gold rush. A beacon in the San Francisco fog; to step into Tadich is to partake of the city's rich gastronomic history.

Thanh Long

Zone 8   Richmond / Avenues
4101 Judah at 46th Avenue
(415) 665-1146

	Vietnamese
	★★★
	Inexpensive / Moderate
	Quality 86 Value B

Reservations:	Recommended on weekends
When to go:	Weeknights
Entree range:	$8.25–20.95
Payment:	AMEX, DC, MC, VISA
Service rating:	★★★
Friendliness rating:	★★★★
Parking:	Street
Bar:	Beer, wine
Wine selection:	House
Dress:	Casual, informal
Disabled access:	Good
Customers:	Local, business, tourist
Dinner:	Every day, 4:30–10 P.M.

Atmosphere / setting: Operated by the An family for over 20 years, Thanh Long has recently renovated its far-out-in-the-avenues dining room in shades of muted green, with one wall papered with tropical flowers. Not that anyone really notices: the food's the star here. Thanh Long is close to the beach, and a neighborhood favorite, so it can get very crowded on warm weather weekends.

House specialties: Whole roasted crab with garlic and lemon butter or sweet-and-sour sauce; soft rice-paper shrimp rolls; crab cheese puffs; butterfly prawns in pastry; Saigon beef broiled paper thin around green onions; squid stuffed with pork and mushrooms; lemongrass chicken; broiled red snapper.

Summary & comments: Thanh Long's soft green ambiance provides a cool backdrop for the vibrant, flame-colored platters of whole crabs shimmering from the kitchen. Crab is the main event here, and everyone orders it in one form or another; some say it's the best to be had in a town famous for its crab purveyors. The shrimp rolls are also excellent, as are the grilled pork, beef, and squid. Thanh Long is a good dinner stop after a day at the beach, but reserve ahead to avoid a wait.

Thep Lela

Zone 10   Suburban Marin
411 Strawberry Village, Mill Valley
(415) 383-3444

Thai	
★★★½	
Inexpensive	
Quality 88	Value B

Reservations:	Accepted
When to go:	Any time
Entree range:	$6.95–10.95; lunch specials, $3.95–6.95
Payment:	AMEX, MC, VISA
Service rating:	★★★★
Friendliness rating:	★★★★
Parking:	Shopping center lot
Bar:	Beer, wine
Wine selection:	House
Dress:	Casual
Disabled access:	Limited
Customers:	Local, business
Lunch:	Every day, 11:30 A.M.–3 P.M.
Dinner:	Every day, 5–10 P.M.

Atmosphere / setting: Intimate and tranquil, Thep Lela twinkles like a lovely little jewel in its rather mundane shopping center location. High beamed ceilings, white walls trimmed with carved and gilt woodworking, green leaf carpeting, a colorful mural of Thai village life, fresh flowers, and crisp napery all contribute to the restful ambiance. Remove your shoes to sit at the platform footwell tables, or choose standard seating; more than any other Thai restaurant in Marin, Thep Lela weaves a graceful Asian spell.

House specialties: Muntodd, coconut-dipped slices of fried sweet potato with dipping sauce; hot and sour seafood soup; roasted boneless duck with chili, mint, cashews, and lime; Thai barbecue pork or chicken; rice noodles in broth with prawns, chicken, and cilantro; calamari salad with onion, chili, lemongrass, and mint; grilled fish with spicy sauce.

Other recommendations: Red, green, or yellow curries; Thai noodles; pad graw praw; stir-fried beef, pork, chicken, seafood, or vegetables with chili, garlic, and basil leaves; vegetarian dishes.

Summary & comments: Thep Lela is a lesson in the virtue of atmosphere. The menu offers standard Thai selections, but they're thoughtfully presented, and the gracious service and decor set this tiny hideaway apart. The efficient kitchen provides quick and excellent service, but you'll want to linger anyway, just to soak up the charm.

Ti Bacio

Zone 13   Oakland
5912 College Avenue
(510) 428-1703

Italian	
★★★	
Moderate	
Quality 85	Value B

Reservations:	Accepted
When to go:	Any time
Entree range:	$10.95–14.95
Payment:	VISA, MC
Service rating:	★★
Friendliness rating:	★★
Parking:	Street
Bar:	Full service
Wine selection:	Very good
Dress:	Casual
Disabled access:	Good
Customers:	Local, tourist, student
Dinner:	Every day, 4–10 P.M.

Atmosphere / setting: Like walking into an Etruscan museum. The walls are painted with murals, and numerous urns and other artifacts dot the interior landscape.

House specialties: Italian without red meat or veal. "Heart conscious" fare. Daily specials often include entire meals prepared without any animal or dairy product, no fat or oil, and little or no salt, e.g., penne estate, pasta with assorted vegetables in a tomato, garlic, and wine sauce. In other dishes, turkey stands in for veal, as in tacchino scallopini or piccata. Meat entrees are served with roast potatoes, whole grain rice, and seasonal vegetables.

Other recommendations: Special orders are gladly prepared to conform to restrictive diets. Orders to go at 20% off menu price.

Entertainment & amenities: Patio dining in summer.

Summary & comments: The composition of the menu can be distressingly PC, and the restaurant's constant theme of the hyper-healthy and the wholesome can be tiresome to a God-fearing, meat-eating, fat-loving, salt-pouring American diner. But the proof is in the pudding. None walk away thinking they've had a bad meal. Though one looks for it, tofu does not appear on the menu. The thoughtful, well-balanced wine list is ample evidence that highly developed palates are at work here. And while the staff are willing and able to discuss the nutritional evaluation of the menu, they won't hit you over the head with it.

Ti Couz

Zone 7   SOMA / Mission
3108 16th Street
(415) 252-7373

	Crêperie
	★★
	Inexpensive
	Quality 74 Value B

Reservations:	Not accepted
When to go:	Before or after the movie
Entree range:	$2–6.50
Payment:	Major credit cards
Service rating:	★★
Friendliness rating:	★★★
Parking:	Street
Bar:	Beer, wine
Wine selection:	Adequate
Dress:	Casual
Disabled access:	Yes
Customers:	Locals, movie-goers
Open:	Monday–Friday, 11 A.M.–11 P.M.;
	Saturday, 10 A.M.–11 P.M.;
	Sunday, 10 A.M.–10 P.M.

Atmosphere / setting: Clean, bright, polished blue and white. Simple decor befitting the simple yet very good fare. Located across from the Roxie Theater, it's often peopled by a boisterous and friendly mob of film fans and bookstore denizens.

House specialties: Crêpes, crêpes, and more crêpes. Crêpes of every description and kind and possible filling. Sweet crêpes, savory crêpes, plain and fancy crêpes. Fillings include seasonal fruits and butter or chocolate; mushrooms with sauce; seafood with sauce; cheese and crème fraiche.

Other recommendations: A pretty good selection of beers.

Summary & comments: It's quick, it's good, and the surroundings are undemanding of the discriminating diner. And that's meant in the nicest way. You don't have to put on the dog or your best clothes to have a good feed here.

Tommy Toy's

	Chinese
	★★★½
	Moderate
	Quality 85 Value B+

Zone 4   Financial District
655 Montgomery Street
(415) 379-4888

Reservations:	Accepted
When to go:	Any time
Entree range:	$6.95–18.95
Payment:	Major credit cards
Service rating:	★★★★
Friendliness rating:	★★★
Parking:	Street
Bar:	Full service
Wine selection:	Good
Dress:	Business
Disabled access:	Yes
Customers:	Local, tourist
Lunch:	Monday–Friday, 11:30 A.M.–3 P.M.
Dinner:	Every day, 6–9:30 P.M.

Atmosphere / setting: It looks like you've just walked into the state dining room of the Emperor of China. Gilt and magnificent draperies, carved screens, and panels flank a huge collection of Chinese antiques and a garden of flowers.

House specialties: Sometimes called "Pacific Rim," a cuisine that brings out natural flavors and presents the dishes in a manner in keeping with the magnificent decor: minced squab imperial served in lettuce cups; beef soup with scallops in a coconut shell; Peking duck with buns; Maine lobster dismembered, prepared with spices, and reassembled on the plate; rich filet of beef with oyster sauce and forest mushrooms.

Other recommendations: "Chinese with just a soupcon of French." The items so described on the menu are of the classical Chinese repertoire with influence from traditional French applications: crêpes filled with spicy duck; fried chicken coated with crushed almonds; sautéed lamb with spicy sauce.

Summary & comments: You can get a set-piece banquet for two for $70–90, depending on season and selections, or order à la carte. Many people recommend putting yourself in the hands of the very capable and friendly staff. They know all the items on the menu and what goes best with what, what will fill you up and what will whet your appetite for more. Service is so attentive that you might begin to suspect that the emperor is watching. Tommy Toy and the headwaiter are indeed watching, though, and they are likely to make a call on your table to welcome you and see that all is well.

Tommy's Joynt

Zone 2   Civic Center
1101 Geary Street
(415) 775-4216

American	
★ ★	
Inexpensive	
Quality 75	Value A

Reservations:	Not accepted
When to go:	Any time
Entree range:	$3.50–8
Payment:	Cash
Service rating:	★ ★
Friendliness rating:	★ ★
Parking:	Lot
Bar:	Full service
Wine selection:	Fair
Dress:	Casual
Disabled access:	Poor
Customers:	Everybody
Open:	Every day, 10–2 A.M.

Atmosphere / setting: Crowded, noisy, crazy place with everything conceivable on the walls and ceiling. If you've ever lost anything, you might well find it here.

House specialties: Hofbrau, deli, and here you can find what roams on the range: genuine buffalo stew and, as an added treat, buffalo chili. Also famous for their pastrami and corned beef. The Irish come here on St. Patrick's Day.

Other recommendations: Cheesecake. A wide selection of international beers.

Summary & comments: This is one of the older places in the city that survived the earthquake of 1906. Don't come here to relax; the patrons and the decor are too loud. Come for the beer, the buffalo, and the boisterous fun.

Town's End Restaurant and Bakery

	New American
Zone 7 SOMA/Mission	★★★
2 Townsend Street, Building 4	Moderate
(415) 512-1749	Quality 84 Value B+

Reservations:	Recommended
When to go:	Any time
Entree range:	Breakfast or brunch, $4.75–8; lunch and dinner, $6.75–11.50
Payment:	All major credit cards
Service rating:	★★★
Friendliness rating:	★★★½
Parking:	Street, metered during day
Bar:	Beer, wine
Wine selection:	Limited but good
Dress:	Casual, informal
Disabled access:	Good
Customers:	Local, business, tourist
Breakfast/Brunch:	Tuesday–Sunday, 8 A.M.–2:30 P.M.
Lunch:	Tuesday–Friday, 11:30 A.M.–2:30 P.M.
Dinner:	Tuesday–Thursday, 5–9 P.M.; Friday and Saturday, 5–10 P.M.

Atmosphere / setting: Town's End doesn't command a view, but feels as though it does, with its azure trompe l'oeil mural, glass walls, and the bridge twinkling in the distance. The dining area has an airy feel, an open kitchen, and a Zen approach to flower arrangement.

House specialties: Baskets of house-baked breads; homemade pastas; and house-smoked red trout and salmon. Niçoise salad; grilled salmon with corn and tomatillo relish; curried lamb stew with pecan-currant couscous; grilled chicken marinated in garlic, lemon, and lime with organic greens, pears, Roquefort, and walnuts. Lemon meringue pie with raspberry sauce; white chocolate Napoleon.

Other recommendations: Brunch: fritatta scamorza with smoked mozzarella, wild mushrooms, sun-dried tomatoes, and fresh herbs; Dungeness crab cakes; Swedish oatmeal pancakes with pears and almonds.

Summary & comments: Town's End is another SOMA venue with moderate prices and a tasty, freshly prepared menu. The unusual waterfront location, with neighboring gardens and park, offers an idyll away from, but still within, the boundaries of city life. The bakery section, with a few small tables, is open all day for coffee and pastry.

Tu Lan

Zone 7   SOMA / Mission
8 Sixth Street
(415) 626-0927

	Vietnamese
	★½
	Inexpensive
	Quality 69 Value A

Reservations:	Not accepted
When to go:	Any time
Entree range:	$2.50–8
Payment:	Cash
Service rating:	★★
Friendliness rating:	★★
Parking:	Street
Bar:	Beer, wine
Wine selection:	House
Dress:	Casual
Disabled access:	No
Customers:	Local, business
Open:	Monday–Saturday, 11 A.M.–9 P.M.

Atmosphere / setting: A scruffy old downtown diner with no friends. Old wooden floors, a long formica counter, and rickety old wooden tables and chairs, none which have four legs of the same length.

House specialties: Some really outstanding Vietnamese fare considering the price: hot and spicy soup dotted with pineapple bits; pounded shrimp wrapped on split sugarcane sticks and broiled; spring rolls; imperial rolls; ginger fish or chicken; pork shish kebab; lemon beef salad.

Other recommendations: Curry potatoes.

Summary & comments: You can't miss Tu Lan. It's the tacky place on the corner with all the newspaper and magazine reviews taped up to the window. There is only one reason to come here: to get what is, for the money, one of the best Vietnamese meals you can find outside of Saigon. It's located in what has been for a long time a tough and seedy neighborhood. The local denizens will likely be hanging out along your route, but if you walk by quickly, they won't bite.

Venezia Cafe & Ristorante

Zone 12 Berkeley	Italian
1799 University Avenue	★★★
(510) 849-4681	Moderate
	Quality 85 Value B

Reservations:	Accepted
When to go:	Early; pre-/posttheater
Entree range:	$8.50–13.50
Payment:	Major credit cards
Service rating:	★★
Friendliness rating:	★★
Parking:	Free lot evenings only
Bar:	Beer, wine
Wine selection:	Good
Dress:	Casual
Disabled access:	Good
Customers:	Local, regular
Lunch:	Monday–Friday, 11:30 A.M.–2:30 P.M.
Dinner:	Monday–Thursday, 5:30–10 P.M.;
	Friday and Saturday, 5–10 P.M.;
	Sunday, 5–9:30 P.M.

Atmosphere / setting: A large dining area painted and decorated to recall a working-class street scene in Venice. Laundry hangs from a line in the corner and a fountain gurgles in the middle. It could have been tacky, but the decorators have made it work well.

House specialties: Robust and rustic Italian fare featuring pasta, a few grill items, and specials of meat, fish, and poultry. Malfatti con funghi, a dish hardly ever seen outside Italian homes, is good here. Spaghetti ala rustica with eggplant, grilled peppers, tomato, and spicy sausage; fettuccini with four cheeses; linguine marinara; osso buco; roasted chicken with spinach and potatoes; chicken sausage.

Summary & comments: Near Berkeley Repertory Theater, Venezia began as two restaurants, across the street from each other and under the same ownership. Neither was large enough to accommodate the crowds they eventually began to draw, and the lines of waiting patrons outside were blocking foot traffic. So they were consolidated under one roof, their menus combined, and the total floor space increased by one-half. There is still some waiting on weekends, but it's all inside at the pleasant wine bar. The menu is short, making for easier choices, and allowing the kitchen staff to hone their skills on these particular dishes. The wine bar, too, doesn't have a giant selection, but it's a very nice place to sit and relax over wine, beer, or aperitif while waiting to be seated.

Vlasta's

Zone 5   Marina
2420 Lombard street
(415) 931-7533

Czech	
★★½	
Inexpensive	
Quality 79	Value A

Reservations:	Accepted
When to go:	Any time
Entree range:	$8.50–16
Payment:	Major credit cards
Service rating:	★★
Friendliness rating:	★★★
Parking:	Street
Bar:	Beer, wine
Wine selection:	Fair
Dress:	Casual
Disabled access:	Yes
Customers:	Local, business
Dinner:	Tuesday–Sunday, 5:30-10 P.M.

Atmosphere / setting: Very warm and welcoming, almost like walking into someone's country lodge. Heavy dark wood and gilt. Some very good paintings gracing the walls. This is old world, nothing trendy here.

House specialties: Crispy, Bohemian herb-roasted duck with red cabbage and dumplings; sauerbraten; Viennese schnitzel; chicken paprika; beef stroganoff; roast pork.

Other recommendations: Simple but superior salads; superior apple strudel.

Summary & comments: A slow easy pace in pleasant surroundings; warm and almost matronly. A place for a really good Central European meal at a good price. You can stagger from the table here. It's that old designation "hearty," but done well and with a lot of love.

Washington Square Bar and Grill

Italian	
★★★	
Moderate	
Quality 88	Value B+

Zone 6 North Beach
1707 Powel Street
(415) 982-8123

Reservations:	Accepted
When to go:	Any time
Entree range:	$9.50–18.95
Payment:	Major credit cards
Service rating:	★★★
Friendliness rating:	★★★½
Parking:	Validated
Bar:	Full service
Wine selection:	Good
Dress:	Casual
Disabled access:	No
Customers:	Eclectic, local, celebs
Lunch:	Monday–Saturday, noon–3 P.M.;
	Sunday, 2–4 P.M.
Dinner:	Monday–Thursday, 5:30–10:30 P.M.;
	Friday and Saturday, 5:30–11:30 P.M.;
	Sunday, 5–10 P.M.

Atmosphere / setting: Wood, brass, and white tablecloths. Nothing too much or too little. A very cordial, clubby atmosphere where anybody can come and feel like a member. People like their tipple and food here abundantly. Affectionately known by its acronym: The WASHBAG.

House specialties: If you're lucky, cioppino. It's a tomato-based fish stew that takes the diner to unmatched heights of gustatory experience. Food writer Roy Andreis De Groot called it the best recipe in America. It can only be made with the best ingredients and a lot of time, so it's only available occasionally. If you're not lucky that night, have a big steak, roast chicken with garlic, or crab Louie.

Summary & comments: It's not quite accurate to call the washbag an Italian kitchen. It has a number of items on its menu that you would find in eateries all over the country. But it's the Italian muse that inspires the cook. Many local celebs hang out here, but they don't come to be seen, just to be, and of course to eat and drink. Political rivals leave their differences at the door (well, for the most part) and hobnob with local artists and writers and ordinary folk. The view of Washington Square, where kids are often at play or on their way to and from school, gives the place a neighborhood feel.

WATERFRONT CAFE

American
★ ½
Inexpensive
Quality 69   Value B

Zone 9   Waterfront Crescent
85 Liberty Ship Way,
   Schoonmaker Point, Sausalito
(415) 332-5625

Reservations:	Not necessary
When to go:	Sunny days
Entree range:	$2.90–4.50
Payment:	Cash
Service rating:	★★★
Friendliness rating:	★★★
Parking:	Free public lot
Bar:	Beer
Wine selection:	None
Dress:	Casual
Disabled access:	Limited
Customers:	Local, tourist, local business
Breakfast:	Monday–Friday, 7:30 A.M. for coffee and pastry; Saturday and Sunday, 8 A.M.
Lunch/Dinner:	Monday–Friday, 7:30 A.M.–6 P.M.; Saturday and Sunday, 8 A.M.–6 P.M.

Atmosphere / setting: A small waterfront cafe at the edge of one of Sausalito's marinas, with indoor and outdoor seating. The decor is somewhere between high tech and punk; red, orange, black, and gray with slate flooring, exposed pipes, and aluminum siding. But the swaying masts, the clink of riggings, and the smells of the sea are the main attraction here. The Waterfront Cafe is hard to find: heading north on Bridgeway out of Sausalito, take the downhill right at Liberty Ship Way, and follow the road out to Schoonmaker Point. Kayak, water-bike, scull, and jet ski rentals are available next door.

House specialties: Daily special salads: curry chicken with rice; pasta with sun-dried tomatoes and goat cheese; grilled chicken with papaya. Daily soups and quiches; sandwiches.

Other recommendations: Coffee drinks, sodas, hot chocolate.

Summary & comments: The Waterfront Cafe is a great stop for a casual outdoor lunch during a bicycle ride on Sausalito's bike path, or before or after an afternoon of sailing or kayaking. The clientele are mainly sailors and other outdoor, watery types. The salads and sandwiches are savory and fresh tasting.

Whole Foods

Zone 10 Suburban Marin	American
414 Miller Avenue, Mill Valley	★★½
(415) 381-1200	Inexpensive
	Quality 79 Value C+

Reservations:	Not necessary
When to go:	Any time
Entree range:	$3.25–5.25
Payment:	MC, VISA, ATM
Service rating:	★★
Friendliness rating:	★★
Parking:	Free lot, street
Bar:	Beer and wine shop
Wine selection:	Good
Dress:	Casual
Disabled access:	Good
Customers:	Local, business, tourist
Open:	Every day, 9 A.M.–8 P.M.

Atmosphere / setting: Mecca for the natural foods set: large, well-stocked store with juice bar; coffee bar; bakery; salad, soup, and hot entree bar; and deli. Located near the main road to Marin County beaches and hiking trails. In-house booth seating at the front of the store.

House specialties: Tofu, tempeh, and vegetable burgers; burritos; deli and specialty sandwiches: try the provolone, olive salad, and roasted red peppers; the roasted eggplant with goat cheese on focaccia; or grilled rosemary chicken breast with red peppers and aïoli. Entrees include grilled salmon steaks; barbecued chicken; polenta tapenade torte; baked meat loaf with eggplant. Salads and sides: Jamaican jerk seitan on skewers; grilled new potatoes; spicy Thai noodles; apricot lemon quinoa; roasted butternut squash with cherries and citrus.

Other recommendations: Salad bar, soup, and fresh-squeezed juices and smoothies from the juice bar, baked goods, cheeses, breads, and a thoughtful selection of domestic and imported wines by the bottle, including organic ones.

Summary & comments: "The revolution is over, and we have won!" exulted the hippies in the 60s; this somewhat tunnel visionary sentiment is alive and well at Whole Foods, where New Age meets old, middle, and teenagers to shop, shmooze, and swap survival strategies. And, you can get anything you want, from chocolate-tofu torte to wheat-grass juice, from oil-free carrot ginger soup to organic meat loaf with garlic mashed potatoes.

Woodward's Gardens

Zone 7   SOMA/Mission
1700 Mission
(415) 621-7122

	French
	★★★
	Moderate
	Quality 83 Value B

Reservations:	Required
When to go:	Any time
Entree range:	$13.50–15.50
Payment:	Cash only
Service rating:	★★★
Friendliness rating:	★★★
Parking:	Street
Bar:	Beer, wine
Wine selection:	Fair
Dress:	Casual, informal
Disabled access:	Limited
Customers:	Local, business, tourist
Dinner:	Wednesday–Sunday: seatings at 6, 6:30, 8, and 8:30 P.M.

Atmosphere / setting: Dwarfed and nearly invisible in its dark, under the freeway, Mission Street location, Woodward Garden's interior replicates a miniature Parisian bistro, with lace curtains veiling the traffic outside; open kitchen; banquettes; and velvet counter stools. This is real togetherness; there's infinitesimal space between the tables and clamor and smoke from the kitchen.

House specialties: Weekly changing menu, with bounteous portions, possibly including: garden salad with mango, grapefruit, kumquat, pecans, and goat cheese; warm white beans with grilled mussels, scallops, clams, cured salmon, and Meyer lemon aïoli; braised lamb ravioli with tomatoes, fresh oregano, and feta; gumbo of prawns, duck breast, and andouille sausage over basmati rice; roasted chicken with cucumbers, ricotta salatta, tomatoes, olives, arugula, and frisee; New York steak with five-onion marmalade.

Other recommendations: Raspberry crème brûlée; chocolate torte.

Summary & comments: There's something slightly heartbreaking about Woodward's Gardens, like watching Cinderella toiling away in a smoking scullery when she deserves to be at the ball. This diamond buried in the asphalt should be popped into a pumpkin coach and whisked to the palace. Chefs Dana Tomassino and Margie Conard bring forth an astonishing array of sprightly, original cookery in magnanimous portions with a minuscule kitchen and bare-bones crew. One can only hope that Woodward's current rousing success will lead to much bigger and better located things.

Yank Sing

Zone 4   Financial District
427 Battery Street
(415) 362-1640

Chinese	
★★	
Inexpensive	
Quality 76	Value B

Reservations: Accepted
When to go: Lunch
Entree range: $4–6
Payment: Major credit cards
Service rating: ★★½
Friendliness rating: ★★
Parking: Street
Bar: Beer, wine
Wine selection: House
Dress: Casual
Disabled access: Yes
Customers: Local, business
Lunch: Monday–Friday, 11 A.M.–3 P.M.;
               Saturday and Sunday, 10 A.M.–4 P.M.

Atmosphere / setting: A modernly furnished restaurant, its white table-cloths and impeccable service make it a step above the usual dim sum house. A class act for simple fare.

House specialties: Dim sum and yet more dim sum, constantly issuing forth fresh from the kitchen. Wheeled about on trollies, you can choose barbecued pork buns; shrimp moons; silver wrapped chicken.

Other recommendations: Small portions of Peking duck. A wide variety of vegetarian dim sum including pea leaves, sautéed eggplant, and mustard greens. Chrysanthemum blossom tea.

Summary & comments: Selections are cooked with less fat than usual. Yuppies love it here. They can stuff themselves without having to spend any extra time at the gym.

YaYa Cuisine

Zone 8   Richmond/Avenues
1220 Ninth Avenue
(415) 566-6966

Iraqi/Mesopotamian	
★★★½	
Moderate	
Quality 88	Value B

Reservations:	Recommended on weekends
When to go:	Any time
Entree range:	Lunch, $7–9.50; dinner, $10.50–14
Payment:	All major credit cards
Service rating:	★★★½
Friendliness rating:	★★★½
Parking:	Street
Bar:	Beer, wine
Wine selection:	Fair
Dress:	Casual, informal
Disabled access:	Good
Customers:	Local, business, tourist
Lunch:	Tuesday–Friday, 11:30 A.M.–2 P.M.
Dinner:	Tuesday–Sunday, 5:30–10 P.M.

Atmosphere / setting: Sandwashed walls and deepest blue mosaic arches; Persian carpets and Mesopotamian murals; a private dining area with woven cushions and floor seating; YaYa is a Middle Eastern restaurant with no small sense of style.

House specialties: Armenian flatbread dipped into olive oil flavored with sesame, thyme, and sumac; grilled Japanese eggplant with coriander cucumber relish; date-filled ravioli with cardamom, cinnamon, and walnuts; grilled quail with hummus and tahini; grilled salmon with saffron sumac sauce; eggplant stuffed with lamb, coriander, and pine nuts with tamarind tomato sauce; beef and rice with almonds, onion, raisins, and sun-dried lime.

Other recommendations: Vegetarian specialties: sorrel, spinach, feta, and shiitake mushrooms in phyllo with red bell pepper coulis; grilled vegetables with rice, almonds, and cardamom in phyllo with berry sauce.

Summary & comments: Yahya Salih, who cooked with Jeremiah Tower at the Balboa Cafe, brings a designer's sensitivities to the use of ingredients traditional to his homeland near Ninevah. Yahya is an exuberant, inquisitive host, interested in comments from his guests, as well as recommendations for his changing wine list, and ready with information regarding the intriguing murals gracing his establishment. His is inventive, unusual cooking, with sweet-and-sour notes, crisp clouds of pastry, pungent pools of sauces. Portions are enormous and artistically presented.

Yoshi's

Zone 13 Oakland	Japanese
6030 Claremont Avenue	★★½
(510) 652-9200	Moderate
	Quality 78 Value B

Reservations:	Accepted
When to go:	Any time
Entree range:	$11–14.50
Payment:	VISA, MC, AMEX, DC
Service rating:	★★
Friendliness rating:	★–★★★, depends on who's working
Parking:	Free lot
Bar:	Full service
Wine selection:	Fair
Dress:	Casual
Disabled access:	Good
Customers:	Local, student, musical
Dinner:	Every day, 5:30–9:30 P.M.
	(sushi bar till 10:45 P.M.)

Atmosphere / setting: A spacious Japanese restaurant cum nightclub. Here the spare and airy quality of a Japanese temple combines with the exuberance of a smokin' jazz club. High ceilings and bright lights in the large bar, a little more intimate and dimmer in the main dining room downstairs, and upstairs a traditional sit-on-the-floor Japanese sushi restaurant. Adjoining the bar is the jazz club.

House specialties: All the things one associates with a Japanese restaurant: sashimi and tempura, sukiyaki, eels and gyoza. A good bargain are the combination dinners.

Other recommendations: Sushi.

Entertainment & amenities: Live jazz in the auditorium.

Summary & comments: The original building first housed a French laundry. The current owners bought it and operated it as a sushi bar. Success followed, and the first of many additions to the structure were built. It is now a large, rambling gastro-culinary-musical cultural complex. The East-meets-West quality is less of a mixture of cultures and more of a juxtaposition. Some of the biggest names in jazz appear here, and many a good time and good meal are to be had. The service is generally quite friendly and prompt, but the odd surly bartender is strangely tolerated.

YUET LEE

Zone 1   Chinatown
1300 Stockton Street
(415) 982-6020

	Chinese
	★★½
	Inexpensive / Moderate
	Quality 78 Value A

Reservations:	Not accepted
When to go:	Any time
Entree range:	$3.50–16
Payment:	Cash only
Service rating:	★★★
Friendliness rating:	★★★
Parking:	Street, public pay lots
Bar:	Beer, wine
Wine selection:	House
Dress:	Casual
Disabled access:	Good
Customers:	Local, business, tourist
Open:	Monday–Sunday, 11–3 A.M.

Atmosphere / setting: Nondescript, clangorous formica-tabled seafood and noodle shop on a busy corner in North Chinatown, with fresh seafood tanks, chartreuse framed windows, and an open kitchen with flying cleavers.

House specialties: Fresh seafood specialties: seasonal lobster; pepper and salt prawns; crab with ginger and onion; fresh boiled geoduck or razor clams; steelhead fillet with greens; sautéed fresh and dried squid. Clay pots: salted fish with diced chicken and bean cake; roast pork, bean cake, and shrimp sauce; oyster and roast pork with ginger and onion. Roast squab; braised chicken with abalone; fresh New Zealand mussels with black-bean sauce; steamed live rock cod with ham and shredded black mushrooms. Also, a vast assortment of noodles and noodle soups: wontons and dumplings; braised noodles with beef stew; Amoy- or Singapore-style rice sticks.

Other recommendations: Rice soups or plates; roast duck.

Summary & comments: There are basically two kinds of people in the world: those who believe salvation can be found in a bowl of Chinese noodles, and those who do not. If you are among the former, you will not care about Yuet Lee's fluorescent lighting, linoleum floors, and slambang service. You will forsake soft music and cloth napkins and candlelight. You will know that each vessel of glistening dumplings swimming in broth perfumed by star anise and ginger and scattered with emerald scallions contains all the mysteries of the universe. You will want to taste every item on the menu; stay until closing time at 3 A.M. just to watch the fragrant platters come steaming from the kitchen, yea, verily, to become one with the noodles and the fishes.

Zarzuela

Zone 5   Marina
2000 Hyde Street
(415) 346-0800

Spanish	
★★★½	
Moderate	
Quality 83	Value A

Reservations:	Recommended
When to go:	Any time
Entree range:	Tapas, $2.75–5.25; entrees, $8.50–13.95
Payment:	MC, VISA
Service rating:	★★★★
Friendliness rating:	★★★★
Parking:	Street
Bar:	Beer, wine
Wine selection:	Limited but good
Dress:	Casual
Disabled access:	Good
Customers:	Local, tourist, business
Lunch:	Monday–Saturday, 11:30 A.M.–3 P.M.
Dinner:	Monday–Saturday, 5:30–10 P.M.

Atmosphere / setting: Disarming warmth beckons as piquant aromas of garlic and seafood waft over the sidewalk from within. Modest appointment inside: tawny walls and tiled floors, beamed ceilings and arched windows, hand-painted dishes on the walls, and the music of soft guitars. The nuances of Spanish culture and charm softly beguile.

House specialties: Thirty-eight different types of tapas: mussels or clams with white wine and garlic; grilled shrimp; poached octopus with potatoes and paprika; snails baked on croutons; grilled scallops and chard with red pepper sauce; Spanish sausage with wine; cold roast veal with olives; grilled vegetables; rolled eggplant with goat cheese. Entrees include zarzuela, a Catalan seafood stew; pork tenderloin in raisin and pine nut sauce; paella; loin of lamb in thyme and red wine.

Other recommendations: Sangria, gazpacho; romaine salad with roasted garlic; caramel flan; Alicante Muscatel dessert wine.

Summary & comments: Oranges and olives, garlic and olives, red wine and sherries. Spanish cuisine presents a provocative departure from French and Italian in its colorful little plates of tapas and the substantial offerings issuing forth from Zarzuela's kitchen. Dishes here are as refined as they are close to the earth. Prices are soothing as the ambiance, and a small group of diners can sample a wide assortment of dishes without having to run to the ATM. Sangria is darkly sweet and spicy and poured into large goblets. The small selection of sherries is being widened. Zarzuela is a quintessential neighborhood restaurant: low key, low priced, and welcoming.

Zuni Cafe and Grill

Zone 2   Civic Center
1658 Market Street
(415) 552-2522

	Italian
	★★★
	Moderate
	Quality 89 Value B+

Reservations:	Accepted
When to go:	Any time
Entree range:	$9–28
Payment:	Major credit cards
Service rating:	★★★
Friendliness rating:	★★★
Parking:	Street
Bar:	Full service
Wine selection:	Superior
Dress:	Casual, business
Disabled access:	Yes
Customers:	Local, business, tourist
Open:	Every day, 7:30 A.M.–midnight

Atmosphere / setting: Lots of bustle. A happy and exuberant place full of people coming and going, eating and enjoying at all hours of the day and into the night. There's a long copper bar just right for bellying up to and holding forth to all who will listen, and excellent views of busy Market street.

House specialties: The menu changes every day, and only the best stuff is purchased for Zuni. Examples include: rib-eye steak (frequently recurring item); roast chicken; grilled tuna; braised cod; pasta dishes simply but expertly prepared; any soup; vegetable fritters.

Other recommendations: Regularly available hamburgers and pizza.

Summary & comments: This is a place that concentrates on perfecting the simple. The kitchen team, and it is a team, will mine a single ingredient or recipe for the most that it can give while still retaining its essential character. An example is the use of Meyer lemons. They are grown almost exclusively in the backyards of East Bay homes, rather than commercially, and are sweeter and more aromatic than other lemons. They are to lemons what truffles are to mushrooms.

Zza's

Zone 13   Oakland
552 Grand Avenue
(510) 839-9124

	Italian
	★★
	Inexpensive
	Quality 75 Value B

Reservations:	Accepted for 6 or more
When to go:	Early or late
Entree range:	$7.50–10.95
Payment:	VISA, MC
Service rating:	★★★
Friendliness rating:	★★★
Parking:	Street
Bar:	Beer, wine
Wine selection:	Fair
Dress:	Casual
Disabled access:	Good
Customers:	Local
Dinner:	Wednesday–Friday, 11 A.M.–10 P.M.; Saturday–Monday, 4:30–10 P.M.

Atmosphere / setting: A cavernous place full of families and other groups of all kinds. Kids can be kept amused with the crayons provided for drawing and coloring on the paper tablecloths. A few video games are in the rear, but nothing egregious. It's a fun place with lots of color.

House specialties: Pizza, calzone, and pasta. A good selection of toppings and fillings including cilantro pesto; spinach and gorgonzola; roasted garlic; eggplant; corn, zucchini, and leaks.

Other recommendations: After 5:15 P.M., rosemary-roasted chicken; veal special of the night.

Summary & comments: It can be hard to get a table here as it is extremely popular. A 40-seat banquet room is available nearby with a great view of Lake Merrit. There is a room charge and the management can work within your budget. Catering is also offered at very good prices.

Eclectic Gourmet Guide to San Francisco
Reader Survey

If you would like to express your opinion about your San Francisco dining experiences or this guidebook, complete the following survey and mail it to:

Eclectic Gourmet Guide Reader Survey
P.O. Box 43059
Birmingham, AL 35243

	Diner 1	Diner 2	Diner 3	Diner 4	Diner 5
Gender (M or F)	___	___	___	___	___
Age	___	___	___	___	___
Hometown	___	___	___	___	___

Tell us about the restaurants you've visited . . . .

You're overall experience:

Restaurant	👍	👎
_____	___	___
_____	___	___
_____	___	___
_____	___	___
_____	___	___
_____	___	___
_____	___	___

Comments you'd like to share with other diners:

_____
_____
_____
_____
_____
_____
_____
_____
_____